Routledge Revivals

Latin Explorations

Latin Explorations, first published in 1963, offers a fresh approach to Roman poetry from Catullus to Ovid. Traditionally, the period is divided for specialist studies – Lyric, Epic and Elegy. In each of them, techniques of interpretation prevail, isolated from contemporary ideas about poetry and dominated by barriers between 'textual', 'exegetical' and 'aesthetic' criticism.

Kenneth Quinn discerns in Roman poetry of this period the adolescence, maturity and decay of a single coherent tradition whose internal unity surpasses differences of form. His argument attempts to reverse the dissociation of purely academic research from appreciative criticism, whilst also incorporating the work of textual scholars. Each chapter is supported by a detailed analysis of the texts: nearly 700 lines of poetry are discussed and translated.

Latin Explorations will be of significant value not only to students of the Classics, but also to the 'Latinless' general reader who is interested in Roman literature.

Latin Explorations
Critical Studies in Roman Literature

Kenneth Quinn

First published in 1963
by Routledge & Kegan Paul Ltd

This edition first published in 2014 by Routledge
2 Park Square, Milton Park, Abingdon, Oxon, OX14 4RN
and by Routledge
711 Third Avenue, New York, NY 10017

Routledge is an imprint of the Taylor & Francis Group, an informa business

© 1963 Kenneth Quinn

The right of Kenneth Quinn to be identified as author of this work has been asserted by him in accordance with sections 77 and 78 of the Copyright, Designs and Patents Act 1988.

All rights reserved. No part of this book may be reprinted or reproduced or utilised in any form or by any electronic, mechanical, or other means, now known or hereafter invented, including photocopying and recording, or in any information storage or retrieval system, without permission in writing from the publishers.

Publisher's Note
The publisher has gone to great lengths to ensure the quality of this reprint but points out that some imperfections in the original copies may be apparent.

Disclaimer
The publisher has made every effort to trace copyright holders and welcomes correspondence from those they have been unable to contact.

A Library of Congress record exists under LC control number: 63006179

ISBN 13: 978-1-138-01400-8 (hbk)
ISBN 13: 978-1-315-79489-1 (ebk)
ISBN 13: 978-1-138-01402-2 (pbk)

Latin Explorations

*Critical Studies in
Roman Literature*

by
KENNETH QUINN

ROUTLEDGE AND KEGAN PAUL
London

*First published 1963
by Routledge & Kegan Paul Ltd
Broadway House, 68–74 Carter Lane
London, E.C.4*

*Printed in Great Britain
by Western Printing Services Ltd
Bristol*

© *Kenneth Quinn 1963*

No part of this book may be reproduced in any form without permission from the publisher, except for the quotation of brief passages in criticism

Contents

	PREFACE	*page* ix
	ABBREVIATIONS	xi
1.	HORACE'S SPRING ODES	1
	Horace's Ode to Virgil (iv, 12)	7
	The Spring Meditations for Sestius and Torquatus (i, 4 and iv, 7)	14
2.	VIRGIL'S TRAGIC QUEEN	29
3.	EMERGENCE OF A FORM: THE LATIN SHORT POEM	59
4.	DRAMATIC MONOLOGUE IN THE ODES OF HORACE	84
5.	TACITUS' NARRATIVE TECHNIQUE	110
6.	PROPERTIUS, HORACE, AND THE POET'S ROLE	130
	The Importance of Propertius	130
	The Crisis in Roman Love Poetry	141
	The Elegiac Compromise	148
	Horace's Assault on Love Elegy	154
	The Search for Fresh Solutions	162
7.	PROPERTIUS AND THE POETRY OF THE INTELLECT	167
	The Power of Love (ii, 12)	168
	Death of the Lover (ii, 27)	182
	The Lover's Dream (ii, 26a)	187
8.	THE TEMPO OF VIRGILIAN EPIC	198
	Elliptical Narrative	202
	Interweaving	212
	Allusion	216
	The Narrative Sentence: Tenses	220
	The Death of Priam (ii, 506–58)	229

Contents

9. PERSISTENCE OF A THEME: THE PROPEMPTICON 239
    Propertius, the Passionate Lover (i, 8) 242
    Horace's Cautionary Tale (*Odes* iii, 27) 253
    Ovid, the Poseur (*Amores* ii, 11) 266

   LIST OF POEMS AND PASSAGES DISCUSSED 275

   INDEX 277

Preface

Latin Explorations, like my previous book, *The Catullan Revolution* (1959), is concerned with the critical discussion of Roman poetry. The main difference is one of emphasis. In *The Catullan Revolution* my aim was to offer a preliminary reassessment of the surviving work of one poet. A revision of common views about the nature and quality of the poetry of Catullus seemed to me overdue, and easiest brought about by a simple statement of the main issues. In *Latin Explorations* the sweep of the inquiry is broadened—half a dozen writers are discussed instead of one. But the focus is narrowed, to pick out aspects of these writers where a fresh approach seemed most needed; or general issues that had, I felt, to be clarified (by fairly full discussion) before a proper understanding could be reached of a single, rich literary tradition running from Catullus to Ovid—a movement that represents Roman literature's major, perhaps sole, contribution to serious poetry. From the unity of that tradition the book derives its unity: the topics of the individual chapters are not dealt with in isolation but in the context of an intensely cohering pattern of poetic experiment.

Six of the nine chapters deal with the Roman personal poets —a department of Roman poetry that has suffered almost as much from the practice of dividing a single literary tradition into three separate fields of research (Catullus, Horace and elegy) and two literary epochs (republican and Augustan) as from conventions of interpretation that sacrifice the spirit of the poetry to a rigorous scrutiny of the letter. The two chapters on Virgil illustrate different ways of applying the same method of responsive interrogation of the text to the study of a poet the vastness of whose canvas is apt to make us suppose—wrongly— that his techniques have nothing in common with those of the personal poets. I have added a chapter on Tacitus as a tentative demonstration of what a similar approach can reveal of

Preface

the work of a historian whose poet's instinct led him back to Virgil.

In making the English versions I have had chiefly in mind those who will want to read the Latin but may need help where the original is unfamiliar. But the versions are intended also as an interpretation of the Latin. My aim has been to express the original in English as natural as is appropriate. Here and there I have straightened out an obscurity, or simplified a detail where a literal translation was likely to do the reader a disservice by denying him the clue he needed. In a few places, too, where differences in idiom or in the connotations of words would have meant a literal translation that misrepresented the original, I have allowed myself more liberty than is customarily taken in the examination-room. The reader with little or no Latin will not, I think, be seriously misled; and he will find it more possible, I hope, to sense what the original is like.

A book like this owes much to others. In the first place to the commentators and interpreters whose industry and perspicacity reduce to manageable proportions the task of making sense of a Latin poem. I have been helped, too, by friends in many countries—in Europe, in the United States and Canada as well as in Australia and New Zealand. They will recognize much in these pages that shows the influence of their criticisms. I shall not expect them to lend their assent to every idea put forward in a work that cannot claim to offer more than the results of a fresh reconnaissance of ground long familiar but still very inadequately explored.

K. Q.

Melbourne
August 1962

Abbreviations

A.J.Ph.	*American Journal of Philology.*
A.P.	*Anthologia Palatina.*
Aumla	*Aumla: Journal of the Australasian Universities Language and Literature Association.*
Austin	R. G. Austin, *Aeneidos Liber Quartus* (1955).
Bailey	D. R. Shackleton Bailey, *Propertiana* (1956).
Butler and Barber	H. E. Butler and E. A. Barber, *The Elegies of Propertius* (1933).
Campbell	Archibald Y. Campbell, *Horace: A New Interpretation* (1924).
C.J.	*Classical Journal.*
Collinge	N. E. Collinge, *The Structure of Horace's Odes* (1961).
C.Ph.	*Classical Philology.*
C.Q.	*Classical Quarterly.*
C.R.	*Classical Review.*
Enk	P. J. Enk, *Sex. Propertii Elegiarum Liber I (Monobiblos)* (1946).
Fordyce	C. J. Fordyce, *Catullus: A Commentary* (1961).
Fraenkel	Eduard Fraenkel, *Horace* (1957).
Heinze	*Horaz*, Kiessling's commentary re-edited by R. Heinze; *Oden und Epoden* (8th edn. 1955).
Heinze *V.E.T.*	Richard Heinze, *Virgils Epische Technik* (3rd edn. 1914).
J.Ph.	*Journal of Philology.*
Mackail	J. W. Mackail, *The Aeneid* (1930).
N.G.G.	*Nachrichten der Akademie der Wissenschaften in Göttingen.*
N.J.	*Neue Jahrbücher für das klassische Altertum.*
N.J.A.B.	*Neue Jahrbücher für Antike und deutsche Bildung.*
Pasquali	Giorgio Pasquali, *Orazio Lirico* (1920).

Abbreviations

P.C.Ph.S.	*Proceedings of the Cambridge Philological Society.*
Pease	Arthur Stanley Pease, *Publi Vergili Maronis Aeneidos Liber Quartus* (1935).
Ph.	*Philologus.*
Quinn	Kenneth Quinn, *The Catullan Revolution* (1959).
R.A.L.	*Rendiconti della Classe di scienze morali e storiche dell'Accademia dei Lincei, Roma.*
R.E.	Paulys *Real-Encyclopädie der classischen Altertumswissenschaft;* neue Bearbeitung von G. Wissowa *et al.* (1894–).
R.E.L.	*Revue des études latines.*
Rothstein	M. Rothstein, *Die Elegien des Sextus Propertius* (Vol. i, 2nd edn. 1920).
T.A.Ph.A.	*Transactions of the American Philological Association.*
T.L.L.	*Thesaurus linguae latinae* (1900–).
Wilkinson	L. P. Wilkinson, *Horace and his Lyric Poetry* (1945).
Williams	R. D. Williams, *Aeneidos Liber Quintus* (1960).
Y.Cl.S.	*Yale Classical Studies.*

1

Horace's Spring Odes

To what extent can we judge a Latin poem the way we judge poems in our own language? The poem's meaning in the humblest sense we usually can decide, more surely than we can tease a meaning from the words of many English poems. But a good poem offers the reader things subtler than plain communication. To these his reaction also must be subtle. Upon it may depend his ability to grasp the poem's real meaning. When we read a poem written two thousand years ago in Latin, can we hope to react as the poet intended to the elements in his poem transcending plain communication? If we cannot, is it not presumption to sit in judgment upon the poet's success? May we as much as pronounce his poem good or bad? As for pretending to found our judgment upon intimate contact with the poem—attempting the sort of structural analysis and appraisal of detail that the critic of modern poetry employs to reinforce initial impressions—does this not demand a feeling for a dead language we cannot honestly claim to possess?

The intervention of the literary critic in classical studies is regarded by many, understandably, with suspicion. There are at least three things that are said against him. The first is that his is a game scholars shouldn't play—because it involves a subjective approach to classical literature incompatible with the impersonal role of scholarship. It is a point of view that is often held, but it is really quite untenable. For clearly, even in the course of the most scholarly tasks, scholars must make subjective decisions. Indeed if they didn't, classics would be a laborious and arid discipline, doing little to sharpen the faculty of judgment, or our ability to measure quality in the statement, or representation, of human values—not worth anyone's trouble except the specialist's. The scholar-critic antithesis is a false one—and a comparatively recent one in the long history of classical studies. It dates from the rise in nineteenth-century Germany of a tradition of scientific scholarship that soon established itself throughout Europe and in America. In England the specially English tradition of the scholar who was also a critic worth listening to, a man who claimed the right to exercise culture and taste as well as learning, was challenged, and attempts were made, which never wholly succeeded, to impose on classical studies the stringent limitations of a new dispassionate professionalism.

A second objection to the classical literary critic deserves more attention. Those who put it forward admit the scholar is faced constantly with subjective decisions. They agree the interpretation of literature cannot be divorced from the appreciation of it. But they assert that this particular game, literary criticism, is not worth playing. It looks too much, they feel, like the intrusion of a fresh professionalism, hardly more to be desired than the other. It involves techniques they view with suspicion, even when applied to contemporary literature. The techniques produce clever people, they argue, but not people whose perception of human values, or even of quality in literature, is noticeably developed. Like Dr. Leavis they detect often 'a glib superficiality'[1] in the professional appraisal of literature; but they are not, like him, convinced that the profession has more substantial contributions to make to humane studies. They find unsettling the notion that good literature is hard to appreciate. Yet I doubt if their objections deserve much attention either. They boil down often to the well-known fact that some forms of ignorance are more comfortable than some forms of knowledge, especially those forms of knowledge that compel us to recognize factors which cannot be dealt with by the exercise of logic or the display of learning.

[1] F. R. Leavis, *Education and the University* (new edn. 1948), p. 8. Cf. the words of another distinguished critic, Lionel Trilling, 'The sense of the past', in *The Liberal Imagination* (English edn. 1951), p. 183:
> We often feel of them that they [the critics] make the elucidation of poetic ambiguity or irony a kind of intellectual callisthenic ritual.

Horace's Spring Odes

The most troubling objection raises the questions with which this chapter opens, and answers them by asserting that in classics literary criticism is a game that cannot honestly be played at all. The arguments here include those to which Virginia Woolf lent the weight of her persuasive eloquence in a famous essay, 'On not knowing Greek.'[1] However subjective we are prepared to be, it is maintained, however ingenious, we just can't get a grasp of things written in Latin or Greek tight enough or sure enough to permit worth-while critical opinions. Everything is too blurred, to put it another way, for us to see clearly. Everything becomes too blunt, if you like, to have any bite. The odd thing about this third objection is the ready acquiescence it wins from most scholars not irrevocably committed to either of the previous positions. Put it to them, and they will agree that they don't know Latin well enough to pass judgment on what they read. Yet the rest of the time it is obvious that these scholars (being men who like the classics) do allow themselves to pass judgment, publicly as well as privately, on what they read in Latin. Undoubtedly we miss a lot, are left unsure by things that did not trouble the contemporary reader, make mistakes he wouldn't have made. But all these things happen to the present-day English reader of Shakespeare, or to the American reader of Dylan Thomas—not to mention the French reader: can *he* really make as much of Dylan Thomas as we might of Virgil? Usually, of course, with a Roman poet it *is* harder. But the scholar who makes this third objection regards himself as belonging to a class of reader so specially under-privileged that criticism is not just prone to error but impossible. And he is apt to assume (wrongly, surely) that contemporary readers of Virgil missed nothing, knew *all* the things he realizes he doesn't know, made *no* mistakes.[2]

My purpose in this chapter is not to refute any of these three lines of objection by argument, for these are not issues where

[1] Virginia Woolf, 'On not knowing Greek', in *The Common Reader* (uniform edn. 1929), pp. 39–59.

[2] The case is well put in a recent article by Mr. Niall Rudd, 'Patterns in Horatian lyric', *A.J.Ph.*, lxxxi (1960), pp. 375–6:
> We need not imagine that a poem is some sort of concrete entity of which we could give a final and definitive account if only we had the necessary evidence. Certain aspects of the *Odes* eluded even the best-informed and most sympathetic of Horace's friends. . . . A poem will not be located. The most a critic can do in any age is to describe the area in which it moves.

Horace's Spring Odes

argument is effective. It is to show literary criticism in action, dealing with three poems about which evaluative judgments can hardly be avoided by any who claim to read Latin with pleasure. If we are sensible, we shall not expect final answers from our exercise in practical criticism; but we may hope to discover what answers are possible, and to explore methods of arriving at answers. We may then proceed to the application of these methods in the subsequent chapters to a variety of problems.

Horace wrote three odes about spring. In our texts they are numbered i, 4 (*Soluitur acris hiems grata uice ueris et Fauoni* ...), iv, 7 (*Diffugere niues, redeunt iam gramina campis* ...) and iv, 12 (*Iam ueris comites, quae mare temperant* ...). Two are famous, the third seldom much praised.[1] That looks already like the beginnings of critical discrimination, and as a matter of fact scholars have passed judgment on the poetic quality of the three poems with some assurance. Unhappily they disagree. A. E. Housman, who made a fine poem of his own out of iv, 7, pronounced it, we are told, in an unguarded moment, 'the most beautiful poem in ancient literature'. Mr. L. P. Wilkinson thinks he is right.[2] Dr. Eduard Fraenkel is less sure. He is reluctant to contradict two eminent Cambridge Horatians openly; but his enthusiasm for iv, 7 is lukewarm. '*Diffugere nives* ... is certainly an accomplished poem,' he admits; 'but,' he goes on, 'we should not use its perfection to slight its lovely forerunner.'[3] On the other hand this sneaking preference for the gracefulness of i, 4 abates when a closer look at both reveals the greater seriousness of iv, 7.[4]

---

[1] A cautious rehabilitation is attempted by Fraenkel, p. 418:
This ode, *Iam veris comites*, is not distinguished by depth of feeling or novelty of detail, and yet it is one of Horace's truly felicitous poems. Several traditional topics merge into a graceful whole.

[2] The wording of Housman's remark given by Wilkinson, p. 40, differs slightly. I have quoted it in the version given by a former student in a letter to *The Times* (5 May 1936), quoted by Grant Richards, *Housman 1897-1936* (1941), p. 289:
... One morning in May, 1914, ... he reached in his lecture Ode 7 in Horace's Fourth Book. ... This ode he dissected with the usual display of brilliance, wit, and sarcasm. Then for the first time in two years he looked up at us, and in quite a different voice said: 'I should like to spend the last few minutes considering this ode simply as poetry.' Our previous experience of Professor Housman would have made us sure that he would regard such a proceeding as beneath contempt. He read the ode aloud with deep emotion, first in Latin and then in an English translation of his own. 'That,' he said hurriedly, almost like a man betraying a secret, 'I regard as the most beautiful poem in ancient literature.' ...

[3] Fraenkel, p. 419.   [4] Ibid., pp. 420-1.

Horace's Spring Odes

We may put down Fraenkel's noble volume, and its many tributes to the greatness of Horace's poetry, not seriously disturbed. He agrees after all with Housman as much as we might expect two very different men to agree about a poem both clearly liked. It is when we come to consider what has been written in Germany about these odes that we feel the first spasm of apprehensive despair in our pursuit of scholarly guidance. Wilamowitz, that giant of *klassische Philologie*, is no less sure, but his opinion of the poem his English counterpart was to call (a few months later) the most beautiful in ancient literature is poor indeed. He thought no better of iv, 12. In a discussion of the odes of Book IV published in 1913, he dismissed both impatiently as 'unimportant poems about spring' (*unbedeutende Frühlingslieder*), and passed on quickly to discuss, with more enthusiasm and sympathy, the eleventh and thirteenth odes of the same book.[1] Turn now to the standard German commentator on Horace, Richard Heinze. He is more cautious, but admits he finds iv, 7 'poetically weaker' (*poetisch ärmer*) than i, 4. The words occur in his discussion of i, 4.[2] When he comes to deal with iv, 7, he seems to find reasons for preferring that poem.[3]

We need hardly pursue further our consultation of eminent scholars. Others will continue, if with less authority, the disagreement we have noted between Housman and Wilamowitz, commonly reckoned the two greatest classical scholars of our century. Is this then really, perhaps, a situation where only personal fancy is arbiter and plain assertion the only means of communicating judgment? We should pause a moment before we smile at Housman and Wilamowitz. Both perhaps believed one liked a poem, or didn't, and that was the end of it. *De gustibus non est disputandum*, they might say, contemptuous of our efforts to push the matter further. It was a position commonly adopted, during much of the nineteenth century and after, by Romantic critics (and, in so far as they were critics at all, both

[1] U. von Wilamowitz-Moellendorff, *Sappho und Simonides* (1913), p. 321 (quoted by Wilkinson, but the context is worth looking at to see how plain Wilamowitz's enthusiasm is for iv, 11 and 13): 'Ungleich schöner klingt die Mahnung an die verrauschende Zeit in den beiden Mädchenliedern.'

[2] Heinze, p. 26.

[3] E.g. ibid., p. 424:
Während in der Sestiusode neben der zum Lebensgenuss lockenden Frühlingslust der Gedanke an den Tod als zweites Motiv auftritt und somit die Komposition auseinanderklafft, ist hier Einheitlichkeit gewonnen.

Horace's Spring Odes

Housman and Wilamowitz were that). Of the period Mr. F. W. Bateson has written:

> To the Romantics, with their predilections for 'ecstasy' and 'magic', poetic preferences were necessarily reduced to a matter of private, personal taste. There could be no *theoretic* basis for any critical standards at all. On one man the 'magic' worked; on another it didn't.[1]

Mr. Bateson's logic perhaps nudges the Romantics further than most of them would have gone of their own accord. Even the Romantics, one suspects, recognized common agreement on the more obvious issues, while reserving the right to conscientious objection at the inexplicable promptings of taste. All the same the Romantic position is one that hardly any literary critic today would accept. The classical scholar, if he pleads *De gustibus non est disputandum*, must be prepared to live in intellectual isolation. If he is sensible, he will fall back on the sounder argument (our third objection) that the special difficulties of his subject make judgment impossible. But in that case he will have to admit that both Housman and Wilamowitz were wrong in expressing an opinion at all.

We can, of course, explain the clash in their opinions with some completeness in terms of things external to the poems discussed. It is not difficult to recognize in Wilamowitz's attitude the effect of Goethe's doctrine of lyric poetry as personal confession, a quality not apparent in Horace's odes, unless one takes his love poems *au pied de la lettre*, as presumably Wilamowitz did not.[2] Goethe's opinion of Horace's poetry is well known, if not vouched for beyond dispute: technical perfection, but no real poetry, apart from a terrible realism (*eine furchtbare Realität*).[3] There is *furchtbare Realität* in iv, 13, as we shall see

[1] F. W. Bateson, *English Poetry: A Critical Introduction* (1950), p. 62.

[2] The orthodox German view since Lessing's *Rettungen des Horaz* is that Horace's love poetry is pure fiction. See T. Zieliński, 'De Lydia Lalageque et aliis', in Polska Akademija, *Commentationes horatianae* (1935).

[3] The authority for Goethe's opinion of Horace's lyric poetry is a record of a remark made in conversation in November 1806 (F. Frhr. von Biedermann, *Goethes Gespräche*, [1909], i, p. 458):
Sein poetisches Talent anerkannt nur in Absicht auf technische und Sprachvollkommenheit, d.h. Nachbildung der griechischen Metra und der poetischen Sprache, nebst einer furchtbaren Realität, ohne alle eigentliche Poesie, besonders in den Oden.—*Note cont'd opposite*

Horace's Ode to Virgil (iv, 12)

in Chapter 4. It is not difficult, therefore, to understand why Wilamowitz, who after all honestly wanted to like his Horace, should have been impatient to get to grips with something that his standards, based on Goethe, would allow him to regard as good, and a little closer to the note the master struck in his *Römische Elegien*. Housman, on the other hand, is an English Romantic of the Keatsian kind, 'half in love with easeful death'. His own preoccupation with death, so prominent in his poetry, attracts him to those odes that reveal Horace's intimations of mortality; though Horace's realistic Epicureanism, tinged with a characteristically Roman sadness (one thinks of Virgil), has in fact little in common with Housman's more morbid melancholy.

Horace's Ode to Virgil (iv, 12)

Of course the real answer must lie in the three poems themselves, in their characteristics, not in the characteristics of their critics. Are the impressions they produce on sensitive readers bound to be arbitrary and contradictory? At this stage a look at the poems may help to clear the air. Even before we are sure what sort of competition we are organizing between them, I think we can pretty easily place one of the competitors. The ode to Virgil (iv, 12) is surely weaker than the other two. Let us look at it quickly stanza by stanza, and see if we should not be justified in eliminating it as not up to competition standards. Actually it begins well:

> Iam ueris comites, quae mare temperant,
> impellunt animae lintea Thraciae;
> iam nec prata rigent nec fluuii strepunt
>   hiberna niue turgidi.

> *See! spring's entourage, the living breath of Thrace,*
> *assails canvas on an ocean that it calms.*
> *See! no more are meadows stiff, no rivers din,*
> *bloated with winter snow.*

For *furchtbaren*, E. Grumach, *Goethe und die Antike* (1949), p. 366, ingenuously conjectures *fruchtbaren*.

    Though much interested in certain departments of classical literature (e.g. the Homeric question and Propertius), Goethe appears to have known mainly the hexameter essays of Horace (which he read in a German translation) and to have interested himself hardly at all in the odes.

Horace's Spring Odes

The excitement of early spring is quickly and simply caught by the opening *iam* of the first and third lines—a device borrowed from Catullus.[1] With the coming of spring, gentle westerly breezes (the Greeks called them Zephyrs) succeed the equinoctial gales, appearing to calm the sea in readiness for the resumption of navigation (suspended during the winter). The breezes also warm the land, hastening the return of vegetation, and bringing the thaw in the mountains. There is little scope for originality in a description of the spring scene, as Pasquali's collection of Greek epigrams, in which these clichés keep recurring, shows.[2] More vividly than these, the Roman reader would recall Lucretius' detailed development of the theme in his opening hymn to Venus. Horace's first aim, then, is the deft manipulation of these clichés, the economical, oblique evocation of the stock ideas I have listed with the loose, flat explicitness of prose. He employs the opposite technique to Lucretius' rich, full dignity. His second aim is to transform these evocative fragments of clichés into fresh verbal poetry of his own. He sets out from one of those half-personifications congenial to the Roman mind.[3] Spring arrives, like an important official, with his retainers (*comites*; the idea was taken up by Charles d'Orléans in the fifteenth century in his charming lyric '*Les fourriers d'Esté sont venus . . .*'). The personification of the winds is reinforced by a nice piece of verbal poetry: the retainers are spoken of as *animae Thraciae*—a pun on ἄνεμοι, the ordinary Greek word for winds. Horace has in mind very likely the purple passage in *Iliad* xxiii where Iris summons the winds to kindle the pyre of Patroclus (*Iliad* xxiii, 192–230). Their work done, the winds make their way home:

οἱ δ' ἄνεμοι πάλιν αὖτις ἔβαν οἰκόνδε νέεσθαι
Θρηίκιον κατὰ πόντον.[4]

Horace, of course, sacrifices geography a little for the sake of literary allusion. But *animae* also depends on the Lucretian phrase *animae uentorum*, which gives its support to the idea of the

---
[1] In Catullus' spring poem (46), four lines of the eleven begin with *iam*.
[2] Pasquali, pp. 331–2.
[3] For Roman habits of half-personification, see the discussion of Propertius ii, 12 in Chapter 7.
[4] Apollonius uses the phrase ἀνέμοισιν Θρηικίοις (i, 954–5).

Horace's Ode to Virgil (iv, 12)

winds as something living (*ueris comites*). In line 2 we have the image of the swelling sails: the expressive word *lintea* suggests the spreading canvas much better than the everyday word *uela*.[1] The winds' urgent energy, too, is well suggested in *impellunt*. We then pass to the land. The fairly bald *iam nec prata rigent* expects perhaps rather much of the reader, who has to draw upon his memory of spring clichés and remember that the *ueris comites*, by their warmth, soften the frozen fields. The last line of the stanza is better: we can see the snow melting into the river. The only real blemish in the stanza is the weakish relative clause *quae mare temperant*: what it says is relevant (the winds appear to calm the sea), but it says it flatly and we do not feel that the clause has been properly incorporated in the otherwise tight verbal organization of the stanza.

The relative clause looks in fact like one of the consequences of a decision, fatal to the poem's success, to group its statements in seven blocks of sense, each occupying a stanza.[2] We see this more clearly in stanza 2:

> nidum ponit Ityn flebiliter gemens   5
> infelix auis et Cecropiae domus
> aeternum opprobrium, quod male barbaras
> regum est ulta libidines.

> *Mourning Itys sadly, his luckless swallow-mother*
> *builds her nest, symbol everlasting of the shame*
> *for Cecrops' house—at retribution misapplied*
> *to king's barbaric lust.*

---

[1] Actually *lintea* seems to be a technical term rather than a literary word. Horace perhaps got it from Catullus (Poems 4, 5; 64, 225 and 243). Horace uses it a couple of times more in *Epodes* 16, line 27, and *Odes* i, 14 line 9—perhaps another of his calculatedly unpoetic words. See B. Axelson, *Unpoetische Wörter* (1945), pp. 98–113.

[2] The unusualness of this in Horace is noted by Fraenkel, p. 418, Note 3, but he regards as one of the poem's merits 'the neat separation of each stanza from the subsequent one'. Here is a good example of one of the critic's difficulties: the near impossibility of drawing attention to a detail of a poem's structure without describing it in words loaded with the critic's approval or disapprobation. It seems to me clear that Horace went to some trouble in this poem to secure stanza-by-stanza organization of the sense. To me that in itself seems a weakness in the poem— one that Fraenkel glosses over when he says 'several traditional topics merge into a graceful whole'. This is perhaps slippery ground, though, and one's reactions are liable to vary according to whether one takes iv, 12 as a comparatively early poem or a late poem. Along with Bowra and Rand (but not Fraenkel) I regard the poem as early. My objection to the way in which the sense of several stanzas is filled out by clumsy, or otiose, phrases is, I hope, independent of assumptions about date.

Horace's Spring Odes

We feel that last line and a half stumble on with something less than Horace's customary restraint. (Lack of restraint is perhaps the main thing wrong with this ode.) The stanza passes from the actual to the mythological scene (a regular device and one Horace is fond of), to make verbal poetry out of another spring cliché, the return of the swallow. The touch of fanciful cleverness in showing us a swallow making its nest and assuming this particular swallow is unhappy Procne comes off quite well. But the *quod*-clause that completes the stanza is otiose. Horace has made his moral point by the middle of line 3. The *quod*-clause introduces an unnecessary emphasis, a strained rhetorical note, that bear again the marks of padding.

Another consequence of making a whole stanza out of the swallow cliché (instead of, say, a one-and-a-half-line glance) is that the emotional incitement of stanza 1 has not been maintained, and can no longer contribute, therefore, to the effect of spontaneity which the invitation at the beginning of stanza 4 should produce.

Stanza 3 amplifies the rural scene implied by the previous stanza:

> dicunt in tenero gramine pinguium
> custodes ouium carmina fistula   10
> delectantque deum cui pecus et nigri
>   colles Arcadiae placent.

> *Stretched out upon the young grass, among*
> *their plump sheep, the shepherds pipe their songs,*
> *gladdening the god, whose joy is herds and those*
> *sombre hills of Arcady.*

But once more there is obvious padding. Horace has decided to make a stanza out of this pastoral vignette (in which only the young grass reminds us his theme is spring), but has failed to back up his decision with an adequate flow of invention. The first two lines are elegantly-phrased pastoral cliché, the dactylic rhythm underlining the pastoral echoes. The opening words of the next line, *delectantque deum*, neatly introduce the notion of divine approval. The trouble is the relative clause at the end. Some identification of the god is needed, of course. But Horace's gauche circumlocution does not earn its keep. Moreover *placent*

Horace's Ode to Virgil (iv, 12)

needlessly repeats *delectant*, and *nigri colles Arcadiae* is going to get Horace into trouble by starting us thinking about a scene that turns out to be remote from the dramatic scene of the next stanza, which contains the poem's central idea and presumably the scene Horace wants as his central scene.

The real reason for stanza 3 is revealed when we come to stanza 4. It opens with a good vigorous phrase and appears to bring in the name of Virgil naturally after a stanza filled with echoes of the *Eclogues*:[1]

> adduxere sitim tempora, Vergili;
> sed pressum Calibus ducere Liberum
> si gestis, iuuenum nobilium cliens,   5
> nardo uina merebere.

Days like these, Virgil, raise our thirst. But,
if a draught of wine pressed in Cales is what you want
(intimate of our nation's young elite), you must
barter wine with scent.

Unfortunately, by the time those pastoral echoes have been worked in, along with all the spring clichés, Horace has lost contact completely with the mood of excitement at spring's coming aroused by the opening stanza. After the sombre hills of Arcady, particularly, the statement *adduxere sitim tempora* does not carry conviction. What is wanted is a build-up of bright sun, the midday warmth of a spring day, shepherds if you like, but lying down in the shade to escape the sun. Then Horace might convincingly say 'days like these raise our thirst'. Moreover the jocular tone introduced in this stanza and continued in stanzas 5

[1] For details of these reminiscences of the *Eclogues* see C. M. Bowra, *C.R.*, xlii (1928), pp. 165–7, and E. Adelaide Hahn, *T.A.Ph.A.*, lxxvi (1945), pp. xxxii–xxxiii. Most scholars, including Fraenkel, deny the Virgil addressed is the poet; a notable recent exception is Collinge, pp. 75–6. To assume Vergilius is not the poet seems to me (*a*) *a priori* improbable and in clear contradiction of Fraenkel's dictum that 'Horace, throughout his work, shows himself both determined and able to express everything that is relevant to the understanding and the appreciation of a poem' (p. 26); how could Horace not expect us to assume Vergilius is *the* Vergilius? (*b*) negligent of the obvious echoes of the *Eclogues*; (*c*) needless, if we assume, as we easily can, that iv, 12 is an early poem, revived for inclusion in Book IV. See my arguments, 'Two crises in Horace's poetical career', in *Aumla*, No. 5 (1956), pp. 34–43. Those who claim to find offensive the publication of these light-hearted *uersiculi* after Virgil's death seem to me over-sensitive.

and 6 is not convincingly reconciled with the seriously poetic tone of the first three stanzas.[1]

The poem's ostensible object, an invitation to a party, now emerges. The next two stanzas need concern us less. Their object is to build up a picture of the poet keen to entertain his friend, but short of the wherewithal to do so. Stanza 5 is nicely done, as a piece of badinage:

> nardi paruus onyx eliciet cadum,
> qui nunc Sulpiciis accubat horreis,
> spes donare nouas largus amaraque
>   curarum eluere efficax.   20

> *A modest flacon will serve to coax a jar for you*
> *that's reposing now in* Cellars of Sulpicii,
> *generous hope-provider, active neutralizer*
> *of the bitter cares of life.*

But observe that the second line appears to fix the dramatic scene of the poem beyond argument at Rome and not in the country as we might have expected from the preceding stanzas —unless we are to take this line, too, as irrelevant embellishment, on the same footing as the sombre hills of Arcady.[2]

---

[1] Mr. N. E. Collinge has recently argued that this 'extraordinary passage of back-slapping heartiness' (as he calls lines 13–24) forms part of 'a neat triadic plan of thought'. When we get to the final stanza, he maintains, 'the bluffness of 13–24 is seen to be an assumed, unnatural, over-drawn pose, revealing here and there the real pessimism beneath'. (Collinge, pp. 74–7.) His arguments deserve attention, but they seem to me to illustrate another of the difficulties that face the critic of poetry: that of keeping his criticism of a poem focused on what the poet actually wrote. Examination of the *argumentative structure* of a poem may reveal an attractive intellectual pattern—here the contrast in mood. But this contrast in mood is only potentially a quality of the poem until it has been successfully embodied in the *poetic structure*. In the present example the transitions in mood seem to me clumsily contrived, and the mood of the first three stanzas too alien to that of the next three for the whole to be welded into any satisfying artistic unity by stanza 7. Collinge in other words seems to me to be praising some of the ideas behind the poem, not the poem.

[2] Or involve ourselves in improbable assumptions, like Pasquali, p. 331, Note 1:
> A me sembra almeno probabile che il poeta inviti Virgilio in campagna: solo se s'intende così, il carme acquista vera unità.

Yes, but the jar of wine,
> il bariletto . . .sarà stato trasportato per mare da Minturno a Roma, per esser poi carreggiato di lì fino alla villa Sabina di Orazio.

When we have to resort to conjecture on this scale, we should start to suspect bad craftsmanship on the part of the poet.

Horace's Ode to Virgil (iv, 12)

Horace's desire to work in complimentary allusions to a fellow poet and to demonstrate his own talent for pastoral has seriously damaged the poem's coherence. Once more we get the impression of early work: Horace, full of admiration for Virgil, his own reputation as a lyric poet not yet established, is just a little too keen to show Virgil what he can do (hence the seriously poetic stanzas) and to show us how well he knows Virgil (hence the forced note of intimacy).

Stanza 6 is weak:

> ad quae si properas gaudia, cum tua   21
> uelox merce ueni: non ego te meis
> immunem meditor tingere poculis,
>   plena diues ut in domo.

> *Does a party tantalize? Come soon and*
> *bring your wares. I have not the least intention*
> *of plying you with cups brimmed unpaid,*
> *like rich man entertaining.*

To some extent Horace holds himself in check perhaps in order to round things off with a strong final stanza. But one suspects he has laid out his poem on the basis of three stanzas leading up to the invitation stanza, and then three more, and has run a little short of material for stanza 6: *ad quae si properas gaudia*, another relative clause, unnecessarily echoes *si gestis* and clashes with *uelox ueni*, and even more awkwardly with *uerum pone moras* in the next stanza.

The final stanza, judged on its own merits, is on the whole adequate:

> uerum pone moras et studium lucri,   25
> nigrorumque memor, dum licet, ignium
> misce stultitiam consiliis breuem:
>   dulce est desipere in loco.

> *No putting off, materialist! Recall instead*
> *the murky pyre's flames and (too late soon),*
> *planning dropped, act the goat a while:*
> *fooling, in its place, is fun.*

True, *studium lucri* (Horace perhaps means haggling over the

Horace's Spring Odes

bargain he proposes) is a bit obscure—as we can see from the way it has worried commentators.[1] True, the phrase *dum licet* is awkwardly placed: it looks as though it goes with *memor* (which would make very poor sense), but goes in fact with the following line. Against this, set two nicely memorable phrases, neatly juxtaposed so that one occupies the penultimate, the other the concluding line of the poem, the two achieving between them an acceptable moral note—in between profitless gloom and irresponsibility.

Here then is a poem which has obviously a lot wrong with it. Horace has not reached his customary high standard of compression or grace. The mood of the poem wanders, lacking Horace's usual economical drive. It is, after all, probably no more than an elaborate invitation to a party, on the model of Catullus' Poem 13, a piece of light-hearted virtuoso writing for Virgil's benefit. But even judging the poem at the level on which Horace intends it, we have frequent cause to be dissatisfied. Everything in fact is consistent with the assumption that this is an early poem included here by Horace in order to fill out the fourth book, still a slender collection, to something approaching acceptable dimensions.

The Spring Meditations for Sestius and Torquatus
(i, 4 *and* iv, 7)

The other two spring odes produce a very different initial impression. To the sensitive reader they are, obviously and immediately, poetry in a way that iv, 12 is not. To begin with, the writing is tighter: we do not notice so readily phrases that are unessential and detachable—the sort of thing that left us with a feeling of padding in iv, 12. More important than that, these are not poems pretending to be invitations or witty argument with a friend. They have a single serious purpose: to hold our attention as poems should, by making a worth-while claim upon our emotions and our thoughts.[2]

---

[1] The neatest suggestion is Walter Wili's (*Horaz und die augusteische Kultur* [1948], p. 358), that Virgil is invited to bring a poem with him.

[2] I am not suggesting a hierarchy of poems according to their philosophical content. Poems are poems, not sermons, or anything else. But a poem in which the thinking is loose, casual or frivolous usually does not result in that effort for intense, complete expression that we find in a good poem.

The Spring Meditations for Sestius and Torquatus

The two have enough in common to make it convenient to discuss them together. A word of warning is needed however. Their obvious similarities should not lead us to regard them as more or less alternative versions of the same poem. Heinze's words in introducing iv, 7 are typical of the approach of those more impressed by what the poems have in common than by their individual features:[1]

> We might hazard a guess that Torquatus [the addressee of iv, 7], . . . attracted by the other poem [i, 4], has asked his friend for a similar one for himself: in the way we approach a painter for the repetition of a favourite picture in someone else's possession.

If there are differences between the two odes, Heinze goes on to suggest, it only goes to show 'what the artist has learnt in the interval' (*was der Künstler inzwischen hinzugelernt hat*).[2]

Now, firstly, there are poets with whom it would be reasonable to look for special circumstances if one found two poems resembling one another as much as these two. With Horace this is scarcely called for. One of the most striking features of the odes is the way Horace several times makes more than one poem out of a particular theme or set of ideas.[3] Secondly, a little careful attention shows how superficial one's reading of the two poems must be to regard one ode as a repetition (*Wiederholung*) of the other, differing only because of 'what the artist has learnt in the interval'. There are clear and important differences in the two poems, not only in their structure (about which

---

[1] Heinze, p. 424:
Man möchte vermuten, dass Torquatus . . . , von jenem Lied begeistert, den Freund um ein ähnliches für sich selbst gebeten habe: wie man wohl einen Maler um die Wiederholung eines in anderem Besitz befindlichen Lieblingsbildes angeht.
(Observe the influence here of Heinze's view of the odes as occasional poetry—see Chapter 4.)

[2] Yet on p. 26 Heinze found iv, 7 'poetically weaker' than i, 4.

[3] Heinze's statement on iv, 7, therefore, that it is '*mit . . . I 4 so nahe verwandt, wie kein anderes Paar horazischer Oden*' (which seems to me, incidentally, quite wrong on the fact explicitly stated: ii, 3 and ii, 14 for example are at least as closely related) is misleading in its implication that there is something unusual about the relationship of i, 4 and iv, 7, something calling for excusal.

On Horace's fondness for using the same theme more than once, see E. Howald, *Das Wesen der lateinischen Dichtung* (1948).

Horace's Spring Odes

Heinze says something) or even their tone (as pointed out by Fraenkel), but even in what they explicitly communicate, the statements made, the theme itself.

Let us deal with this last point of difference first. There are at least three reasons why we should begin with the theme. First, the differences in theme are commonly disregarded. Second, it is the differences in theme that justify the differences in structure: we shall see that the simpler structure of i, 4 and the more complex structure of iv, 7 are determined by what the poems have to say, and not necessarily (or at all) a consequence of the poet's having learnt his business better in the interval between the two. Third, the failure to observe how different the poems are in what they say has caused them to be regarded as alternatives. The assumption generally made that, in discussing either, we must make up our minds whether or not we prefer it to the other, is largely founded on the belief that the poems are two shots by Horace at the same thing.

What happens in fact is interesting enough to divert our attention for a moment. The scholar who knows his Horace intimately usually feels he somehow likes one of these poems more than the other. Believing they are two shots at the same thing, he is naturally inclined to believe that the poem that appeals less should be rejected. When we realize, however, that the odes are too unalike to be regarded as alternative versions of the same thing, the position becomes different. The individual reader may well prefer one to the other, but there can be removed from his preference any critical rejection of the poem not preferred. And, actually, as far as preferences go, a more intimate, and therefore more discriminating, possession of the two poems and a clearer perception of their individuality may lead to a reversal of our initial preference.

The poems are about spring, but the moment the two describe is quite different. In i, 4 spring is just beginning:

> Soluitur acris hiems grata uice ueris et Fauoni,
>   trahuntque siccas machinae carinas,
> ac neque iam stabulis gaudet pecus aut arator igni,
>   nec prata canis albicant pruinis.
>
> (i, 4, 1–4)

The Spring Meditations for Sestius and Torquatus

Winter's grip relaxed, spring's quickening winds are welcome back.
The winches drag the dry hulls.
Beasts now are not happy in their stalls, ploughman at his fire, fields not white with hoary frost.

It is the moment when we suddenly realize, from the evidence about us, from something in the air, that spring is here and winter on its way out. Everywhere activity is beginning to succeed the inertia of winter. One image in this stanza crowded with images looks forward: the winches drag down to the water the dried-out hulls of ships laid up for the winter. Then two images, cattle herded in the stalls, ploughman sitting idly by the fire, presented neither as things still present nor as things already gone, for the emphasis is on that something in the air which makes man and beast impatient (*neque iam gaudet*) with the warm laziness they enjoyed during the winter months. Finally an image of something already gone: the fields white (and inert) with heavy frost.

In iv, 7, on the other hand, spring is well advanced:

> Diffugere niues, redeunt iam gramina campis
>   arboribusque comae;
> mutat terra uices, et decrescentia ripas
>   flumina praetereunt.
>
>   (iv, 7, 1–4)

The snow's all fled away, the grass returns in the meadows, the trees wear their leaves again.
Earth runs through its changes: streams, not swollen now, slide between their banks.

No longer any trace of snow. The fields are lush with grass, the trees are regaining their foliage. The rivers which had been swollen at the thaw (as in iv, 12) have now fallen again to normal levels. Things are in process of happening in nature (*mutat terra uices*), not just starting to happen. The opening word *diffugere* ('escaped in different directions') is exact, though one does not get the image clear until the stanza is complete: it aptly describes the masses of mountain snow that sank into, and swelled, the streams which are only now beginning to regain

Horace's Spring Odes

their normal level after the thaw (lines 3–4). It is the one striking word in an otherwise flattish stanza. Housman's fine translation, at times admirably accurate, does the opening stanza more than justice.[1]

The natural scene gives place in both poems to a scene of fancy. More fully and more naturally in i, 4,

> iam Cytherea choros ducit Venus imminente Luna,
> iunctaeque Nymphis Gratiae decentes
> alterno terram quatiunt pede, dum grauis Cyclopum
> Vulcanus ardens uisit officinas,
>
> (i, 4, 5–8)

Cytherean Venus leads her dance now beneath a hanging moon;
together nymphs and graces neat
tap the ground, first one foot then the next; Vulcan ruddy-faced
inspects his busy Cyclops' factory,

because we can think of the Venus that dances beneath the hanging moon as the *alma Venus* of Lucretius' opening hymn to the spring goddess (i, 2–4):

> alma Venus, caeli subter labentia signa
> quae mare nauigerum, quae terras frugiferenteis
> concelebras . . .

> *fostering Venus, who beneath the sliding stars*
> *the ship-laden ocean, the fruitful land,*
> *crowdest with life. . . .*

And Vulcan, of course, is Venus' husband, who goes off to get his factory working again after the long sleep of winter. (Virgil,

---

[1] In Housman's first stanza,

> The snows are fled away, leaves on the shaws
>   And grasses in the mead renew their birth,
> The river to the river-bed withdraws,
>   And altered is the fashion of the earth,

'shaws' sets a Romantic, 'poetic' note that is misleading. There is no specially poetic flavour in the words Horace uses, beyond a trace perhaps in *comae*, and 'mead' would have done enough to get that amount of poetic flavour in the English. Then 'renew their birth' introduces into the opening stanza a first statement of the poem's philosophical theme that is absent from the original. On the other hand, Housman's past participle in line 4 obscures the argument—Horace is talking of change in progress, not change completed.

The Spring Meditations for Sestius and Torquatus

perhaps, remembered Horace's vivid vignette when he came to describe Vulcan arriving in the forge of the Cyclopes in *Aeneid* viii to forge the arms of Aeneas.)

The corresponding section of iv, 7 is less convincing:

> Gratia cum Nymphis geminisque sororibus audet
>   ducere nuda choros.
>
> (iv, 7, 5–6)

A Grace, with her the nymphs and her twin sisters, dares naked to lead the dance.[1]

The opening *mood* of the two poems is also different. It is, in fact, the difference between joy and resignation. For i, 4 expresses the world's joy at earth's awakening after the near-death sleep of winter. The opening lines are full of activity, or impatience to be active. The opening couplet sketches in the scene vividly. Then the mood is sharpened in the next two couplets by the repeated *iam* (lines 3 and 5) and sustained by the repeated *nunc* (each time beginning a line) in lines 9 and 11. The dance, words and sound suggest, is a vigorous, strongly rhythmical, joyous one: *alterno terram quatiunt pede* (the words suggest both sound and picture). There is none of this mood in iv, 7. No activity of man or beast in the natural scene, only steady change in nature. The dance of the Graces and nymphs has all suggestion of emotion withheld. Their function is to point to the mildness of mid-spring weather, not to mark the excitement of spring freshly come.

In i, 4 the scene is dramatic, full of an impulse to joy that reflection will quickly show to be unjustified. Sudden joy is followed, we shall see, by an equally sudden foreboding of grief. In iv, 7 there is nothing dramatic in the mid-spring scene. It is only gradually, as a result of reflection, that we find dictated a mood of resignation as we inwardly contemplate the continuing procession of the seasons and piece together their message that nothing lasts. In i, 4 Venus, Vulcan and their entourage build up to a climax alien to Horace's purpose in iv, 7.

---

[1] Heinze's explanation, p. 425, brings out the inherent prosiness of the idea: Das Epitheton [*nuda*] besagt natürlich nicht, dass die Grazien sic him Winter wärmer kleiden, sondern . . . wagen sie sich erst jetzt in die freie Natur.

Horace's Spring Odes

Once this is realized, we can understand how the *lay-out* of the two poems is necessarily different. I, 4 began with a juxtaposition: that moment, between winter and spring, when the two seasons confront one another. Now we have four more lines of fresh details of scene (the real one again, not the fanciful one), in which a more personal note emerges in the poem's mood of joy and thankfulness for life's goodness:

> nunc decet aut uiridi nitidum caput impedire myrto
> aut flore terrae quem ferunt solutae;
> nunc et in umbrosis Fauno decet immolare lucis,
> seu poscat agna siue malit haedo.
>
> (i, 4, 9–12)

Now's the time to twine green myrtle in hair that's sleekly groomed,
or a flower the softened earth has born.
Now's the time for sacrifice to Faunus in a shadowy grove,
whether he demand a lamb, or prefer a kid.

Then unexpectedly (but spring, too, and the joy it brought came unexpectedly to those who did not look ahead) Horace introduces a juxtaposition on another plane. The reflective observer's joy at the coming to life again of the world after the sleep of winter needs restraining by thoughts of another sleep, from which there is no awakening; and of how the passage to it, too, can be abrupt and unforeseen:[1]

> pallida Mors aequo pulsat pede pauperum tabernas
> regumque turris.
>
> (i, 4, 13–14)

Pale death's blow comes steady at door of poor man's shop
and prince's tower.

The two parts of the poem are set side by side, with no transition. The device is brutally effective, though one that needs

---

[1] The proximity in the Roman calendar of the festival of Faunus and the festival of the dead, the Feralia, may have been in Horace's mind; but I find it unnecessary to suppose, with William Barr, *C.R.*, xii (1962), pp. 5–11, that the transition in Horace's poem depends on the reader's remembering this.

The Spring Meditations for Sestius and Torquatus

delicate handling and one to be used sparingly. On subsequent readings we see the two parts are linked by a sound effect which the sensitive reader perhaps caught subconsciously in earlier readings. The words *alterno pede* and their joyous context are caught up by the words *aequo pede*, the knock of death that comes, soon or late, to every man's door.[1] Horace brings off a discreetly calculated ambiguity: *aequo* suggests first the impartiality of death. Then, with *alterno terram quatiunt pede* working on our subconscious, *aequo* suggests the even, dispassionate knock of the pale visitor (*pallida Mors*) whose appearance, too, contrasts with the ruddy countenance of Vulcan just evoked and the faces of the dancers, flushed with excitement, that we have been picturing to ourselves.[2] These details, once observed, help us to perceive the structural unity of the poem, despite its abrupt change of mood: Pale Death stalking the streets is the last of Horace's spring tableaux—a joyless figure among the joyful figures.

Early spring, then, is the season of hope tempered with foreboding. A warning is necessary against letting hope run too far into the future:

o beate Sesti,
uitae summa breuis spem nos uetat incohare longam.
(i, 4, 14–15)

Sestius, fortune smiles, but
life's petty sum precludes initiating hopes that stretch ahead.

The key word is *incohare*—it implies often 'to begin and leave unfinished'. The bulkier, precise word stands out with stark

---

[1] Rudd, art. cit., pp. 379–80, in the course of a sensitive study of i, 4 discusses the structural effect of the echo *alterno pede . . . aequo pede*.

It is sometimes asserted that kicking at the door was the normal ancient equivalent of knocking. See O. Tescari's note in his edition, *I Carmi et gli Epodi* (1936); but it seems better to agree with Heinze, pp. 28–9, that in all the passages cited the demand for admittance is unusually imperious or sinister.

[2] Horace a number of times discreetly ties the parts of a poem together with a verbal echo. A good example is *Odes* iii, 30, where the north wind that is *impotens* ('possessing ineffectual strength') is contrasted with Horace himself, who (in his poetry) is *potens* ('possessing effective strength'). Another example is *Odes* i, 33, where *iungentur* (line 8) provides the overtones Horace wants for *iuga aenea* in line 11.

The words *alterno pede* ('first one foot, then the next') suggest primarily, I think, a visual picture—feet alternating along the line of dancers (for *alterna*, cf. Virgil *A.* v, 376: *alterna iactat bracchia*—of a boxer); but, bound up with that, a tempo and probably a rhythm very different from the steady kick of death.

Horace's Spring Odes

solemnity in a long line made up otherwise of words of one or two syllables.

The reflections in iv, 7 are more complicated: not an abrupt checking of hope and joy before they run too far, but a vague melancholy now the first joy of spring is over, which the poet proceeds to analyse. He starts with the observation that spring keeps changing. That observation carries his thoughts first back to winter, then forward to summer. He reflects then how summer will be followed by autumn, and autumn by winter once again.

> immortalia ne speres, monet annus et almum
>   quae rapit hora diem:
> frigora mitescunt Zephyris, uer proterit aestas
>   interitura simul
> pomifer Autumnus fruges effuderit, et mox
>   bruma recurrit iners.
>
> (iv, 7, 7–12)

Against immortal aspirations the year warns, and time that snatches off the life-bringing day:
the warm west wind mellows cold; summer tramples spring, soon itself to die, once
fruit-laden autumn has poured her produce out; soon then sluggish winter courses back.

The thoughts are not original but the scene in which they arise confers on them an inevitability, and the poet's personality an integrity (this is no poetaster, we feel, manipulating a commonplace), that convince us of their profundity and truth with a force and an economy unattainable by any intellectual statement of the propositions implied. This is one of the great functions of poetry and the quality of the writing here is admirably adequate to the demands made on it. Observe, for example, how *effuderit* with its suggestion of the prodigal abundance of life contrasts with *proterit* and its suggestion of life's ruthless brutality. How the opening word *immortalia* with its fine confident sound raises hopes that alternately fall and rise again during the next six lines, until dashed by the awful last word *iners*. Nothing in nature lasts, but, whereas the seasons form a cycle,

The Spring Meditations for Sestius and Torquatus

> damna tamen celeres reparant caelestia lunae
> (iv, 7, 13)

Yet the swift moons make good the wastage of the sky,[1]

it is not so with us:

> nos ubi decidimus
> quo pater Aeneas, quo Tullus diues et Ancus,
> puluis et umbra sumus.
> (iv, 7, 14–16)

*When we go down though
to join father Aeneas, rich Tullus and Ancus,
we are dust and shadow.*[2]

We can now begin to relate lay-out to mood and moment. Both poems pass from observation of nature to reflections on human mortality. But the different scenes provoking these reflections dictate different courses to the development of an idea that is fundamentally the same: man is mortal.

In the joy of beginning spring, the reflective man may bear in mind the imminence of death:

> iam te premet nox fabulaeque Manes
> et domus exilis Plutonia.
> (i, 4, 16–17)

*Soon night will be about you, the storied ghosts,
and Pluto's unsubstantial home.*

---

[1] The line has provoked an extraordinary amount of argument which we could well neglect to mention, if it were not symptomatic of a kind of feeling of guilt among scholars that asserts itself whenever they are confronted with a passage the literal prose meaning of which is unclear. The passage is only obscure to them, they imagine. The poet's contemporaries must have known what he meant. Collinge, pp. 96–7, says of this line:
  Horace is making the point that from day to day the loss from the visible zodiac at the western horizon... is balanced by the emergence of a fresh and equal section at the eastern, and from moon to moon the loss of a twelfth part by the appearance of a new twelfth.

[2] The reference to *pater Aeneas* is sometimes pointed to as a sign the poem was written after the publication of Virgil's *Aeneid*, and alludes to it. This is perfectly possible, but the legend of Aeneas as the founder of the Roman race had long been current, as the opening words of Lucretius' poem (*Aeneadum genetrix*...) show.

Horace's Spring Odes

It would be morbid, however, for him to dwell on the thought, or to allow more than a tinge of melancholy to infuse itself into his enjoyment of the simple, shallow pleasures of existence:

> quo simul mearis,
>   nec regna uini sortiere talis,
>   nec tenerum Lycidan mirabere, quo calet iuuentus
>   nunc omnis et mox uirgines tepebunt.
>
> (i, 4, 17–20)

> *And when you've made your journey there,*
>   *no drawing lots to organize a spree,*
>   *no admiring looks at young Lycidas; all you men today*
>   *he's hotly*
>   *drawn, and girls will soon feel tepidly attracted.*

The frivolous note that some object to in the ending of this poem is in fact nicely calculated to fulfil a double purpose. First of all Horace wishes, paradoxically, to deepen our enjoyment of the more trivial things in life by making us aware how precarious our grasp on them must be. At the same time he does not want to weaken his poem by an explicit condemnation of young men for wasting precious life on trivial distractions. The contrast between the lightness of the last three lines and the five that precede is warning enough. If the reader wants to take the poem as incitement to frivolity (despite the grim irony one can hardly miss in Horace's pose of tolerant indulgence), Horace is too reticent to protest, confident that those for whom he writes, while not rejecting life's pleasures, will want listed in their life's short *summa* other items than these.

Horace's purpose in the last twelve lines of iv, 7 is harder to follow. Clearly the more subdued mood with which this poem began allows a sterner note in its conclusion. Horace can permit himself here more than a touch of pathos:

> cum semel occideris et de te splendida Minos
>   fecerit arbitria,
>   non, Torquate, genus, non te facundia, non te
>   restituet pietas.
>
> (iv, 7, 21–4)

The Spring Meditations for Sestius and Torquatus

> *When once you're dead, when Minos once has passed*
> *his majestic judgment on you,*
> *not birth, Torquatus, not eloquence, not piety*
> *can rehabilitate.*

Observe the noble solemnity of the triple *non* (in asyndeton with increasing predicate). The metre of line 21 pulls us up with an impressive change of tone at the caesura. The first half of the hexameter has light-moving dactyls: *cum semel occideris*. We are not at all downcast by the thought of death, is perhaps the implication, but we should be: after the caesura, three long monosyllables (the heaviest, slowest rhythm possible)—it begins to sink in what death means. But the well-constructed poetry of this sentence is preceded by lines the direction of which is less certain. First comes:

> quis scit an adiciant hodiernae crastina summae
>   tempora di superi?
>
> (iv, 7, 17–18)

> *Who knows if the gods above will add tomorrow's span*
> *to this day's sum?*

The attempt at a motto-couplet is a little fussily phrased, missing the stark simplicity of

> uitae summa breuis spem nos uetat incohare longam.
>
> (i, 4, 15)

Moreover, the reference to the uncertainty of life's span adds nothing to the argument of the poem, which is that death is inevitable and permanent; not that the time of death's coming is uncertain. It is a natural further reflection, but one that weakens the impact of the poem. The satirical note of the following couplet is similarly misplaced:

> cuncta manus auidas fugient heredis, amico
>   quae dederis animo.
>
> (iv, 7, 19–20)

> *Everything you spend on your own dear self escapes*
> *your heir's greedy grasp.*

Horace's Spring Odes

It reads a little too much like two lines from an epistle, done into lyric metre: an idea versified, and overtly satirical; not an idea transformed into poetry and the satire refined to irony.[1]

The structure of the poem suffers as a result of these four intrusive lines. They compel Horace at line 21 to pick up a little lamely the theme he had already launched in lines 14–16: without them he could have avoided the weak rephrasing of *nos ubi decidimus* in *cum semel occideris*—words that anyway are perhaps too facile an echo of Catullus.[2]

The poem ends by reinforcing the statement in lines 21–4 of the finality of death by a series of illustrations from mythology:

> infernis neque enim tenebris Diana pudicum
>   liberat Hippolytum,
> nec Lethaea ualet Theseus abrumpere caro
>   uincula Perithoo.
>
> (iv, 7, 25–8)

Diana, remember, cannot free from the place of shadows her chaste Hippolytus,
Theseus lacks power to break the chains of Lethe from about his dear Pirithous.

The prime object, of course, is to avoid ending on a strident note—a cheap trick Horace is always careful to avoid. The lines are as well (something, I think, that has not been observed) bound by implication to the argument of lines 23 and 24. Hippolytus was *pudicus*, Pirithous was not,[3] but the grip of death is as fast on the lecher as it is on the model of chastity. The lines convey an implied restatement of:

> non, Torquate, genus, non te facundia, non te
>   restituet pietas.
>
> (iv, 7, 23–4)

---

[1] I find that Mr. Rudd, art. cit., p. 383, shares my uneasiness:
I have always been a little puzzled by these lines. . . . It is one thing to conclude a poem with a whole stanza of satire like *absumet heres* (II, 14), but quite another to introduce a greedy *captator* and then relapse at once into profound melancholy.
[2] See Fraenkel, p. 420, Note 2.
[3] For Horace's view of Pirithous, see *Odes* iii, 4, 79–80:
   amatorem trecentae
   Perithoum cohibent catenae.

26

The Spring Meditations for Sestius and Torquatus

They show the proper, integrated use of mythology in poetry. A mythological reference should restate, or expand, the theme of the poem in another kind of poetic language, one that elicits the reader's collaboration from his knowledge of the legend, as Venus and Vulcan do in i, 4; not simply serve as ornament (like the Graces and nymphs at the beginning of this poem), or sound vaguely impressive (like the name-dropping in line 15).

Both poems are complex works of art. We could, and should, spend a great deal more time with them. Discussing, for example, the superbly sharp imagery of i, 4: six clear-cut vignettes in the first eight lines. Whereas the imagery of iv, 7 is less directly visual, doubtless because it is aimed at securing a pervasive melancholy of tone rather than clear-cut reactions to things observed. All I have attempted is to sketch a procedure for working towards intimate possession and real appreciation of the two poems.

In the present case there are perhaps four stages involved. The first is to realize the poems are different and independent, not two shots at the same thing. The second is to observe how they differ. The third, to decide with some finality, when we have experienced the poems more completely, which of the two we prefer: our preference can have only limited absolute validity, but differentiation is an important part of appreciation. The fourth, to decide how much our preference rests upon qualities inherent in the poem we prefer (better craftsmanship; greater freedom from things that jar, confuse or bore; tighter logic; deeper meaning; and so on), and how far upon personal reaction (our preference for sharp images, for rhetorical grandiloquence, for solemnity, or lightness, of tone; whether we respond more to the line of sense, or to the imaginative and incantatory properties of the poem; and so on).

I have given clear hints of my own preference. IV, 7 is undoubtedly a fine poem, but I like it less than i, 4: it seems to me to offer less straightforward pleasure because its imagery is weaker, and to be less firmly controlled in the thrust of its argument. Both poems, however, seem to me, in craftsmanship as well as theme, demonstrably superior to iv, 12.[1] But my object has been to take taste beyond the level of blank assertion;

---

[1] For a preference for i, 4 over iv, 7 based exclusively on craftsmanship, see Collinge, pp. 111–12.

Horace's Spring Odes

to show there can exist a measure of common response among sensitive readers of Latin poetry today, sufficiently substantial to make discussion profitable. By discussion recognition of what we all sense can be elicited and stated for agreement. Through discussion, since readers are not (fortunately) uniformly responsive, it should be possible for one reader to learn occasionally from another. In the last resort, taste rightly still decides.

2

Virgil's Tragic Queen

THE fourth book of Virgil's *Aeneid* is mainly Dido. She speaks one hundred and eighty-eight of the seven hundred and five lines—more than a quarter of the book. Between her return at line 296 to accuse Aeneas of running away and her death at line 692, her words form nearly half the text. She is usually considered Virgil's greatest character; the only character created by a Roman poet, Richard Heinze said, to pass into world literature.[1] She is regarded, indeed, by many as more successful than the poem's hero. Aeneas gets a thin time of it from his critics, not only for the pathetic figure he seems to them to cut in Book IV, but for his whole performance in the poem. The majority, as Professor Perret has shrewdly pointed out,[2] conceive their ideal epic hero in shallow terms: a strip-cartoon superman, assailing with equanimity and mastering without effort the perils that beset him, as untouched by moral anguish as by lethal weapon. These are the standards they unconsciously impose. Equally, they expect an ideal lover, cast in the same mould, his passion always the servant of his chivalry. Aeneas, they feel, hardly meets the case.

But Dido causes the critics no such misgivings. Many,

---

[1] Heinze *V.E.T.*, p. 133:
... die einzige von einem römischen Dichter geschaffene Figur . . ., die in die Weltliteratur übergehen sollte.

[2] J. Perret, *Virgile l'homme et l'oeuvre* (1952). His brief delineation of the character of Aeneas (pp. 133–40) is penetrating and convincing. For a sensible defence of Aeneas as 'a developing character, . . . who grows greater as his responsibilities grow', see D. R. Dudley, 'A plea for Aeneas', *G.R.*, viii, No. 1 (1961), pp. 52–60.

Virgil's Tragic Queen

however, feel compelled to add to their praise of Virgil's heroine their opinion that success came to Virgil by accident. The common view is often held to be neatly summed up in a phrase used by John Conington in the introduction to his edition of Virgil a hundred years ago. In Dido, said Conington, Virgil

> has struck the chord of modern passion, and powerfully has it responded; more powerfully, perhaps, than the minstrel himself expected.[1]

So much of what passes for literary criticism in classics belongs to a kind of patchwork quilt. On it are stitched together the eye-catching pronouncements of scholars and critics whose eminence is taken to compel assent. What Coleridge said about Lucretius;[2] what Housman, or Wilamowitz, or Goethe said about Horace;[3] every classical poet has received his due, and the old aphorisms continue to pass for fresh criticism, their context seldom checked. Yet we should remember the nature of patchwork quilts. They are serviceable, comfortable and warm, evocative of pleasant reminiscences of past days. The patches, however, seldom harmonize, and if we could see rather more of the materials from which the scraps have been salvaged to serve a fresh turn, the stuff might often seem now oddly old-fashioned and perhaps produce a different impression altogether from the one it produces on the quilt; or at any rate one less striking.

When we lift his words from their context, as the slightly flamboyant prose of Oxford's first Corpus Professor of Latin tempts critics to do, it is easy to read more into them than was intended. Remembering Conington grew up when Romantic poetry and criticism reigned supreme (he was ten years old when Coleridge died), we might suppose he had at the back of his mind the conviction that modern (i.e., nineteenth-century)

---

[1] J. Conington, *P. Vergili Maronis Opera* (vol. ii, 2nd edn. 1863, p. 13).

[2] Coleridge, *Collected Letters*, ed. E. L. Griggs, iv (1959), p. 574:
Whatever in Lucretius is poetry is not philosophical, whatever is philosophical is not poetry.

The remark is thrown out in passing by Coleridge in a letter to Wordsworth on 30 May 1815 while discussing a proposed philosophical poem by Wordsworth, 'The Recluse'.

[3] See Chapter 1.

Virgil's Tragic Queen

sensibility far surpassed that of the ancient world; and that, as a consequence, Dido appealed to the modern reader to an extent Virgil could not foresee. In fact, Conington's intention seems to have been to point to a clash, which he thought constant in the *Aeneid*, between the conventions of Homeric epic and what he called 'the poet's modern spirit'. In Dido, he maintained, Virgil inadvertently conceded too much to the modern spirit.

But the idea that Dido had somehow got out of hand caught on, and Conington's dictum was used to set the seal of authority upon it.[1] It seemed to the later English Romantic critics, who rated Virgil highly (one thinks of Tennyson), an attractive explanation for the conflict they felt between Virgil's presumed intention to cast Dido in a secondary role and what seemed to them her manifest domination of the book. The case is strongest put by J. W. Mackail, the last of Virgil's great Romantic critics, writing as recently as 1930:

> . . . art proved greater than the artist; and his human sympathy . . . swept him away irresistibly.[2]

('Irresistibily' because Aeneas is thrust into a role that cannot

---

[1] Conington's words are quoted, e.g., by Sir Paul Harvey, *Oxford Companion to Classical Literature* (1937), s.v. *Aeneid*, in support of his own judgment:
  It is perhaps unintentionally that the poet so powerfully enlists our sympathy for Dido.
Pease quotes an impressive list of authorities for the opinion (which he himself rejects, p. 38ff.) 'that her cause so gained with him [Virgil] the upper hand as to endanger the purpose and unity of the whole poem' (p. 8). A vigorous rebuttal of the common view is attempted by Austin, p. xiii: 'Virgil,' he maintains, 'planned the book on clear firm lines.' Dido is shown plainly as 'a temptress of the flesh, dominated by passion'. Austin's quotation of L. C. Knights on *Antony and Cleopatra* in *Scrutiny*, 1949, p. 322 ('It is one of the signs of a great writer that he can *afford* to evoke sympathy or even admiration for what, in his final judgment, is discarded or condemned') seems to me most just, though he does not reconcile Knights' notion of passing sympathy finally rejected with his own view of Dido, that in the end 'we remember nothing but her nobility'. His short Introduction does not allow space, however, for supporting the assertions made about Dido's character by argument. In his commentary Austin seems to me to miss Virgil's intentions at a number of crucial points, e.g., the '*odi et amo*' note of Dido's fourth speech, lines 416–36, and the significance therefore of the concluding lines of that speech (see my discussion of this speech).

[2] Mackail, p. lxvii. Cf. his Introductory Note to Book IV:
  Yet we may feel that in this episode the lure of his art has carried the artist further than he intended.

Virgil's Tragic Queen

be defended: 'defence of Aeneas is impossible . . .'.) It is important to understand Mackail means to praise Virgil: quality of inspiration meant more to him than quality of structure. For the later Romantic critics, as Mr. F. W. Bateson has put it, 'ideally a poem wrote itself'.[1] They believed poetry *should* get out of hand: inspiration, which alone counted, should take over from the poet, to produce things different from what the poet had planned, and greater than he could have conceived unaided.

We need not, of course, reject the possibility that the character of Dido came to fascinate Virgil so much that he was led beyond what he had originally planned in laying out his poem. It is an attractive hypothesis, but we should not let it draw us into speculating about what the poet might have written, instead of looking at what he wrote. The common view, however, implies more than this. It is argued that Dido by getting out of hand did serious damage to the poem Virgil actually wrote. The damage done is said to be of two kinds. First, her final heroism in the planning and execution of her suicide is said to involve Virgil in inconsistencies in his development of Dido's character. Second, Dido, in rising out of control to these heights of moral nobility, is said to damage Aeneas, the proper hero of the poem, by the role she forces Virgil to assign him. Here are strictures which, if justified, must materially affect our appreciation of the book. They constitute a criticism of its artistic success that must be looked into with care.

Dido's is the story of a woman who died for love. She kills herself, indeed, in a strangely horrible and spectacular form of carefully premeditated suicide. The concluding scenes of the drama of her death are pervaded by a sublimity of tone and a sense of tragic inevitability that provide the reader in abundance with all that most readers require of the tragic experience. Their success conceals in fact from most a question all should ask—because upon our answer our judgment of the structure of the whole book depends. The question is: *Why does Dido die?*

Let us look for a moment at the text. At line 504 a passage begins, describing in some detail the scene that remains the

---

[1] F. W. Bateson, *English Poetry: A Critical Introduction* (1950), p. 43.

Virgil's Tragic Queen

dominant one in our minds during the final act of the three into which Virgil has divided his narrative:

> at regina, pyra penetrali in sede sub auras
> erecta ingenti taedis atque ilice secta,   505
> intenditque locum sertis et fronde coronat
> funerea; super exuuias ensemque relictum
> effigiemque toro locat haud ignara futuri.

> *But the queen in an inner fastness of the palace rears*
> *a great pyre skywards of pine brands and hewn ilex-oak;*   505
> *decks the place with garlands, crowns pyre with foliage*
> *of death; on it places the sword and harness he had*
> *left, and him in effigy, not in doubt of what will be.*

From here to the end of the book no normal reader feels impelled to ask why Dido is killing herself, because the detail of what is happening absorbs his attention. And at the end of the book, moved (as readers from St. Augustine onwards confess they have been moved) by the evident quality of the last two hundred lines and their almost irresistible power over him, the normal reader may not immediately question the plausibility of the events just enacted in his mind.

Yet the question *Why does Dido die?* is clearly a relevant and important question. Not all women deserted by their lovers commit suicide. Few of those who do, kill themselves in so spectacular a fashion. Did Virgil perhaps make a mistake when he decided to keep Dido's suicide upon the funeral pyre as the climax of his story, after introducing quite different circumstances from those which traditionally led up to it? (In older versions of the story, in which Aeneas does not figure, Dido kills herself to avoid marrying Iarbas.) The commentators have little to offer that can be called a convincing, or even an adequate, answer to our question. They seldom attempt to look for the pattern of events and situations which, in the poet's fiction, should act upon his characters; or ask themselves whether those events and situations so act upon Dido as to lead her, convincingly and inextricably, to an end to which events and situations like these could lead a woman like the Dido Virgil draws.

Virgil's Tragic Queen

The commentators are too obsessed with looking for the single tragic error of Aristotle. They claim to find it in Dido's oath to her dead husband not to remarry, and her respect for her oath. The approach is too mechanical. If you want a single tragic error, it lies (as we shall see) in Dido's assumption that Aeneas shared the view she took of their liaison. This is not of course an error we find her acknowledging, as she is not fully aware of it; but it is the main single factor that releases the chain of events leading to her death. It only leads there, however, because Dido is the person Virgil makes her. But this is anticipating.

If *Aeneid* iv were a poem about Dido's death and nothing else, we could afford to ignore such reflections perhaps, regarding them as questioning things that are not an integral part of the poem. It is perfectly possible to write a fine and moving poem about a situation that is artificially contrived. The plausibility of the events leading to the situation in which Hamlet finds himself at the beginning of Shakespeare's play hardly concerns us because those events are not an integral part of the play, but constitute merely a preliminary hypothesis which the poet asks us to accept in order to proceed with his drama.

But in *Aeneid* iv the suicide of Dido is only the final episode of a series of episodes, all of which are part of the poem. It is, in fact, but the third of the three sections into which Virgil has divided his book. He takes some trouble, moreover, to make it clear where each section starts, by beginning each with the same two-word formula, *at regina*, which serves almost as a stage direction, marking the queen's entry. The book opens with *at regina*. The same words bring us back to Dido again at line 296 after a long sequence of scenes in which she does not figure. And they introduce her a third time at line 504, for the sequence of scenes that leads to her suicide.

Virgil spends in fact some five hundred lines leading up to the final two hundred. The moment we realize this, it is clear the question *Why does Dido die?* must indeed form part of our assessment of the book. How far is her death due to tragic inevitability of circumstances, and how far to excesses, clearly pointed to by the poet, in Dido's character? For we have agreed that her action in taking her life is not reasonable, or at any rate not usual; and the poem, we must now agree, purports to

Virgil's Tragic Queen

relate the events that led up to her suicide. Does *Aeneid* iv, in a word, provide the reasons for tragedy as well as the tragic spectacle?[1]

If we find reasons given or suggested and if they are plausible ones, the charge against Virgil that he let his character get out of hand loses much of its force. At best then the charge deals with things that may have influenced the architecture of the book; it does not call in question the quality or the harmony of its design, as built. And if, as we may already suspect, the reasons why Dido took her life are more complex than concentration on the final spectacle caused us to suppose, and if they impute to her a share in the responsibility for the tragedy; then perhaps Virgil has not after all allowed his sympathy for his heroine to blacken his hero beyond defence.

In this chapter we must concentrate on Dido; but we may permit ourselves the passing reflection that those who think ill of Aeneas for deserting Dido are often the same people who think ill of Mark Antony (the historical character) for not deserting Cleopatra. This is not a sophistical rejoinder. We cannot doubt Virgil intended his readers to have at the back of their minds the historical parallel his fiction foreshadowed. As Perret has pointed out, pre-historic legend and the Augustan age (and the historical pageant that linked the two) keep blending into one another throughout the poem.[2]

But Book IV is Dido's book, and our first task must be to understand Virgil's tragic queen. A word however, before we turn to the text, about the formal lay-out. We shall find it convenient to use the terminology of drama; but we must bear in mind that *Aeneid* iv is not a play: It remains in many respects epic poetry. The action of epic, for example, changes in tempo more easily than in a play because the whole is spread, normally, over a period of time considerably longer than the action a

---

[1] Heinze *V.E.T.*, p. 141, is forced to argue it does not. He finds Dido a shallow character and the events leading up to her death (the *Weg zum Tode*) exciting enough, because of Virgil's compact artistry, but lacking convincing motivation:

... diese Kunst zwingt dem Leser unvermerkt das Gefühl der Notwendigkeit des tragischen Schlusses auf, wie es bei andern grossen Dichtern aus den Voraussetzungen eines tief angelegten und individuell gezeichneten Charakters herauswächst.

[2] See Pease, pp. 24–8, for the similarities between Dido and Cleopatra.

Virgil's Tragic Queen

classical tragedy embraces.[1] Epic possesses, moreover, narrative resources tragedy must do without. The poet is enabled to use his authority as narrator to put beyond doubt factors in his plot that might remain doubtful if left to emerge from dialogue. He must use the device discreetly, of course, or he will make things too easy for the reader, and, by rendering alert attention to the dialogue unnecessary, surrender that active collaboration of the reader with the poet upon which all really successful writing depends. Virgil in fact intervenes as narrator at more than one important point in *Aeneid* iv. For example, in line 395 (at the end of the quarrel scene), to tell us what we might otherwise be unsure of, and what many inattentive readers doubt despite Virgil's precaution: that Aeneas is so deeply in love with Dido (*magno labefactus amore*) he almost goes back on his decision to depart.[2]

Nevertheless *Aeneid* iv comes closer to tragedy than any of the other books of the poem.[3] Partly because dialogue bulks so large, and is used to lay bare emotions of a complexity we associate more with classical tragedy than classical epic. Partly, too, because of the book's unusually dramatic structure. It falls, as we have seen, into what we may call three acts, each beginning with Queen Dido on stage.[4] Let us look briefly, before focusing our full attention on Dido, at the unfolding of the story in these three acts. At the beginning of the first, the extent to which she has fallen in love with the handsome adventurer, whose exploits have held her attention, as they have held ours, during Aeneas' recital of them in Books II and III, is rapidly and poignantly revealed. Within the first fifty lines Anna, her sister, has convinced Dido she should not resist her passion, and the two set out to elicit divine approval for what Dido is persuaded can be a *mariage de raison* as much as a *mariage de coeur*. But it is marriage she wants. After the scene of religious ritual (described by Virgil with his crisp relish for the grisly), we see Dido seeking Aeneas' company openly. By line 89 the action of

[1] The question is discussed in Chapter 8.
[2] We may, of course speculate whether Virgil succeeds in creating a character that convinces us, by his words and actions, that he is in love.
[3] The book's formal resemblances to tragedy are listed by Pease, pp. 9–11.
[4] A tripartite structure is found in other books too, e.g., II and XII. On II see R. S. Conway, 'The architecture of the epic', *Harvard Lectures on the Vergilian Age* (1928), p. 134.

Virgil's Tragic Queen

the drama has been prepared for. It is precipitated by a pact between Juno and Venus, ending with the words '*Hic hymenaeus erit*' ('This will be their marriage') after a scene loaded with implications of trickery.[1]

The day of the hunt follows, culminating in the union of Dido and Aeneas in a cave, while a storm rages round them. The emotional climax of

> fulsere ignes et conscius aether   167
> conubiis, summoque ulularunt uertice Nymphae

> *A firmament flashing with fire was witness*
> *of their union, and wail of nymphs from mountain top*

is followed immediately by words that foreshadow disaster:

> ille dies primus leti primusque malorum
> causa fuit.   170

> *That day was first entered on an unhappy road that led to death.*

The reason for disaster is precisely stated:

> neque enim specie famaue mouetur   170
> nec iam furtiuum Dido meditatur amorem:
> coniugium uocat, hoc praetexit nomine culpam.

[1] A word is perhaps necessary on the complex question of Virgil's divine machinery, if only in rebuttal of the curious opinion, occasionally put forward, that *Aeneid* iv is not a tragedy of character at all. E.g., H. E. Butler, *The Fourth Book of Virgil's Aeneid* (1935), p. 24:
    Dido ... is the sport of circumstances, the victim of two designing goddesses, and the poet never seeks to evoke any emotion in our hearts save pity.
The usual (and to my mind most reasonable) view is that the gods serve as an externalized reflection of the natural tendencies of character; that 'divine actions ... merely bring to a focus feelings already latent' (J. MacInnes, 'The conception of *fata* in the *Aeneid*', *C.R.*, xxiv [1910], p. 173; cf. Warde Fowler, *Death of Turnus* [1919], p. 110). The gods, in fact, provide a conventional supernatural source for all that seems (often to us, too) genuinely mysterious in life: accidents of circumstance, sudden and apparently irrational decisions, impulses and intuitions (cf. the two interventions of Mercury in *Aeneid* iv), inspired feats of courage and physical prowess, etc. We may have the feeling that destiny intervenes (the divine machinery serves, too, of course as a relevation of destiny to the reader), even that it plays tricks; but we should not have the feeling that it manipulates automata.

Virgil's Tragic Queen

Unmoved by talk, or how things looked,
it is no clandestine love now that Dido has in mind:
she calls it marriage, cloaking with this word how she failed.[1]

Roman law in Virgil's day did not draw the sharp line we draw between people who are respectably married and people who are not. The old religious marriage had yielded much ground to marriage by common consent. In such a relationship the parties might regard themselves as entering on marriage from the outset; or what began as a liaison might develop into binding marriage after a transitional period, during which the parties might easily have different views or hopes. This is the background to the relationship of Dido and Aeneas.[2] After the cave episode, Dido's goal, respectable marriage, seems within her grasp.[3] She regards herself, not as embarking on a liaison to be kept secret (*nec . . . furtiuum . . . meditatur amorem*), but an effective marriage to be openly acknowledged. For the moment, though, we can imagine she is as anxious as he to avoid explicit discussion of intentions. She must wait till she feels Aeneas willing to sacrifice for her his mission to Italy. But 'she calls it marriage' (*coniugium uocat*). The word slips out, perhaps, in his presence; if it does, he lets it pass. Virgil leaves it all as vague as he wants us to imagine they did. The danger of a misunderstanding when neither wanted to risk a show-down over a word would have been apparent to Virgil's contemporary readers. The Aristotelian-minded can regard this, if they wish,

---

[1] With *coniugium uocat* compare line 431:
  'non iam coniugium antiquum, quod prodidit, oro.'
As Mackail points out in his excellent note on line 19, where Dido herself uses the word, *culpa* means only 'failing' (surrender to passion) and does not imply either criminality or moral obliquity.

[2] For types of Roman consensual marriage, see P. E. Corbett, *The Roman Law of Marriage* (1930), pp. 85–96. For a consideration of their relevance to Dido, see C. Buscaroli, *Il libro di Didone* (1932), 'L'unione fatale', pp. 136–43, especially pp. 141–3, and the comment (in a review of Buscaroli) of A. Guillemin, *R.E.L.*, x (1932), p. 502. I don't mean, of course, that Virgil expects us to view the relationship of Dido and Aeneas in strict accordance with Roman laws of marriage. He does, however, expect his readers to interpret the heroic situation realistically, in terms of what might have happened at Rome.

[3] The symbolic ceremony in the cave scene emphasizes the significance of the cave episode for Dido. It symbolizes, too, of course the hand of destiny, indicating perhaps what we mean when we say of two people 'they were meant for one another'. Obviously no one would suppose an immediately binding religious marriage had taken place.

Virgil's Tragic Queen

as Dido's tragic mistake: she failed to ensure her view of their relationship would be shared by Aeneas, hoping (until the quarrel scene) he shared it already. It was hardly a reasonable construction for a queen to put on their relationship, but we shall see Dido was not a reasonable woman.[1] The plot in a word turns upon a misunderstanding; one, however, that is not merely a tragic device, but, as well as that, a piece of acute psychological insight.

The next hundred lines offer a kind of relaxation in the action. We have a series of scenes (the flight of Fama to spread news of the liaison, the slightly comic episode of Iarbas, the briefing of Mercury), terminating with a bravura passage in the best Hellenistic traditions of pure poetry: Mercury, on his way to Carthage to admonish Aeneas, passes by Atlas, simultaneously described as the mountain and the living giant.[2] The main characters are off stage for only a hundred lines; but when they reappear (we come back first to Aeneas, at line 279), we renew contact with them feeling a lot has happened since we last saw them. Virgil has dextrously manipulated the resources of epic. He has relaxed the tension, but held our interest by three pieces of virtuoso writing. More important, it is with a feeling of time elapsed that we see Aeneas and Dido return. Virgil makes it easy to assume that Aeneas has in some measure compromised himself by acquiescing in Dido's evident view of their relationship. But, by avoiding direct narrative of the liaison, he avoids, too, explicit inculpation of Aeneas, allowing the assumptions we naturally make (as a result of our feeling that time has passed) to perform the work of direct narrative more economically, more discreetly, and, because the reader's collaboration is sustained, more poetically.

Aeneas' admonition by Mercury and his decision to depart from Carthage occupy fifteen quick-moving lines. He suddenly realizes, to rephrase it in naturalistic terms, that he is getting too deeply involved in something incompatible with his obligations to those under his command. The tempo of the narrative

---

[1] Pease's comment, p. 45, that Dido 'consistently exaggerated the closeness of her ties to Aeneas' shows how an able commentator can read his text attentively, and yet miss a vital point.

[2] The whole passage 238–61 is reminiscent of the mannered style of Catullus Poem 64. Even in detail: cf., e.g., the play on *Atlantis* in lines 247–8 with Catullus 64, 19–21. For a similar interlude of pure poetry, cf. *Aeneid* viii, 407–53, Vulcan in his forge.

Virgil's Tragic Queen

is fastest here. In lines 289–94 Virgil resorts to a comparatively rare device: when Aeneas tells his men the reasons for departure, we are not given his actual speech, but a reported summary. Again Virgil's purpose is not only to speed the narrative, but to reduce to a minimum the evidence put on record against Aeneas. In particular Aeneas' responsibility for the disaster that is to come is underplayed. He promises his men to take the first favourable opportunity to tell the queen he is leaving—and then understandably procrastinates until it is too late. The soundness of Virgil's psychological insight is once more evident.

In fact Dido finds out they are going before Aeneas gets round to telling her. Act 2 begins with her confrontation of him. The quarrel scene—her first long speech, Aeneas' brief reply, her long rejoinder—occupies not quite a hundred lines (to line 387). It marks the end of their liaison, although again Virgil avoids underlining facts that must tell against Aeneas. But clearly we are to suppose that Dido and Aeneas have been living together, till the moment of the quarrel, in the royal *thalamus*. After the quarrel Aeneas takes up residence with his men at the harbour and preparations for departure become open and frantic (to line 415). Although the action moves so fast, we must not miss Virgil's explicit statement at line 395 that Aeneas is deeply in love with Dido. It does not occur to Dido that Aeneas could love her and still leave her. Their alienation, like their liaison, rests on a misunderstanding. He loves her, but she believes he despises her. It is against the background of these facts that we have to think of Aeneas in the great tree simile. Dido has been trying through Anna to get Aeneas to consent to a meeting with her. But though Anna tries repeatedly to arrange the interview, she cannot sway Aeneas:

> ac uelut annoso ualidam cum robore quercum
> Alpini Boreae nunc hinc nunc flatibus illinc
> eruere inter se certant; it stridor, et altae
> consternunt terram concusso stipite frondes;
> ipsa haeret scopulis et, quantum uertice ad auras   445
> aetherias, tantum radice in Tartara tendit:
> haud secus adsiduis hinc atque hinc uocibus heros
> tunditur, et magno persentit pectore curas;
> mens immota manet, lacrimae uoluuntur inanes.

Virgil's Tragic Queen

Imagine an oak-tree, strong with years of growth:
about it rage the Alpine blasts, now this way, now that,
struggling to overthrow it; leaves from its howled-round
top strew the ground and the tree's trunk shakes;
but it holds fast to the rock, for its roots stretch   445
as far Hellwards as its top does skywards into the air:
just so the storm of words beats this way, that way, around
Aeneas. His great heart feels the full impact of anguish.
The mind remains unshaken. Ineffectual tears fall.[1]

This brings us to line 450. Dido conceives her plan for death and gives Anna a version of it that conceals her real intentions. Her unnatural calm contrasts with the turmoil of her thoughts just after, as she lies awake on the eve of suicide. At line 552 Aeneas receives a second warning from Mercury—an intuition,

---

[1] Whose are the tears? Unless we are prepared to believe Virgil spoilt the coherence of his simile in its last three words, we must give the tears to Aeneas. Three things about the oak-tree are relevant to the comparison: (1) Its trunk is tossed around. (2) Its foliage falls to the ground. (3) Its roots are firm in rock. Obviously (3) corresponds to the *mens immota*: the innermost fastnesses of Aeneas' resolution are unshaken. The trunk of the tree (1), corresponds to Aeneas' *pectus*, tossed about by the emotional storm to which it is exposed. Aeneas is not an unfeeling brute: *persentit* shows this and we have already been told at line 395 that he loved Dido deeply. (There is a deliberate ambiguity involved in *magno pectore*, which is (*a*) visual—the great manly frame of Aeneas [compare Dido's remark at line 11, *quam forti pectore et armis!*] which we can think of as resembling the oak-tree's massive trunk; (*b*) it equals 'in his great heart', the abstract notion, reinforced by echoes of *magno animo*, etc.) When this is realized, it seems hard to doubt that the tears (as Rand suggested) correspond to the falling leaves—the only external sign of damage wrought by the stress imposed. See Viktor Pöschl, *Die Dichtkunst Virgils* (1950), pp. 76–80.

The tears can hardly be Dido's, as many (including Austin) have rather carelessly supposed. Aeneas and Dido are not together again after line 392, and Virgil would hardly ruin his image at its climax by asking us without warning to take in simultaneously an extraneous image of the absent Dido. Anna certainly cries. But are the tears of a minor character relevant at the climax? When Aeneas meets Dido in the underworld, it is he who cries (vi, 455).

A final word on *inanes*. If the tears were Anna's (or Dido's), *inanes* would mean 'ineffectual', i.e. unable to shift Aeneas. Used of Aeneas' tears, the word implies tears of frustration because Aeneas is not free to go against fate. Just as in *Aeneid* x, line 465, Hercules is unable to prevent the death of Pallas:

audiit Alcides iuuenem magnumque sub imo
corde premit gemitum lacrimasque effundit inanis.

It may seem to us to weaken the impressiveness of Aeneas' *mens immota* if Aeneas is acting under fate's compulsion. But this, I think, is not how Virgil looked at it. Aeneas is the good Stoic whose merit is the strength of will to place himself on the side of destiny, however much the passions pull in another direction.

Virgil's Tragic Queen

if we prefer to think of it that way, that disaster will come if he does not sail at once. He departs hurriedly. As dawn rises on the departing fleet, Dido breaks into a passionate denunciation of Aeneas (lines 590–629). The death scene follows soon after. Dido dies in Anna's arms, and the book ends with a brief epilogue.

It is clear from an examination of the lay-out of the book that it is constructed around two main themes, the disintegration of the liaison and Dido's suicide. These form the second and third of the three acts and occupy about four hundred lines out of seven hundred. The events leading to the liaison and those determining its rupture are sketched in quickly and precisely in the first act, along with clear hints about the nature and progress of the liaison and Dido's view of it. Act 1 in terms of action therefore embraces much more than the other two. Its structure is also different: after opening dramatically, it proceeds more in narrative form, relieved by short speeches. It is in short more representative of the normal epic structure of the remainder of the poem.

In Acts 2 and 3 dialogue predominates. In them, nearly everything turns on the speeches. We notice how fast, and how much, the character of Dido develops from speech to speech. The speeches are, as it were, detailed reflections of successive states of mind. The mood of each is clear cut, the moods so different they justify Mercury's warning:

> 'uarium et mutabile semper
> femina.'   570

> *'A thing that changes, always different,
> that is woman.'*

Though the speeches are often preceded or followed by brief sketches of Dido's emotional state or appearance on the poet's own authority (stage directions, as it were), it is to the speeches themselves that we must look if we are to understand the character Virgil is creating and the portrait he gives of her emotional disintegration. It will help if we tabulate for reference the nine speeches Dido makes, the position they occupy in the text

Virgil's Tragic Queen

and their length, rather as though they were the arias of an opera. Our tabulation will read like this:

Act 1

I: *'Anna soror, quae me suspensam insomnia terrent! . . .'* (9–29; to Anna; 21 lines; there is an interval of 276 lines, mainly narrative, between Speech i and Speech ii).

Act 2

II: *'dissimulare etiam sperasti . . .'* (305–30; to Aeneas; 26 lines).
III: *'nec tibi diua parens . . .'* (365–87; to Aeneas; 23 lines; narrative interval between Speeches ii and iii: 35 lines).
IV: *'Anna, uides toto properari litore circum . . .'* (416–36; to Anna; 21 lines; narrative interval between Speeches iii and iv: 29 lines).
V: *'inueni, germana, uiam (gratare sorori) . . .'* (478–98; to Anna; 21 lines; narrative interval between Speeches iv and v: 42 lines).

Act 3

VI: *'en, quid ago? rursusne procos inrisa priores . . .'* (534–52; soliloquy; 19 lines; narrative interval between Speeches v and vi: 36 lines).
VII: *'pro Iuppiter! ibit . . .'* (590–629; soliloquy; 40 lines; narrative interval between Speeches vi and vii: 38 lines).
VIII: *'Annam, cara mihi nutrix, huc siste sororem . . .'* (634–40; to Barce; 7 lines; narrative interval between Speeches vii and viii: 5 lines).
IX: *'dulces exuuiae, dum fata deusque sinebat . . .'* (651–62; soliloquy; 12 lines; narrative interval between Speeches viii and ix: 11 lines).

Let us now consider these nine speeches. The book begins magnificently with eight lines tersely describing Dido's brooding passion. Her opening speech to Anna reveals a woman deeply in love, so emotionally tense she must talk to someone. Her exclamation

'quis nouus hic nostris successit sedibus hospes?'   10

'Who is this stranger with us now in the palace?'

(note how the s's fix its tone in an urgent whisper) is a transparent excuse for talking, as the following line

> 'quem sese ore ferens, quam forti pectore et armis!'   11
>
> *'How confident he looks! What a chest on him, what shoulders!'*

shows more clearly still. Dido is already starting to think of marriage to Aeneas, as indeed she might, for she is a widow. She has exceptional standards however: those of the Roman matron who aspired to the proud claim at her death that she died *uniuira*, one man's wife. To Dido any remarriage seems a dereliction of *pietas*, a 'failure' (*culpa*), an act of surrender to passion, hitherto rejected, now for the first time half entertained:

> 'huic uni forsan potui succumbere culpae!'   19
>
> *'For this man, no other, I might have come to fail, and yield!'*

She wants Aeneas desperately and would like to find a way of convincing herself that remarriage can be justified. Virgil here uses the tragic device of the confidante with skill. Anna is not merely on stage to be told what the reader-audience must know. Nor is she really there to make up Dido's mind for her. Dido's mind *is* made up, unconsciously, and Anna is there to find for her the arguments from expediency that Dido's pride will not allow her to explore for herself. How great the tension is in Dido is shown by the way in which the passionate protestation of fidelity to her dead husband that bursts out after the ominous admission, *agnosco ueteris uestigia flammae*, is followed first by a desperate effort at calm statement,

> 'ille meos, primus qui me sibi iunxit, amores   28
> abstulit,'
>
> *'He who first joined me to him stands now between me and love,'*

and then by collapse into tears.

What may we expect of the woman Virgil draws in this opening speech? Much of her nature is clear. It will be natural for such a woman to find a way of yielding to passion. We may

Virgil's Tragic Queen

expect she will allow herself to be convinced that remarriage *is* possible; and Anna soon convinces her. But—and again this is a type we know—hers is a scrupulousness that fixes on the letter, not the spirit. And in fact we shall soon see her (at the end of Act 1) ready to regard as assured marriage, and not mere surrender to passion, what no one else, least of all Aeneas, could seriously be expected to regard as certain to develop into marriage:

> neque enim specie famaue mouetur   170
> nec iam furtiuum Dido meditatur amorem:
> coniugium uocat, hoc praetexit nomine culpam.

> *Unmoved by talk, or how things looked,*
> *it is no clandestine love now that Dido has in mind:*
> *she calls it* marriage, *cloaking with this word how she failed.*

Here is a woman who can easily accept private standards of her own rightness of conduct, and maintain them by flagrant self-deception. This is the character Virgil wants, and that is the person we feel Dido is after her first speech.

A character like this is more than usually prone to moral disintegration. Each speech now brings that disintegration closer. The Dido of the second speech is as remote from the conscience-stricken widow, tormented by love's renewal, of the first speech as she is from the transparently love-sick woman who a while ago resorts to any pretext that brings her lover to her side:

> Iliacosque iterum demens audire labores   78
> exposcit pendetque iterum narrantis ab ore;

> *and mad to hear a second time what Troy endured,*
> *she demands the tale, hangs on his lips when he tells it;*

or from the radiant queen, all golden, who sets out on the morning of the hunt, aware she will spend the day at her lover's side:

> tandem progreditur magna stipante caterua   136
> Sidoniam picto chlamydem circumdata limbo;
> cui pharetra ex auro, crines nodantur in aurum,
> aurea purpuream subnectit fibula uestem.

Virgil's Tragic Queen

At last she emerges with her great entourage,
an embroidered Phoenician cloak thrown about her.
Her quiver is of gold, her hair is tied with gold,
a golden brooch clips up her bright red dress.

When Dido reappears at the beginning of Act 2, all that seems far away. Now she is reeling under the impact of the knowledge that Aeneas is leaving. Observe how the narrator has intervened to fix the tone of Dido's speech. When she learnt of Aeneas' plans to leave, she did not rush straight to him, as we might have expected if love for him were all she felt. Instead, she stormed through the city:

> saeuit inops animi totamque incensa per urbem   300
> bacchatur, qualis commotis excita sacris
> Thyias . . .

Seething, aflame, at her wits' end, the city's width
and breadth she storms, like some Bacchante when she feels
the frenzied rites begin . . .

Her mood is not so much despair as anger: the angry thought 'he can't do this to me!'. At the moment the liaison begins to disintegrate, we have Dido's impetuous pride hinted at. It will become an important ingredient in the tragedy. For the moment it is underplayed.

In the speech that follows (Speech ii, *'dissimulare etiam sperasti . . .'*) Virgil wants us on Dido's side. When it ends, she has gained a clear moral ascendancy. The angry opening sentence is followed by a reasoned appeal to pity. She keeps emotion under control, though her words make clear the effort it costs her. Even in the truly moving conclusion,

> 'saltem si qua mihi de te suscepta fuisset
> ante fugam suboles, si quis mihi paruulus aula
> luderet Aeneas, qui te tamen ore referret,
> non equidem omnino capta ac deserta uiderer,'   330

> *'If at least I had had a child of you before*
> *you ran away, a baby Aeneas playing in the*
> *palace whose looks yet brought you back to me,*
> *I'd not then feel a prisoner, utterly alone,'*

Virgil's Tragic Queen

pride adds dignity and restraint to her appeal. The strength of the speech comes partly from Dido's queenly bearing, partly from her confidence in her moral claim upon Aeneas (Virgil catches both in the superb *mene fugis?*). It is important to observe that a moral claim is all Dido feels she has. She takes it for granted that, if Aeneas is deserting her, it means he does not love her. But he should pity her, and he is (in her view) really under an obligation to her. She goes on to say, 'We're as good as married' (*per inceptos hymenaeos*, line 316), and thus assert her moral claim. It is perhaps the first open statement Aeneas has of Dido's view of their liaison, and that may contribute to the embarrassed reticence with which he takes up the point (*nec praetendi taedas*, lines 338–9) in his reply.

The appeal to pity carries with it the first hint of the course disaster will take:

'nec moritura tenet crudeli funere Dido?'   308

'Dido will die a cruel death: does not that hold you back?'

In part, Virgil gets in the threat of death by a kind of linguistic trick: the convention, embedded in words such as *pereo*, that violent unrequited love destroys its victim.[1] Virgil, however, has perhaps tried to extract too much from the device of dramatic irony in this line, by making it serve as well (at the outset of the disintegration of the liaison) as a hint that Dido will die in reality a cruel death.

Aeneas makes a brief rejoinder. He is in that common situation where a morally right decision cannot be made to appear more attractive by defending it. The less said the better. The speech serves, too, as an emotional contrast, Aeneas' quiet realistic dignity opposed to the sublime tragic dignity of Dido. Scorn has been heaped upon Aeneas for his inadequate defence, but his reticence appears to me dramatically convincing.[2] He is aware he cannot help matters now by talking, and he is aware, too, of his moral responsibility. He has procrastinated when he should have told Dido he was going. Worse, he has got out of

---

[1] See the discussion of Propertius ii, 27 in Chapter 7.

[2] Any commentary will provide or quote instances. Sound defence of Aeneas is harder to find. The best perhaps is T. S. Eliot's, in 'Virgil and the Christian World', *On Poetry and Poets* (1957), p. 129.

Virgil's Tragic Queen

step with destiny—as he had done once before in Book II (an occasion treated more leniently by the commentators) when he plunged into useless fighting on the night of Troy's destruction, instead of heeding Hector and making the salvation of his people and their gods his first care.[1] Here is the real answer to the critics who protest that, by letting Dido get out of hand, Virgil damaged the hero of the poem. Virgil is too good a poet to pretend that Aeneas' conduct is beyond reproach, and his delineation of Aeneas is sensitive enough to show a hero aware of his share of blame. More than that, Virgil is prepared to have Aeneas misjudged, as in real life (Virgil wants us to think, perhaps, of some of the ugly decisions Augustus took in the civil war) courageous, unsentimental decisions are often misjudged. He even allows for this view of his hero within the poem, in the vivid opening scene of Book V: Aeneas standing silent watching the flames on the horizon which the reader, though not Aeneas, knows are the flames of Dido's funeral pyre, apart from his men, emotionally separate as well. For, though they do not know the rights and wrongs of the 'great love that was polluted', they silently judge their leader in their thoughts. One of the functions of Book V is to heal this alienation of commander from his men.

Virgil now contrives a dramatic *tour de force* which seems to me extraordinarily successful, and with it the rehabilitation of Aeneas begins. By the end of the first of the two speeches she makes in the quarrel scene, Dido has won our complete sympathy. That speech marks, however, the climax of Dido's moral ascendancy. From now on it is Virgil's purpose to detract from the stature of the character he permitted, temporarily, to play the role of heroine. In her second speech in the quarrel scene (Speech iii, *'nec tibi diua parens . . .'*) Virgil makes Dido lose every trick. First of all her appearance (again the narrator intervenes): instead of anger just contained, anger blazing forth, eyes rolling. Yet nothing she says this time really tells. The words seldom seem to us to justify the mood. Most of the speech is taken up with filling out clichés: the first is the customary accusation that Aeneas is not the son of his father;[2] the second a statement of Dido's *benefacta* toward Aeneas. A self-

[1] See the discussion of this point in Chapter 8.
[2] Compare Priam's words to Pyrrhus, *Aeneid* ii, 540 (discussed in Chapter 8).

Virgil's Tragic Queen

righteous note is introduced that helps to alienate us from Dido. She recovers, it is true, some of her stature with the curse with which she ends the speech, bitterly picking up Aeneas' '*Italiam non sponte sequor*' (line 361) with '*i, sequere Italiam uentis*' (line 381) and again with '*sequar atris ignibus absens*' (line 384). Then, before she can finish, she faints and is taken back to the *thalamus* from which she had emerged so happily at line 133.

Virgil is careful of course not to draw in this other aspect of Dido explicitly too soon. It is sufficient if we are left with the feeling that her second speech in the quarrel scene evokes our embarrassment more than our sympathy. This is the moment Virgil chooses for what he has till now withheld: a clear emphatic statement on the poet's own authority that Aeneas is in love with Dido. The reader's collaboration is dextrously exploited. Told earlier that Aeneas loved Dido, his reaction to the first half of the quarrel scene would have been mixed. He could not have sided with Dido as whole-heartedly as Virgil wished him to—at that stage. But told now that Aeneas really loves Dido, when the pendulum of his sympathy has begun to swing away from Dido, the reader feels the swing accelerate, noting with grudging approval Aeneas' restrained anguish[1] and reluctantly contrasting it with Dido's lack of self-control. And, when Dido is carried off-stage in a faint, Aeneas seeks *his* release from pent-up emotion in action, the comfort offered by the routine of a job to do: he goes to prepare the fleet for departure (line 396). It is the end of the liaison.

By the beginning of her next speech (Speech iv, '*Anna, uides toto properari litore circum . . .*'), Dido has already been brooding for some time and watching Aeneas' preparations for departure. The flaming anger of Speech iii has hardened into a dull bitterness, mixed with a residual attraction to Aeneas that she cannot shake off. It is a mood familiar to the reader of Roman love poetry, summed up tightest in Catullus' famous antithesis, *odi*

---

[1] The anguish is restrained, but not suppressed. We see him *multa gemens*. For the expression, cf. Aeneas in *Aeneid* i, 220-2, quietly grieving by himself for comrades he thinks he has lost in the storm:

> nunc Amyci casum gemit et crudelia secum
> fata Lyci, etc.

Observe, too, that Aeneas is called *pius* (line 393) to emphasize his feeling for Dido. It is the only occurrence of the formula *pius Aeneas* in Book IV.

Virgil's Tragic Queen

et amo. We can imagine the effort it would cost Dido to plead with a man who, as she believes, does not love her; particularly after the curse of lines 384–7. We know, of course, Aeneas does love her, and the tragic irony goes a little way toward restoring our sympathy for Dido, but on a new basis: not as a woman pitilessly deserted, but as a woman piteously self-tormented. Using of herself the language appropriate to one who has been conquered by an enemy in battle (*uicta,* line 434), she now asks Anna to approach 'the enemy' with a request on behalf of the conquered. Her petition is not for love, which she no longer hopes for; not for marriage or that Aeneas should abandon his voyage to Italy (to remain as her unloving consort); but for 'a little time' (*tempus inane peto,* line 433). Line 431 shows how far she has retreated since line 316:

'non iam coniugium antiquum, quod prodidit, oro,'   431

'*I plead not for what once was marriage, by him betrayed.*'[1]

Her request needs a word of explanation. Though Dido hates Aeneas, she wants desperately to be with him, at any rate until she can compose herself to face death. The conflict in her feelings is resolved by a bitter irony of expression. 'Let him lend me a little of his time,' the speech ends, 'and I shall repay him with interest':

'extremam hanc oro ueniam (miserere sororis),   435
quam mihi cum dederit cumulatam morte remittam.'[2]

She regards Aeneas, not merely as causing, but as desiring her

[1] The close-packed ambiguity in this line needs considerable expansion in interpretation: (1) 'I do not ask him to restore the marriage that was ours till he betrayed it (*antiquum* = 'former', and *oro* = 'ask back'); (2) 'I do not ask for old-fashioned, honourable marriage—he was false to that ideal' (*antiquum* = 'old and honourable', and *oro* = 'plead to get') .The second is the generally acknowledged marriage she hoped Aeneas would consent to—sanctified perhaps by a religious ceremony. She has abandoned hope of that. The first is her version of their relationship before the quarrel. She no longer hopes even for a restoration of the *status quo*. For the first meaning of *antiquum,* see Austin, p. 131, for the second Mackail, p. 150. Professor Jackson Knight in his Penguin translation (*Virgil: The Aeneid* [1956], p. 110) attempts to bring out both: 'I do not now beg him to restore our honoured marriage as it was before he betrayed it.' But, put plainly in prose, the statement sounds too rational—and just not true; whereas the ambiguity of Virgil's line well represents Dido's emotional indignation and her failure to distinguish in her own mind between what she had actually lost and what she had only hoped to get.

[2] Nearly all editors reject the reading *dederis,* reported by Servius as an alternative to *dederit.*

Virgil's Tragic Queen

unhappiness, and she will continue to believe this till the end. In her last speech of all she imagines Aeneas' satisfaction at the spectacle of her funeral pyre (line 661). (How he really feels then, Virgil tells us at the beginning of Book V, as we have seen.) All the same, she wants now to borrow back a little illusory happiness by being in his company. For this she is prepared to pay, not merely with renewed unhappiness when Aeneas finally goes, but with something she bitterly regards as likely to give Aeneas greater satisfaction and which she can only hint at in speaking to Anna—her death. The conclusion of her speech (especially line 436) has much puzzled the commentators, because it has not occurred to them that Virgil wants us to think of Dido as simultaneously hating Aeneas and desperately wanting his presence.

In this fourth speech, too, the plan to take her life begins to fall into shape. Her thoughts have naturally to be veiled in speaking to her sister. Indeed, the progress of Dido's thoughts towards a decision to take her own life needs careful examination, if we are to understand how her suicide is a consequence of her character. It began, as we have seen, with a fairly idly expressed cliché in her first speech in the quarrel scene:

'nec moritura tenet crudeli funere Dido?'   308

'Dido will die a cruel death: does not that hold you back?'

Then, in accordance with Virgil's conception of Dido as a noble woman made foolish by passion, the idea of a violent end steadily becomes an obsession. We have the cliché again near the end of the same speech:

'cui me moribundam deseris?'   323

'Whom do you leave me to, to die?'

By the end of the quarrel scene, the idea of death has already begun to embed itself:

'et, cum frigida mors anima seduxerit artus,   385
omnibus umbra locis adero.'

'And, when cold death subtracts my body from the living me, a ghost of me, omnipresent, will attend you.'

Virgil's Tragic Queen

She has reached the point where she practically thinks of death as a way of getting her own back. There is still no indication of imminent suicide. Little more than the rhetorical gesture: 'I'll haunt you when I'm dead.'

However, by the time Dido reappears at line 416 for her speech to Anna, she *has* begun to think seriously of killing herself. Virgil emphasizes this by the words of comment with which he introduces Speech iv:

> ne quid inexpertum frustra moritura relinquat. 415
>
> *lest she leave a way untried, and die in vain.*

And the ominous ambiguity of her own words quickly reveals the way her mind is working:

> 'hunc ego si potui tantum sperare dolorem,
> et perferre, soror, potero.' 420
>
> *'If I could bring myself to hope for this great passion,
> then, sister, I'll bring myself to face it out.'*

In line 419 *potui* has its common meaning of 'I brought myself' (to do something). There is a clear echo of the *potui* in line 19:

> 'huic uni forsan potui succumbere culpae.'
>
> *'For this man, no other, I might have come to fail, and yield.'*

When Dido now says *'et perferre, soror, potero'*, for Anna this simply means 'and I'll endure it'. For Dido and us the same words have a grimmer note: they mean 'and I'll see it through to the end'—to the only conclusion there can be, death. Her decision is partly the outcome of despair and partly an hysterical gesture, in which two subconscious objectives may be discovered. The first is to keep an Aeneas who does not love her at Carthage by the threat of suicide if he leaves. The second a confused desire to 'punish' Aeneas, by imposing on him the responsibility for her death. They are the melodramatic thoughts of a woman made foolish by despair, who might say: 'It will serve him right if I kill myself.' With them, however, is introduced an aspect of

Virgil's Tragic Queen

Dido's character that enables Virgil to reverse further her earlier moral ascendancy over Aeneas, by removing—temporarily—some of her tragic stature. A woman who behaves hysterically ceases to be truly tragic.

The structure of the action from now on needs to be looked at closely. What happens is that in a sense Dido's bluff is called. Somehow she had expected to influence Aeneas by talk of death; but Aeneas, though deeply moved, cannot abandon his decision to depart. In order, therefore, to maintain her belief in her own dignity (pride was, from the outset, an important element in her character), Dido is really forced to go ahead on the level of reality with a plan that had been embarked upon on an essentially rhetorical level.

The interesting thing is how the decision to take her life, once firmly entered upon, enables Virgil to restore to Dido the tragic stature he has so steadily taken from her. In different ways Dido and Aeneas are equally heroic in the end. Aeneas by reason of a resolute facing of realities. Dido by a resolute acting out, not under the impetus of a momentary impulse, but deliberately over a period of time, the consequences of a position hysterically assumed. Each has his concept of personal dignity and each is faithful to it.

Dido's plan is given shape in her fifth speech. It begins on a note of bitter, pathetic irony:

  'inueni, germana, uiam (gratare sorori).' 478

'I have found a way, dear Anna, congratulate your sister.'

She unfolds her plans for the construction of a great pyre, and the magic ceremony that will, so she tells Anna, restore Aeneas to her. The reader finds it impossible not to guess her real purpose. Having failed to wring from Aeneas the brief respite for which she pleaded, feeling death close in upon her, she starts actually to look forward to it:

  tum uero infelix fatis exterrita Dido 450
  mortem orat; taedet caeli conuexa tueri,

Dido now, in terror at the direction fate is taking
prays for death, sick of looking on the curve of heaven.

Virgil's Tragic Queen

Again the narrator intervenes to fix the tone of Dido's words. Frightful portents, terrifying dreams (an odd mixture—to us—of ancient conventional belief, exploited by Virgil for gruesome effect, and modern insight: the symbolism, for example, of the dreams), all seem to her to reveal the direction fate is taking. Act 3 begins with thirty lines of eerie descriptive writing showing Dido's plan being put into effect:

> at regina pyra penetrali in sede sub auras
> erecta ingenti taedis atque ilice secta, 505
> intenditque locum sertis et fronde coronat
> funerea; super exuuias ensemque relictum
> effigiemque toro locat haud ignara futuri.

> *But the queen in an inner fastness of the palace rears*
> *a great pyre skywards of pine brands and hewn ilex-oak;* 505
> *decks the place with garlands, crowns pyre with foliage*
> *of death; on it places the sword and harness he had*
> *left, and him in effigy, not in doubt of what will be.*

In both Speech v at the end of Act 2 and the narrative that opens Act 3 Virgil's purpose is complex. He wants first to suggest the icy determination with which Dido goes ahead with her plan now she realizes she *must* kill herself. On the other hand we have seen enough of Dido to accept that she is the woman to make a spectacle of suicide. Her determination finds expression, therefore, in a macabre piece of hocus-pocus. Yet, as she places on the great pyre the effigy of Aeneas, the sword she gave him and which he left behind when they quarrelled, and then proceeds with the magical rites, the conviction grows that this is more than spoof; and, intermingled with our judgment that what we are watching is the behaviour of a wilful exhibitionist, we feel a mounting flood of pity. On the more rational level, the magic is all supposed to be an elaborate subterfuge: she wants to commit suicide dramatically, but keep her plan concealed. At the same time it is clear that Dido half believes irrationally in the power of the hocus-pocus, somehow, to stave off the inevitable and keep Aeneas.[1]

---

[1] Dido's half-belief in the power of magic may be compared with that revealed by Propertius in his opening elegy, i, 1, 19-24 (see Chapter 6): as in Dido's *odi et amo* Speech iv, we see Virgil applying the psychological subtleties of Roman love poetry to epic.

Virgil's Tragic Queen

This is her mood in Speech vi (*'en, quid ago? rursusne procos inrisa priores . . .'*), her soliloquy as she lies sleepless in her bed. She must prove to herself there is no other way. Of course there is. Dido is much more the victim of character than the victim of circumstance. Presumably this is always the rational view of a situation that has led to suicide. But it cannot be Dido's. To tighten her resolution now in the shadow of the act, she must prove to herself there is no other way out. She does this by considering only alternatives that are clearly out of the question. For *her* there is no way out save death. She must go on with her plans.

Speech vi concludes with lines in which Virgil allows Dido an insight that is deeply touching into the reasons for her downfall:

> 'non licuit thalami expertem sine crimine uitam   550
> degere more ferae, talis nec tangere curas . . .'

> *'I was not allowed to leave marriage out of it, to live*
> *reproachless, animal-like, untouched by grief like this. . . .'*

Dido frames it, of course, in terms of inevitability of circumstance. But we can understand 'I was not allowed' in the most general, allusive sense. Dido was not allowed by fate, by herself, by others, by the standards incumbent on a queen. Then *thalami expertem* evokes a complicated pattern of ambiguity. The more obvious meaning is the abstract one, 'marriage', and Virgil had prepared us for this meaning of the word already in line 18:

> 'si non pertaesum thalami taedaeque fuisset'

> *'Had I not come to loathe marriage, weddings.'*

Disaster has come to Dido because she could not leave marriage out of it. Because her concept of queenliness demanded marriage. Because, thinking she had got marriage, she went ahead:

> coniugium uocat, hoc praetexit nomine culpam.   172

> *She calls it* marriage, *cloaking with this word how she failed.*

Virgil's Tragic Queen

The other meaning of the words *thalami expertem* is more subtle, but beyond doubt. This time *thalamus* is the room in the royal palace that Dido shared with Aeneas. The *thalamus* in which we saw her linger on the morning of the hunt (*thalamo cunctantem*, line 133). The *thalamus* to which we saw her carried back when she fainted at the end of the quarrel scene (line 392). The *thalamus* from which, in her speech to Anna giving directions for the building of the pyre (Speech v), she had directed all should be taken that reminded her of the departed Aeneas (line 495). By this triple occurrence of the word in prominent contexts emphasizing its concrete meaning, Virgil has got that meaning established for use here in an implied contrast with *more ferae*.

If only, Dido means, there hadn't had to be the civilized marriage of a queen, if only she and Aeneas had been free as animals are free. As *they* would have been free if things had been left as things might have been left, with the liaison kept on the basis on which it began when they met *more ferarum* in the cave. If it seems strange that Dido's words should be so tight-packed, so many-sided, we should remind ourselves of the nature of poetic tragedy: the characters are real in the sense that their motivation is convincing, and they offer us, if we like to call it that, a psychological experience. Their *words* are poetry, and unrealistic, offering us the special complex, compact pleasure poetry affords. And, understandably, when the psychological experience is more than usually intense, the poetic experience is also likely to be unusually intense.

The sublimity of the concluding scenes has already been discussed. They have little more to contribute to our investigation of Dido's character. All that remains now is to translate decision into deed. A second apparition of Mercury precipitates the action. Aeneas departs the same night. As dawn breaks, Dido sees the Trojan ships sailing out of the harbour of Carthage. It takes a while for her to grasp that an unaccustomed scene, a harbour empty of ships, has taken the place of the accustomed one, a harbour filled with ships. Then she breaks into her seventh speech (*'pro Iuppiter! ibit . . .'*), ablaze with an indignation that is as illogical (because Aeneas' going was settled) as it is convincing. We do often react, when confronted with the spectacle of something happening that we knew would happen, as though what we saw were totally unexpected. There is just a hint that Dido had at the back of her mind some form of vengeance. Or was the vengeance she planned that Aeneas should witness the spectacle of her suicide? We must not allow ourselves to be trapped into discussing what might have happened. The only details of the story are those the poem gives.[1]

Dido's short speech to the old nurse follows (Speech viii, '*Annam, cara mihi nutrix, huc siste sororem . . .*')—a brief interval of calm while she pulls herself together after the near frenzy of Speech vii. The discipline she exercises on herself here at the very moment of her death enables Virgil to make convincing the dignity that her dying words restore to his tragic queen. They follow immediately (Speech ix, '*dulces exuuiae, dum fata deusque sinebat . . .*'):

> 'dulces exuuiae, dum fata deusque sinebat,   651
> accipite hanc animam meque his exsoluite curis.'

> '*Relics sweet so long as fate and god allowed,
> receive the life in me, and free me from my grief.*'

As she speaks her words acquire the ring of a formal epitaph, leaning on the familiar Roman convention which made the dead person address the living from the tomb:[2]

> 'uixi et quem dederat cursum fortuna peregi,
> et nunc magna mei sub terras ibit imago.
> urbem praeclaram statui, mea moenia uidi,   655
> ulta uirum poenas inimico a fratre recepi,
> felix, heu nimium felix, si litora tantum
> numquam Dardaniae tetigissent nostra carinae.'

---

[1] The dangers involved in expanding the poet's story for him are discussed by L. C. Knights in a well known, and important, essay, 'How many children had Lady Macbeth?', in *Explorations* (1946), pp. 1–39.

All the same we should not overlook hints the poet gives of complexities not dwelt on; they help to prevent the progress of the action from becoming simply mechanical.

[2] The words *dixitque nouissima uerba* suggest as well that Dido is pronouncing her own funeral oration: cf. the same words of Aeneas farewelling the dead, *Aeneid* vi, 231.

Virgil's Tragic Queen

> *'Life's done, the span fortune granted ended.*
> *And now my great ghost proceeds beneath the earth.*
> *I founded a city of renown, I saw my walls rise.*   655
> *I venged my husband's death (a brother was our foe).*
> *Fortune favoured—ah! too much: if but these shores*
> *had never felt the touch of keels from Troy!'*

Dido's statement of her accomplishments in life is set out in four formal end-stopped hexameters, then a final flood of emotion breaks loose the moment her thoughts come back to Aeneas.

The spectacle that follows is noble and impressive. Nor does it lean intolerably upon its conventional tragic framework. Dido is an exceptional woman. She shows it in her capacity to inspire and return love. But we are left, as we should be left, with the feeling that this is not merely a story of a woman who kills herself because she has lost her lover. Dido is exceptional, too, in the standards she sets herself. It is her standards of queenliness, what is due to a queen, what a queen owes to herself, as much as her passionate despair, that lead her to her end. If there was a point in the drama where the motives that moved her seemed less heroic and more wilful and petty, we may now rightly feel that the pettiness has been transcended in the final grandeur of self-destruction.

3

Emergence of a Form: the Latin Short Poem

We should, I suppose, begin by considering what we mean by 'a Poem'. There will be no shortage of critics eager and competent to tell us. As we are anxious, however, to pass on, in order to get to grips with a problem of more practical concern to the reader of Latin poetry, we should look for a critic who is willing to be brief. If his answer clarifies the approach to our real problem, we should not be cross because it seems light-hearted. The distinguished modern German poet and critic Gottfried Benn, lecturing a few years ago at the University of Marburg on 'Problems of Lyric Poetry', began, like us, feeling it was necessary to secure some agreement about what a Poem was. His definition ran like this. You must have noticed, he said, from time to time when you open your Sunday newspaper (though this is something that can happen during the week too), among the solid columns of type, usually in the top right-hand or the bottom left-hand corner, a block of type different from the rest with a frame round it. Well, that is a Poem. It is usually quite short. In autumn it is about November mists. In spring about crocuses. . . .[1]

Benn, like us, was impatient to clear the air for a more profitable discussion; but there is much to be said all the same for this Wittgenstein type of definition in literary criticism.

[1] Gottfried Benn, *Probleme der Lyrik*, Vortrag in der Universität Marburg (1951), p. 5.

Emergence of a Form: the Latin Short Poem

How often does the more pretentious theoretical definition get us further? So long as the critic can get and keep his bearings, it is not usually necessary to settle every theoretical issue before he starts looking at the poetry. It is probably not even possible. The fundamentals of aesthetics have shown themselves to be pretty insoluble. Too conscientious a battle to solve them is likely to get in the way of our understanding of poetry, in-instead of helping. The real way to get somewhere is by endeavouring to build on a basis of rough working concepts, as Benn does, remaining prepared to modify or abandon them when the actual study of literature throws doubt on their validity or their usefulness. It may sound logically messy to advocate such a complicated process of interaction between progressively clarifying approximations, but in most human situations this is the way to keep in touch with reality.

As a matter of fact, we may learn two things of value to our present enquiry from Benn's seemingly frivolous definition. The first is that most people are pretty clear, really, in their own minds about what 'a Poem' is. Implicit in the concept are limiting factors of length, style, social significance and likely range of theme. Automatically involved in any judgment of a poem is an assessment of the degree to which it measures up to our expectations on these counts. Our thinking in fact, not only about 'Poems' but about poetry in the more general sense, tends to be shaped and restricted, without our being fully aware of this, by a pattern of preconceptions built up from the sort of poetry with which we are most familiar. And today it is that kind of short poem, the more external of whose formal characteristics Benn indicates.

This is easy to see. So, too, is the second point, but it is more readily lost sight of, and liable to do more damage if we do lose sight of it. It is that such a concept of 'a Poem' is plainly an unhistorical one. It depends too much on the present habits of poets, publishers and readers to possess permanent validity. A moment's thought tells us these habits are largely determined by the present structure of society. There are obvious dangers in applying, even unconsciously, a pattern of preconceptions based on them to the literature of a society whose social structure differs significantly from ours. We must particularly beware of these preconceptions in approaching a past literature. For there

Emergence of a Form: the Latin Short Poem

the sort of poem described by Benn was not always the usual manifestation of poetry. In Roman literature, for example (to take an obvious difference), the long epic poem was commoner in all periods than the kind of short meditative 'lyric' that we know best today. For an educated Roman in the time of Augustus, 'poem' (*carmen*) would suggest the sort of poetry we discussed in Chapter 2 rather than the sort we discussed in Chapter 1. The poets or poetasters he knew were much more likely to write the former than the latter. The odes of Horace probably seemed odd and unconventional to him in ways that they can't, automatically, to us.

Our preconceptions, then, our working concepts pretty certainly need readjustment in a number of respects. In many cases there will not be the clear intimations of things alien that the sensitive student of modern drama experiences on his first encounter with a Greek tragedy. But the briefest reflection can hardly fail to convince us that our thinking about a Latin poem must be accompanied by some comparable process of reorientation.

At this stage it is important to resist a twinge of panic. Was our study of the Spring Odes of Horace a waste of time after all, we may ask—not because we 'didn't know Latin', but because the odes were just not the kind of poetry we took it to be? The reasonable reader, recalling our discussion of them, will surely feel this is too extreme a position to be adopted seriously. On the other hand we must allow that some systematic reorientation is almost certainly necessary before we can put an ancient poem alongside a modern poem and expect it to stand on its own feet; or before we can regard both the ancient and the modern poems as attempts that may usefully be compared at solving similar difficulties of poetic statement or expression. How do we make this reorientation? That is the problem it will be the object of this chapter to discuss.

We may seem, despite protestations of dislike for theory, to be raising questions that are primarily theoretical. Yet our aim is strictly practical. If we have posed a theoretical problem, it is because the issue it raises is too often sidestepped in discussing Roman poetry, and sidestepping the problem looks like involving us in very real dangers. It is liable, for example, to cause us to misunderstand a great deal of Catullus and Horace.

Emergence of a Form: the Latin Short Poem

Similar problems probably concern all who deal with the poetry of older literatures, perhaps all who deal with any poetry where Benn's definition is not immediately applicable.

There may be said to be two prevailing attitudes to the problem of the short Latin poem. A common attitude among professional scholars is to dismiss the problem from consideration. For them the difficulties a Latin poem presents lie in fixing the text and settling the sense of the words. Neither pursuit should be derided. Both are of capital importance. We may, however, question the assumption that, when these tasks are discharged, nothing requiring the scholar's attention remains to be done.

The indifference of this type of scholar to the problems of reorientation that a Latin poem poses is in part due to the fact that the weight of his attention is most often concentrated on a painstaking scrutiny of short passages, taken in isolation. He seldom allows himself more than a casual enquiry into what the poem as a whole is about. The features of poetry which make it different from prose seem to him frills. They can cause the statements poetry makes to be less clear than prose statements, but they are not an integral part of the statements. Once the text and the sense of the bits are fixed, the only important ingredient of the poem remaining is the line of meaning, the logical connection that exists, or does not exist, between the bits. The rest calls usually for no more than brief *obiter dicta* which sensible people can be expected to accept without argument, due allowance being made for the mysteries of taste. The people who deal with Latin poetry in this way do not always say this in as many words, but this is the attitude implied by what they do say. Possibly they feel the same way about modern poetry. Their attitude may fairly be described as scholarly only in the sense that it reflects their determination to concentrate on things sealed off from the experience of poetry.

The first attitude, then, is that no particular readjustment need be attempted. A second attitude is that the readjustment necessary is total. This is asserted not so much by classical scholars as by professional critics of modern literature—people strenuously concerned with the discussion of poetry. We may suspect they tend to accept the professional classic's judgments about Latin poetry and regard it, understandably, as—by their

Emergence of a Form: the Latin Short Poem

standards—pretty childish stuff. Aware of the complexity of the poetry they know more intimately, they assume ancient and modern poetry are utterly unalike, and the latter obviously superior.[1] We may wonder whether the often-asserted superiority of modern poetry is in fact to some extent a matter only of more responsive readers, better trained to appreciate poetry, and more sensitive critics. The idea sprang originally, however, from Romanticism. Up to the end of the eighteenth century the modern world was content to rival the ancient; the nineteenth felt it had at last overtaken antiquity, in literature as it had materially. We find the idea that modern poetry is quite unlike ancient poetry given pretentious expression in Coleridge.[2] In the German literary tradition it seems the responsibility of Goethe, whose opinions have profoundly influenced German literary critics and classical scholars. While it is today an attitude found primarily among literary critics, it is reflected by that type of classical scholar who breaks off from a scholarly discussion to invite our assent to the proposition that Latin poetry is totally unlike poetry written nowadays.

The representatives of this second attitude reproach Roman poetry in the main with two things. The first is a lack of that lyrical depth which, in the view of the Romantics, could come

---

[1] An example is provided by Mr. Bateson. Discussing a trend away from classical studies, he writes:
   Since 1920 or so the number of serious readers of the classics has decreased. . . . The change is sometimes deplored, not on the ground that English literature is inferior to the classics—*poet for poet it is obviously better*—but because the reading of English poetry, or so it is asserted, does not provide the intellectual discipline of the classics.
(F. W. Bateson, *English Poetry: A Critical Introduction* [1950], p. 263, italics mine.)

[2] A difference in 'fundamental characteristics' between ancient and modern poetry is a recurring theme in Coleridge's *Essays and Lectures on Shakespeare*, e.g.:
   I will note down those fundamental characteristics which contradistinguish the ancient literature from the modern generally. . . . The ancient was allied to statuary, the modern refers to painting. . . . The Greeks idolized the finite, . . . the moderns revere the infinite . . . —hence their passions, their obscure hopes and fears, their wandering through the unknown, their grander moral feelings, their more august conception of man as man, their future rather than their past— in a word, their sublimity.
(*Everyman* edn., p. 19; cf. p. 50.) Compare Lecture on Dante (ibid., p. 273), where Coleridge links the difference in fundamental characteristics with a difference between polytheism and Christianity—a distinction which perhaps inspired C. S. Lewis's well-known half-truths about fundamental differences between ancient love poetry on the one hand and medieval and modern on the other in *The Allegory of Love* (1936), p. 4.

Emergence of a Form: the Latin Short Poem

only from genuine worth-while personal experience. The words *Erlebnis-* and *Bekenntnisdichtung* tend to get splashed around by German critics at this point. Catullus, of course, comes off pretty well on this score. It is customary even to call him a Romantic. Horace fares very badly. Once again confusion is produced in the minds of critics who are not professional classics when they come to discuss Roman poetry. They accept the nineteenth century's low opinion of Horace as a 'lyric' poet, not realizing that it sprang from transitory and now largely defunct Romantic conceptions of what made poetry.[1] The fact that an Horatian ode is in many ways remarkably like a modern poem escapes their attention. Another reproach levelled at Roman poetry is its lack of thematic originality and creative imagination. Again these are aspects of poetry brought to the fore by Romanticism. It has become customary to talk of the Roman poets' 'slavish imitation' of their Greek models and to assume this is something permanently alien to modern ideas about poetry.

Enough has been said to hint how hard the nineteenth century found it, by comparison with the sixteenth, seventeenth and eighteenth, to prevent its preconceptions about poetry from getting in the way of its appreciation, its understanding even, of the Latin short poem. It is surely possible to free ourselves from the incubus of past preconceptions. But what about our own present-day preconceptions? Are they also to be guarded against? What differences should we be aware of between Latin poems and the poems we know today?

Actually the present-day notion of what a poem is and of how it works is a lot less liable to lead us astray than the Romantic one. The present fashion is for poetry that is the product of hard work as well as imagination. We can appreciate better, therefore, the painstaking craftsmanship of Catullus, Horace and Virgil because we are accustomed in our own contemporary literature to poems that are the work of painstaking craftsmen; that are carefully fitted together, controlled by intelligence,

[1] An example of nineteenth-century disparagement of Horace so extreme as to appear ludicrous to us today is Tyrrell's lecture on him delivered at Johns Hopkins in 1893. It contains gems like the following appraisal of Horace's style:
 The runnel is exquisitely smooth, but its shallow waters flow where they will, from their natural channel, and end in a puddle.
(R. Y. Tyrrell, *Lectures on Latin Poetry* [1895], p. 199.)

Emergence of a Form: the Latin Short Poem

consciously evocative of a rich literary tradition. We must first, of course, rediscover the presence of these features in Latin poetry; or at any rate reappraise them, ridding ourselves of judgments passed by several generations of critics who did not look for them, or despised them when they found them. When we have done that, we can begin our closer appraisal with an initial impression that Horace, or Catullus, is doing the sort of thing we know poets do. This does not mean, however, that we may dispense with the process of reorientation: it merely makes the task of getting to know a Latin poem more stimulating.

To begin with, we should remember how rare in ancient literature and how comparatively late a development anything like a modern poem is.[1] Nothing in fact really like a modern meditative lyric poem is to be found until we come to the Roman personal poem of the first century B.C. Because so much of Greek poetry has been lost, we may perhaps lend Roman personal poetry a uniqueness and an originality to which it is not entitled. The fact remains that here for the first time we meet with poems that we can recognize as poems comparable to ours. On the other hand no fruitful historical evolution followed Roman poetry of the first century B.C. After passing from a simple to a highly mannered style (compare English poetry of the seventeenth century with that of the sixteenth), the new style failed abruptly and inexplicably almost at the outset of the Empire, rather perhaps as seventeenth-century metaphysical poetry gave way to our English Augustan age.

---

[1] We tend too much to think about classical literature unhistorically, as though all classical writers belonged to a single epoch. What we have, of course, is an evolutionary process (not accompanied by a continuous rise in *quality* from period to period), occupying many centuries, and extending a good deal longer in time than most modern literatures have yet extended. In Greek the short poem was quite unusual. The three great modes of Greek poetry—epic, lyric and dramatic—succeeded one another; they did not co-exist. See Bruno Snell, 'Das Erwachen der Persönlichkeit in der frühgriechischen Lyrik', *Antike*, xvii (1941), pp. 5–34. The simplest forms of song are doubtless primeval. But how far the poetry of Sappho, Alcaeus and Anacreon got beyond this stage is hard for us today to fix. It is almost impossible to read their fragments and take them as they are without attributing to them an emotional and intellectual strength, suggested to us by the words, that the words can hardly have possessed in their historical context. The formal qualities of poems that survive only in fragments are beyond assessment. And when Aeolian lyric passed into the choral lyric of Pindar and Athenian tragedy, we are confronted with forms remote from the short personal poem.

Emergence of a Form: the Latin Short Poem

Tracing the evolution of a style and assessing the degree to which it bulks in a national literature are matters that concern the literary historian rather than the literary critic. But there is a way in which the historical context concerns the literary critic too. Often we find the Roman poet fumbling with problems of expression that we have long ago solved; preoccupied, to a degree that can bore us, with the effective expression of ideas that hardly seem novel enough any longer to justify the poetic energy expended on them. The impression is just, but it needs correction by what Mr. Lionel Trilling calls (picking up the title of an unfinished novel by Henry James) 'the sense of the past'.[1]

Let us take a simple example and endeavour to gain from it some preliminary notions of perspective as a contribution to the sort of reorientation which the practical critic requires before he can usefully practise criticism. Here is a poem of Catullus (Poem 86):

>   Quintia formosa est multis. mihi candida, longa,
>   recta est: haec ego sic singula confiteor.
>   totum illud formosa nego: nam nulla uenustas,
>   nulla in tam magno est corpore mica salis.
>   Lesbia formosa est, quae cum pulcerrima tota est,   5
>   tum omnibus una omnis surripuit Veneres.

> *Quintia's a Beauty, many say. I say she's tall, fair-skinned,*
> *holds herself straight. Each single item I allow.*
> *But is the total Beauty? No. She's no charm, no grace.*
> *There's not a spark in that great frame of wit or fun.*
> *Lesbia? There's Beauty now. Utterly lovely she is, and, too,   5*
> *all charm's incitements she's assumed that any other owned.*

Our initial impression is of a sort of combination of Elizabethan and seventeenth-century lyric. A description of the poet's mistress, held in check by intellectual concentration on a point. The point is one that seems to have fascinated Catullus. What does a woman need to have for you to call her 'a Beauty', *formosa*? Quintia was fair-complexioned—clearly a mark in her

---

[1] Lionel Trilling, 'The sense of the past', in *The Liberal Imagination* (English edn., 1951), pp. 181–97. For a discussion of this question, see my study of Catullus in J. P. Sullivan, ed., *Critical Essays in Roman Literature*, Vol. i, *Elegy and Lyric* (1962).

Emergence of a Form: the Latin Short Poem

favour. Roman gentlemen seem also to have preferred the large, stately woman. Catullus' terse *candida, longa, recta* (he is concerned only for the moment with ticking off Quintia's claims to recognition) can be illuminated by lines of Propertius (ii, 2):

> fulua coma est longaeque manus, et maxima toto   5
>   corpore, et incedit uel Ioue digna soror,
> aut cum Dulichias Pallas spatiatur ad aras,
>   Gorgonis anguiferae pectus operta comis;
> qualis et Ischomache Lapithae genus heroine,
>   Centauris medio grata rapina mero.   10

Yeats' version recaptures the emotional warmth behind the words:

> *She might, so noble from head*
> *To great shapely knees*
> *The long flowing line,*
> *Have walked to the altar*
> *Through the holy images*
> *At Pallas Athene's side,*
> *Or been fit spoil for a centaur*
> *Drunk with the unmixed wine.*[1]

But is that really all a woman needs to be called 'a Beauty'? Of the three common Latin words for 'beautiful', *pulcher* is the standard literary word, *bellus* the term of colloquial praise easily awarded, and *formosus* the warmly passionate word that was to become the favourite of Propertius. Perhaps in Catullus' day it was a word just beginning to be bandied about; Catullus' verse makes free use of the value judgments reflected by the jargon of the smart set to which he belonged—words like *urbanus*, *uenustus*, *lepidus*.[2] At any rate, Catullus uses *formosus* only in this poem, and there is just a suggestion in the phrase *totum illud formosa nego* that the word is not his own.[3] It should

---

[1] W. B. Yeats, 'A Thought from Propertius', *Collected Poems* (2nd edn. 1950), p. 172.
[2] See L. Ferrero, 'La poetica di Catullo', in *Un'introduzione a Catullo* (1955), p. 43ff.
[3] Propertius uses *formosus* thirty-four times, Virgil sixteen times in the *Eclogues* (not at all in the *Aeneid*): the word, perhaps, owes its introduction into love poetry to Catullus' Poem 86. It is used only once by Plautus—of a (symbolic) goat, *Mer.* 229, and once by Terence.

Emergence of a Form: the Latin Short Poem

convey, he maintains, something more than physical loveliness. Lesbia, now, is undeniably lovely (*quae cum pulcerrima tota est*); but about her there is something transcending physical perfection that makes you want to call her *formosa*. The six lines of the poem are devoted to a crisp analysis of this problem. Catullus decides the ideal woman must have *uenustas* and *sal*. After five lines of sober intellectual statement a rush of lyrical enthusiasm floods into the final line, abandoning logic for hyperbole. At the same time *uenustas* is caught up from the end of line 3, and a whole range of fresh overtones abstracted for the concluding *Veneres*.[1]

The primary statement of line 6 is that Lesbia has purloined all the Venuses. We think perhaps of famous statues of the goddess: from each Lesbia has somehow prised something.[2] But now the normal meaning of *uenustas* (a trait of personality rather than appearance) introduces a meaning we should not otherwise give to the plural. Lesbia, Catullus means, has every kind of charm, sophistication, as well as every attribute of good looks. Simultaneously the words *nulla uenustas . . . in tam magno est corpore* acquire new meaning when we are reminded that *uenustas* comes from *uenus*. The abstract meaning of *uenus* closest to the personification Venus (sexual desire) emerges. Line 4 now implies that, despite her good looks, there is nothing physically attractive about Quintia.

How do these lines measure up to our present-day preconceptions of what a poem should be? What adjustments should our historical sense impose? A lot turns on our response to that final line, where, it seems to me, statement soars into poetry, as it often does in Catullus.[3] Something that is really hardly yet a poem, by our standards, suddenly becomes one. Those not responsive to the richness of the final line might prefer to call this an epigram rather than a poem. It is true that the lines (apart from the last) sound dry and matter-of-fact by comparison

---

[1] Catullus connects *Veneres* with *uenustas* again to make a neat point in the opening lines of Poem 3:
   Lugete, o Veneres Cupidinesque,
   et quantum est hominum uenustiorum.

[2] Cf. Lucian's description of Panthea (*De Imaginibus*) in terms of a synthesis of famous statues.

[3] See my study of Catullus Poem 41 in Sullivan, op. cit.

Emergence of a Form: the Latin Short Poem

with Propertius' lines; and tempting, perhaps, to call the one poetry just beginning, and the other true poetry. That Catullus' lines are, however, something more than an epigram is suggested by a comparison with Poem 43:

> Salue, nec minimo puella naso
> nec bello pede nec nigris ocellis
> nec longis digitis nec ore sicco
> nec sane nimis elegante lingua;
> decoctoris amica Formiani,　　　　　　　　　5
> ten prouincia narrat esse bellam?
> tecum Lesbia nostra comparatur?
> o saeclum insapiens et infacetum!

Greetings girl whose nose is not exactly small,
whose ankle's not well shaped, whose eyes not black,
whose fingers are not slender, whose lips not dry,
whose tongue avoids all excess of elegance.
Bankrupt Formianus' friend,
among provincials are tales of your beauty spun?
Is your reputation with my Lesbia's coupled?
Truly these are times devoid of taste and judgment.

Here, despite the more boisterous tone, the words do not rise above the level of exuberant persiflage. The lines pose no problem to draw the poet out.

By comparison Poem 86 is a serious poem. It answers to our concept of what a poem should aim at, and achieve. At the same time some readjustment is called for. In the absence of a sense of the past, the lines are apt to sound flippant, because the problem they solve no longer seems fresh or urgent. We all know nowadays a really attractive woman must have charm and sophistication as well as looks. The idea is commonplace, the words to express it come easily. But in Catullus' day the Latin vocabulary for concepts like this was still relatively unsubtle. Words existed but were only just being given full, precise meanings. Moreover, the idea that their mistresses, too, could possess the easy sophistication that Catullus and his set had themselves so recently won for male society was novel and exciting. Catullus' lines are a serious, analytic statement of a

Emergence of a Form: the Latin Short Poem

new concept of the role of women in smart society that came to be embodied in the slogan *docta puella*.[1]

Suppose now we compare our Poem 86 with an actual Elizabethan poem. John Lyly's little poem for example:

> My Daphne's hair is twisted gold,
> Bright stars a-piece her eyes do hold;
> My Daphne's brow inthrones the Graces,
> My Daphne's beauty stains all faces;
> On Daphne's cheek grow rose and cherry,
> On Daphne's lip a sweeter berry;
> Daphne's snowy hand but touched does melt,
> And then no heavenlier warmth is felt;
> My Daphne's voice tunes all the spheres,
> My Daphne's music charms all ears.
> Fond am I thus to sing her praise;
> These glories now are turned to bays.

Here the note we detect in the last line of *Quintia formosa est multis* is more sustained, but both pieces have an unmistakable air of belonging to the same family. Compare the third line of Lyly's poem,

> My Daphne's brow inthrones the Graces,

with the last line of Catullus',

> tum omnibus una omnis surripuit Veneres.

One might quote any number of short Elizabethan poems to put the point beyond doubt. Most would show, like Lyly's, a verbal richness that Catullus cannot match. He has not the same poetic tradition to lean on. But that this is due more to differences of personality and style than to differences in objective or any difference in fundamental poetic characteristics, is suggested by a further look at Propertius (ii, 3):

> nec me tam facies, quamuis sit candida, cepit
> (lilia non domina sint magis alba mea;   10

---

[1] See Quinn, Chapter v, 'The Catullan experience'.

Emergence of a Form: the Latin Short Poem

```
ut Maeotica nix minio si certet Hibero,
    utque rosae puro lacte natant folia),
nec de more comae per leuia colla fluentes,
    non oculi, geminae, sidera nostra, faces,
nec si qua Arabio lucet bombyce puella            15
    (non sum de nihilo blandus amator ego).
```

It isn't fair complexion merely that has caught me
(though lilies are not paler than my mistress' skin—   10
like snow of Caucasus at war with brilliant Spanish red;
like roses' petals when they float in unskimmed milk).
Not her hair cascading on her shoulders' smoothness.
Not her eyes, twin fires, the stars my life hangs on.
Not silk Arab that half reveals the girl it clothes   15
(let me play the gallant lover—I've a lot to fuss about).

On the other hand most of the Elizabethan lyrics we might look at would lack Catullus' intellectual strength, which does not come in English verse till the seventeenth century. And most would show an Ovidian archness that Catullus does not descend to. Again, perhaps, social factors are involved, and minor readjustments called for. But surely if we call the Elizabethan trifles poems, then we must call *Quintia formosa est multis* a poem, too.

Length, for some the criterion for separating epigram from poem, has in fact not much to do with it. Take Poem 14 of Catullus:

```
Ni te plus oculis meis amarem,
iucundissime Calue, munere isto
odissem te odio Vatiniano:
nam quid feci ego quidue sum locutus,
cur me tot male perderes poetis?                  5
isti di mala multa dent clienti,
qui tantum tibi misit impiorum.
quod si, ut suspicor, hoc nouum ac repertum
munus dat tibi Sulla litterator,
non est mi male, sed bene ac beate,               10
quod non dispereunt tui labores.
di magni, horribilem et sacrum libellum!
```

Emergence of a Form: the Latin Short Poem

  quem tu scilicet ad tuum Catullum
  misti, continuo ut die periret,
  Saturnalibus, optimo dierum!   15
  non non hoc tibi, false, sic abibit.
  nam, si luxerit, ad librariorum
  curram scrinia, Caesios, Aquinos,
  Suffenum, omnia colligam uenena,
  ac te his suppliciis remunerabor.   20
  uos hinc interea ualete abite
  illuc, unde malum pedem attulistis,
  saecli incommoda, pessimi poetae.

If you did not mean to me more than sight itself,
my very dearest Calvus, your present would have led
to my hating you equally as Vatinius does.
What have I done, what word spoken to incur
this plague of rotten poets you inflict on me?   5
May the gods bring all manner of perdition
to the client who sent you this ungodly pack!
It must be, I think, the bellelettristic Sulla[1]
who thought up this novel gift to give to you.
It's not that I'm cross—I'm terribly pleased in fact 10
if your labours go not unrewarded, but
ye gods! what a bloody revolting book it is!
And you deliberately sent it off to your friend
to cause him a day of uninterrupted misery,
and that at the Saturnalia, the happiest of feasts! 15
You're not going to get away with this, you crook.
The moment it is day, I'll race to the booksellers'
stalls. I'll buy the works of chaps like Caesius
and Aquinus, of Suffenus, the whole poisonous lot,
to torture you with them in retribution.   20
Meanwhile, be off with you, depart, return
to where you tottered on your ill-starred journey, you
wretched, wretched poets, the nuisance of our time!

This is much too long to be called an epigram. Yet it is only an expansion, into twenty-three lines, of witty writing at the

---

[1] The unknown Sulla is usually dismissed as 'an elementary schoolmaster', but *litterator* was used by Messalla Corvinus of the poet and critic Valerius Cato. See Fordyce's note on this line, p. 136.

Emergence of a Form: the Latin Short Poem

epigrammatic level. No trace of anything we could fairly call seriously poetic. No sign the writer is straining to put into words an idea for which words are not easily found. Put it alongside *Quintia formosa est multis* and we see at once that the shorter piece clearly has something the longer never aspires to.

While, then, there are a number of reasons for regarding *Quintia formosa est multis* as a poem, our recognition of this at once raises several questions. Is this a fair example? Have we not chosen a piece which has certain qualities of poetry, but is so slight as to make recognition of it as a poem of little significance? How easy is it to find something in Latin a dozen lines long or more that by modern standards can really be regarded as a poem? Then how representative is *Quintia formosa est multis* anyway of the kind of poetry Catullus and his contemporaries wrote? And to what extent, even here, are there aspects of the poem —the manner of its genesis, the poet's intention—which I have perhaps thrust into the background in order to stretch the parallel with modern poetry; but which, if we are to make any critical progress, should compel us to admit that Catullus is playing the game to rules no longer observed?

A few words on two or three points may help in clearing the way. To begin with, there are features of Roman personal poetry that mark it off from the generality of ancient literature, setting the Roman personal poets upon a fresh road that was quickly to take them surprisingly close to modern poetry. One is the new relationship they established between the poet and his audience.[1] They succeeded in wrenching the poet away from his role of entertainer, with the obligations and the limitations that role entailed, leaving him free to concentrate on writing what he felt impelled to write. It is the difference between communication and self-expression. The art of communication was so systematically studied in antiquity that it encouraged in most periods a subservience to audience-reaction incompatible with the writing of serious personal poetry. (Recall Cicero's often repeated dictum that the audience alone is judge of the orator's success.) Quite suddenly and for a short time—really only from Catullus to Horace—there is a break away from the rhetorical tradition. An audience still remains, most often in the shape of a formal addressee (about whom we shall have more to say);

[1] See Quinn, pp. 87–90.

but the need to appeal to the public at large is no longer admitted.

We cannot here explore the social factors that brought about, or rather permitted, this revolution in the poet's status. What concerns us is that, when the poet is thus placed in the foreground of importance and his ultimate audience in the background, it becomes possible to make a poem out of things private to the poet, things linked with, and partly compounded of, his personal thoughts and reactions. It is instructive to compare the Hellenistic Greek epigram, where at first sight we have something that looks like a shorter Roman personal poem. But the Greek epigram, though tied to a personal 'I', uses the 'I' only as a depersonalized peg. Roman personal poetry, on the other hand, is devoid of the polite concern Hellenistic epigram displays to spare the reader a too personal revelation of the individual quirks of its maker.[1]

Talk of the poet's private reactions makes it sound as if the innovation that Roman personal poetry represents lay in the introduction of the poetry of personal experience. While this is true to some extent, it is wise to remind ourselves that the Roman poets were more reticent in their use of poetry as a vehicle for raw personal experience than seemed natural to Romantic poets and critics. Catullus, even in the Lesbia poems, writes, it seems to me, under a pressure that is artistic rather than autobiographical. There has long been, of course, a division between what we might call the formalist critics of poetry, who envisage the poet's secret as a technical mastery of words,[2] and those other critics who regard the poet as devoted to communicating unusually exciting or moving things he has experienced (in life or in imagination). The issue is seen more clearly when we come to Propertius: passion shows in his poetry as clearly as it does in the love poetry of Donne which it often resembles. Yet neither can reasonably be said to be concerned primarily with communicating experience. And in discussing either we should be ingenuous not to suspect a mixture of fiction and actual experience.

[1] See U. Knoche, 'Eine römische Wurzel lateinischer Persönlichkeitsdichtung', *N.J.A.B.*, iii (1940), pp. 238–52.

[2] Robert Graves, *Goodbye to All That* (revised edn. 1957), p. 244, so describes T. E. Lawrence's attitude to poetry. It is interesting to observe that Graves, a strict craftsman himself, clearly regards this formalist approach as inadequate.

Emergence of a Form: the Latin Short Poem

A striking feature, none the less, of the Roman personal poem is the way it suggests often, by its form, that it records an emotional tension present in the poet's mind at the time of writing. The result is a kind of poem remote from anything we can fairly call song, and the term 'lyric', in so far as the term suggests song, is misleading. An inner meditation is not an uncommon form for a modern poem to take, but the Roman meditation is apt to be more voluble than the modern poem. The link here is with drama. A familiar convention of ancient drama was for a character to express in a long set speech the progress of an inward emotional conflict. It was natural to draw on this convention when the short personal poem began to emerge as a poetic form. The impetus came not so much from a moral urge to confess, as an artistic urge to solve the problems involved in finding a technique (in a new style that avoided the grandiloquence and stylization of tragedy) for expressing the veerings, doubts or passions of personal experience, and weaving these into complex succinct form.

Often enough, especially in Horace, the thought process is a casual, languid one, while the poetic form given it is terse and exquisite. The typical Horatian ode is hardly ever a static lyric revolving descriptively round a single idea. It sometimes sets out a logical sequence of ideas; but more often what we have is an organic succession of ideas, one leading out of another and the whole owing its unity to the poet's personality, and not to any logical structure—a characteristic that has often bewildered critics.[1]

The well known *O fons Bandusiae* . . . (*Odes* iii, 13) is an example of a poem based on such an evolving pattern of thought:

> O fons Bandusiae splendidior uitro
> dulci digne mero non sine floribus,
>   cras donaberis haedo,
>   cui frons turgida cornibus

---

[1] Tyrrell again has the merit of putting into words what the more conventional scholar of his day might have hesitated to admit (op. cit., p. 199):
> The theory that the Odes are little more than experiments in the Greek lyric metres, having little or no train of connected thought or feeling, becomes very tempting.

Emergence of a Form: the Latin Short Poem

> primis et uenerem et proelia destinat 5
> frustra: nam gelidos inficiet tibi
>   rubro sanguine riuos
>   lasciui suboles gregis.
>
> te flagrantis atrox hora Caniculae
> nescit tangere, tu frigus amabile 10
>   fessis uomere tauris
>   praebes et pecori uago.
>
> fies nobilium tu quoque fontium,
> me dicente cauis impositam ilicem
>   saxis, unde loquaces 15
>   lymphae desiliunt tuae.

Welling waters of Bandusia, outglittering glass,
just is your claim on sweet strong wine and flowers,
but tomorrow's gift to you will be the goat,
whose forehead lowers with tips of

horns, promise of a lecher's battles he'll   5
not fight: your chill stream instead
will run red with blood the lust-
inheriting youngster shed.

The searing peak of summer heat leaves
you inviolate, free to ministrate a cool   10
loveliness to oxen the plough has tired,
or aimless wandering kine.

Your name to the catalogue of noble springs
I hereby add, citing ilex-oak and the eroded
rocky mass it cloaks, whence your   15
loquacious waters tumble.

The scene is a hot summer's day in the country.[1] Horace finds himself beside a spring gushing out from the rocks, shaded by

---

[1] I take *flagrantis atrox hora Caniculae* as fixing the dramatic moment in midsummer: to suppose the poem was written on the eve of the Fontinalia in mid-October in mid-autumn makes nonsense of a poem filled with the imagery of summer—a good example of how a mistaken assumption can become perpetuated by exegetical tradition and go on bedevilling our interpretation of a poem or passage that was not thought about with sufficient care in the first place. The assumption

Emergence of a Form: the Latin Short Poem

trees—or supposes this. While he relaxes, a rambling train of thought unwinds. Streams and fountains are holy and sacrifices are made to them. This spring deserves such attention, if ever one did. There is a sacrifice tomorrow. A young goat will have to die. If we like, we can imagine a herd of goats as part of the scene Horace is contemplating. At any rate, his thoughts wander to a particular goat, whose appearance suggests a little delicate whimsy about the frustration of the young goat's aspirations as a lover. (Goats were proverbial for their lustiness.) Then back to the waters of the spring, cool and clear today, but tomorrow stained with hot, dark blood.

The third stanza extols the spring's benefactions as a refuge from the cruel heat for man and beast, ending with another discreetly implied contrast: the oxen pulling the plough, whose walking is purposeful and productive, and the other animals who wander idly. Obliquely a picture of the spring is built up in our minds, but overtly the statement of benefactions (adapted from a common cliché of religious hymns) leads to the promise of a reward: immortality. There were springs famous in literature: Castalia on Parnassus, Hippocrene and Aganippe on Helicon.[1] Bandusia is less heroic, just as Horace's poetry is less heroic, but her fame is equally assured. In the final stanza Horace passes to a description of the natural features of the spring, linking these characteristically with an ironically proud reference to his poetry. Or rather to this poem; because what started as a languid train of thought eventually ended as a tightly constructed poem. The effect of *me dicente* is to thrust aside the artistic framework for a moment's unexpected intimacy with the reader—the effect the playwright produces by a line suddenly addressed to the audience.

---

[1] Moreover these names were current in Hellenistic literature as the symbols of different types of poetry. The fashion was imitated by certain Roman poets, notably Propertius.

---

is that the festival Horace alludes to must be a particular festival of springs, the Fontinalia, which we happen to know about from Festus and Varro (see the commentators). Yet how unsatisfactory that assumption is (apart from tying the poem to an inappropriate season of the year) is revealed by Campbell's discussion of the passage, pp. 211-2, especially p. 212, Note 1.

Actually sacrifices to springs appear to have quite a respectable pedigree, at any rate in literature, and there seems no reason to connect them all with the Fontinalia: see Frazer and Bömer on Ovid, *F.* iii, 300. Horace perhaps has in mind a passage in Homer, *Il.* xxiii, 147.

Emergence of a Form: the Latin Short Poem

It will be seen how greatly this little poem gains by our understanding of it as the record of a process of thought. It is equally clear how the process of thought is only the beginning. Indeed the word 'record' needs clarification, perhaps, in order to avoid misunderstanding, now that 'record' increasingly implies the crudely verbatim. The record a poem like this provides is a highly concentrated and polished one, to be compared, say, with the record made by an accomplished historian of a notable battle.

The readjustment called for in getting to know a poem like '*O fons Bandusiae* . . .' is slight. The main thing is to realize that what Horace presents as a dramatic monologue corresponds to what we should expect, if we were reading a modern poem, to have presented as an inner meditation.[1] Turning to details of structure, let us consider a type of poem where a formal difference tends to cast the Roman poem in a mould tighter than that which shapes a modern poem. This is what we may call the poem's formal excuse. Here we have, I think, the vestiges of a real artistic problem whose restraining influence modern poets scarcely feel. When a poet today wants to write a poem, he goes and writes it. I do not mean it is easy: the task may dominate him for days or weeks. What I mean is that his background of poetic tradition is so vast and so varied that he can let it suggest patterns of words, ideas, ways of dealing with ideas, without any danger that what he writes will turn out to be moulded into any clear-cut, recognizable traditional form. He can write a ballade or one of the stricter forms of sonnet if he chooses; he can recall allusively by his theme, or his treatment of it, well-known poems of the past. But he is equally free not to do either of these things, and the chances are the poem he writes will not immediately recall, or greatly resemble, any poem or group of poems already existing.

With the Roman poets the case is often different. In the first place, it is almost as if they felt self-conscious about writing poetry at all. The short personal poem was still something pretty uncommon and it gave public expression to the poet's thoughts with a freedom that seemed to call for justification in a society as yet reticent in self-revelation. Moreover, it was not easy. The uncovering of one's thoughts was made to seem more natural if the poet professed to be uncovering them to somebody

---

[1] This type of Horatian ode is discussed more fully in the next chapter.

Emergence of a Form: the Latin Short Poem

—a friend for example. The reader could feel then he was overhearing a confidence, not witnessing an act of gratuitous exhibitionism. Hence the addressee who is so much more a feature of this kind of Roman poetry than he is today. Even then, to appear justified, the revelation needed some kind of occasion or excuse. The personal poet tended to cling to occasions where the use of verse was justified by tradition: deaths, birthdays, a friend to be welcomed home from abroad, invited to dinner or farewelled,[1] an enemy to be lampooned, and so on. Traditionally these had called only for elegant, light-hearted *uersiculi*; or (deaths particularly) had imposed a rigid, trite formality that excluded the poet's personal reactions. Now they began to serve as a formal—often fictitious—excuse for a serious poem. We can see the transition still in progress often in Catullus; in Horace and Propertius the change in status is usually complete.

Now, the inhibiting effect of having to appear to talk to someone or something, instead of freely voicing one's thoughts about that person or thing, is apparent. To cast thought in the form of a dialogue, with a potential interlocutor always more or less in the foreground, is liable to make frankness look a little odd. It is a situation which threatens to turn reflection into argument. These are all factors which are liable to set the Roman poem on a course that is strange to us. Moreover, we find it hard to take seriously as poems pieces where the writer seems to have let his thoughts slip without resistance into a trite occasional form; particularly if, as in Horace, the casual nature of the occasion appears to conflict with the poet's artistic and moral seriousness.

To some extent, of course, in the infancy of the short personal poem it must have been hard to create something that did not cling more or less closely to some existing type of writing. There is more to the matter, however, than that. We get the impression that the Roman personal poets used the traditional forms beyond what was inevitable, consciously turning a familiar form to an unfamiliar use. Partly this is the result of artistic loneliness in strange poetic territory. Another reason, I think, was in order to give this new Roman poetry, technically so indebted to Greece, roots that bound it to native Roman

[1] For farewell poems see Chapter 9.

Emergence of a Form: the Latin Short Poem

culture through the evocation of Roman institutions, scenes and habits of daily life.

We shall discuss this tendency for established forms to persist in a later chapter (Chapter 9). At present we are more concerned with the emergence of a new form by a process of adaptation of earlier, less ambitious forms. Occasionally a poem succeeds in exploiting the formal pattern, turning it to a new purpose instead of leaning upon it. It becomes important then to understand what is going on in the complex poem that results. This is especially true of a transitional poet like Catullus. In his work there are both poems which merely lean on traditional forms and poems which seek to exploit form. Poem 3, for example, turns the old Roman dirge to a new ironically sophisticated purpose.[1] More interesting is Poem 101, where the exploitation of traditional material is particularly complex:[2]

> Multas per gentes et multa per aequora uectus
>   aduenio has miseras, frater, ad inferias,
> ut te postremo donarem munere mortis
>   et mutam nequiquam alloquerer cinerem.
> quandoquidem fortuna mihi tete abstulit ipsum,   5
>   heu miser indigne frater adempte mihi,
> nunc tamen interea haec, prisco quae more parentum
>   tradita sunt tristi munere ad inferias,
> accipe fraterno multum manantia fletu,
>   atque in perpetuum, frater, aue atque uale.   10

> *Many peoples, many seas traversed,*
> *have brought me, brother, to your poor funeral,*
> *to give that last gift the dead receive*
> *and uselessly address the voiceless dust:*
> *since fate deprives me of your actual self . . .*   5
> *(O my poor brother so wrongly torn from me),*
> *following our fathers' ancient practice and their*
> *grim tomb ritual, these provisional goods*
> *accept (all wet with a brother's tears), and*
> *for all eternity, brother, greeting and farewell.*   10

---

[1] See N. I. Herescu, *R.E.L.*, xxv (1947), p. 74, and Quinn, p. 96.
[2] Cf. Fordyce's comment in his introduction to Poem 101:
Here as elsewhere he has turned a recognized literary form into something more intimate and personal.

Emergence of a Form: the Latin Short Poem

We are to imagine Catullus standing by the grave of his brother in Asia Minor. It seems likely he had journeyed there in order to discharge some form of ceremony that would assure his brother's peace in death. The situation is rather like that in *Aeneid* iii, 62–8, when Aeneas and his followers set at rest the soul of Polydorus. The ritual naturally involved traditional formulae as well as traditional actions. Catullus, however, wished to say something from his own point of view, something transcending the ritual situation. And when later he came to make a poem out of the situation, the poem created problems of expression that no normal expansion of a grave epigram could cope with.

The poem that he did write works clearly on two levels which, I think, Catullus has gone to some trouble to distinguish. The ceremony requires him to address his dead brother and to say certain things. Fragments of these prescribed formulae lie embedded in the poem. For the sake of clarity I have left unitalicized the corresponding sections of the translation. This necessarily makes the distinction rigid and mechanical instead of organic: in reality what the poem aims at is not a staccato jumping from one to the other, but a fusion in which the elements, though fused together, retain their separate identities. There might well be some argument about which element a particular group of words belongs to. These fragments are surrounded by the kind of commentary that might occur in the thoughts of an unusually sensitive person involved in what he feels a necessary, but inadequate, ritual.

To convey this higher level of thought, to which the fragments of ritual are set in ironic contrast, Catullus does two things. First, he turns to the obvious device of addressing his brother in the commentary as well as in the formal utterance, but with a heightened intensity and intimacy. Second, he gives a new meaning to the traditional artistic device of speaking to the dead man by suggesting that it is not an empty device; that there really exists between him and his brother some possibility of communication transcending normal experience. (Poem 96 also reflects this feeling that an unusual degree of sympathy can keep the living and the dead in communication; in Poem 96 the feeling is much more explicit and that poem can serve, therefore, to support our interpretation of Poem 101.)

Emergence of a Form: the Latin Short Poem

The poem opens with a mild rhetorical flourish that creates a note of conventional solemnity. It is not overdone, of course—there can be no question of parody in a poem like this. But the opening hexameter strikes a note which is not supported by the sober realism of the pentameter that completes the couplet. This new, quieter tone continues in the next two lines, which end with a statement of what common sense tells Catullus to be the futility of the occasion; though we see it is a futility that Catullus cannot bring himself to accept. The *postremum munus* of line 3 is probably the ritual handful of dust thrown on the tomb.[1] Line 5 is again a ringing hexameter, enunciating the sort of commonplace inevitable in public utterance on such occasions, and serving as a preamble to the actual ceremony referred to in lines 7 and 8. But the commonplace of line 5 is followed immediately by an intimate parenthesis in line 6. A similar parenthesis interrupts the ceremony in line 9, cutting off the description of the ritual from the concluding line. The last line, which has been often admired, is pretty certainly partly formula (the ritual *aue atque uale*), and partly commentary (*atque in perpetuum, frater*), a trite enough reflection, but freshened somehow and strengthened (in a way it is easier to feel than explain) by the trace of sombre irony that the structure of the poem lends Catullus' words. As he pronounces the final ritual formula, we seem to catch the poet's sad aside to his brother, excusing the shallow rhetoric of a ceremony he feels to be unworthy of the intimacy that still subsists, somehow, between them.[2]

Poem 101 is a success. The traditional elements therefore—

---

[1] Cf. Horace's *pulueris exigui munera*, *Odes* i, 28, 3–4. In line 8, *tristi munere* refers partly to the 'grim ritual' (abstract sense of *munus*); partly to the actual gifts ('in sad offering'), as in Virgil, *Aeneid* xi, 26 (concrete sense of *munus*)—a good example of poetically effective ambiguity.

[2] The sensitive reader need hardly be reminded of our earlier warning against making the separation of the two levels in this poem too rigid. But if he feels less than convinced of their presence, he may turn with profit to Aeneas' speech at his father's grave in *Aeneid* v, 45–71. Virgil, I think, imitates the conflict we have in Catullus between personal grief and what the occasion requires. In Aeneas' speech we have: first, the formal exordium, with elaborate statement (e.g., a vocative periphrasis that occupies a full line) (lines 45–8); then the personal note, hesitantly introduced (*nisi fallor . . .*), the tone disjointed by comparison with the exordium (lines 49–54); then the official tone resumed: the occasion is now described as a happy one (*laetum*) whereas in the personal section it was one for grief (*acerbum*) (lines 55–63); finally, details of the games to be held, rounded off with the reminder to his audience, 'Don't forget this is a religious occasion' (lines 64–71).

Emergence of a Form: the Latin Short Poem

the fragments of the actual words of the ritual and the direct address of his dead brother—do not strike us as unnatural. Once we think about them, however, we should probably admit a modern poet would be more likely to describe the formulae of the ritual (using words such as 'archaic', 'rhetorical', 'inadequate', perhaps) rather than resorting, as Catullus does, to oblique evocation of them. And, while the modern poet might address his dead brother, he is more likely to address his readers in general—or nobody in particular. It is doubtful whether Catullus would have had the linguistic resources to *describe* the ritual with sufficient suppleness. He might have had considerable difficulty in conveying his feelings at all without the help of tradition. He found instead the solution we have in Poem 101. The result is undoubtedly a poem in our sense of the word, but a poem that works in accordance with principles the literary historian needs to uncover before the literary critic can fruitfully take over.

4

Dramatic Monologue in the Odes of Horace

IN May 1922 the Classical Association of Leipzig was privileged to hear an address by the eminent German Latinist Richard Heinze, who a couple of decades previously had succeeded Adolph Kiessling as editor of what is still today the standard commentary on Horace. In his address Heinze attempted to list the essential and distinctive characteristics of Horace's odes—a subject on which his audience were entitled to regard the speaker as the greatest living authority. The address was published the following year and reprinted in 1938 along with other essays by Heinze, who had died in 1929. A new edition appeared in 1960, making Heinze's formulation of the critical presuppositions upon which his commentary rests once more readily accessible.[1] For forty years his ideas have exercised a profound, if often undetected, influence on all systematic discussion of the literary form.[2]

Heinze listed five formal characteristics. He began by pointing

[1] Richard Heinze, 'Die horazische Ode', Vortrag gehalten im Verein für klassische Altertumswissenschaft in Leipzig am 19. Mai 1922, *N.J.*, li (1923), pp. 153–68. Reprinted in *Vom Geist des Römertums* (3rd edn. 1960), pp. 172–89. References below to the 1960 edn.

[2] A response to the original publication of Heinze's address by another eminent German scholar, Richard Reitzenstein ('Eine neue Auffassung der horazischen Ode', *N.J.*, lii [1924], pp. 232–41), attacking Heinze's views has had comparatively little influence—perhaps because Reitzenstein conspicuously lacks Heinze's capacity for clear, simple argument.

Dramatic Monologue in the Odes of Horace

out that the normal Horatian ode has an addressee. From this he deduced two further characteristics, both a good deal less self-evident, which it will be the object of this chapter to discuss. The addressee, he argued, is to be thought of as actually present, hearing the ode spoken, some indication of scene being usually added to round off the dramatic illusion. This was Heinze's second characteristic. The third was that the odes are always the outcome of some practical objective: their purpose is never mere communication, still less self-expression or lyric meditation.[1] To these three Heinze added a fourth characteristic as a kind of rider, pointing out the limitations placed in such a poem upon frankness of utterance: the poet's thoughts are held in check by awareness of an audience.[2] Finally a fifth point: the odes were written to be recited, not sung; references to song and musical accompaniment are mere convention.

Heinze's fifth point, that the odes are poems not songs, has won general acceptance. His first, that the odes are directed to an addressee, is clearly true of the great majority of odes; as far as the fact is concerned, Heinze can only be criticized for being too keen to explain away exceptions.[3] His insistence, however, that an ode is organized around its addressee is another matter.[4] The existence of any real organic connection between ode and addressee is often very dubious. Moreover, Heinze exaggerates the inevitability with which his second, third and fourth points follow from an acceptance of the first.

[1] Heinze, op. cit., p. 180:
Zweck der Ansprache ist aber niemals blosse Mitteilung; der Angeredete soll nicht über den Dichter etwas erfahren oder als Gefäss dienen, in das der Dichter seine Gefühle, Leiden und Freuden ergiesst.

[2] For a discussion of this point, see Chapter 3.
The influence of Heinze's views may be seen from the echoes we find of them in subsequent important work on Horace. E.g., Heinze's first and third points appear in Wilkinson, p. 123, in this form:
... the fact that many of the poems are addressed to an individual gives them a hortatory turn which is alien to the free self-expression of lyric. It takes two to make a normal Horatian ode.

[3] Fraenkel, e.g., pp. 227, 431, rightly speaks of *Systemzwang*.

[4] Heinze, op. cit., p. 173.:
... die angeredeten Personen schweben keineswegs nur der Phantasie des Dichters als anwesend vor, so dass das 'du' nur ein lebendigerer Ersatz für ein 'er' oder 'sie' wäre; sondern die Gedichte geben sich als ganz eigentlich an sie gerichtet, zu ihnen gesprochen oder gesungen, dazu bestimmt, von ihnen gehört zu werden.

Dramatic Monologue in the Odes of Horace

Apart from his zeal for classification, Heinze's discussion suffers from the readiness with which he accepts a number of questionable presuppositions. To begin with, his argument is vitiated throughout by an uncritical acceptance of the Romantic doctrine (discussed in the previous chapter) of a fundamental difference between ancient and modern poetry. What Horace wrote, he argues, is an *Aeolium carmen*,[1] accepting the conventions of the old Aeolic lyric poetry (even pretending to be sung), not a poem in the modern sense at all. He neglects the obvious fact that Horace is putting an old form, which he has drastically revised, to very new purposes. It is misleading to treat as a rigidly applied set of rules what are in fact no more than tendencies inherent in the form Horace is expanding and remodelling. Whatever our view of Horace's relationship to his classical and Hellenistic models—whether we prefer Reitzenstein's progressive classicism, or Pasquali's theory of a classic-Hellenistic tension, or Dr. Walter Wili's Graeco-Roman syncretism (to name three successive theories that all reflect part of the truth)[2]—it is clear the odes are not just *Aeolia carmina*. In any case, Horace does not write to a single recipe as Heinze is apt to suggest: there is a good deal of experimentation, and the odes clearly fall into a number of groups.

It is Heinze's second and third points that I wish to consider. The second is that the ode is a kind of drama, involving the poet and an addressee actually spoken to in a scene. It seems to me that this is indeed the proper way to look at a largish minority of Horace's odes; some we are likely to misunderstand altogether if we fail to observe their dramatic character and take them instead as verse epistles. Heinze would insist that these odes are *dialogues*, with all but one of the actors remaining silent. He rejects the term 'monologue', because monologue seemed to him something peculiar to modern poetry. He was thus enabled to make his third point, that the odes are always concerned with some kind of practical objective, not with the formulation of the poet's thoughts. They are in fact, according

---

[1] Heinze takes up Horace's own phrase (*dicar . . . princeps Aeolium carmen ad Italos deduxisse modos*) in *Odes* iii, 30, 10–14.

[2] Richard Reitzenstein, 'Horaz und die hellenistische Lyrik', *N.J.*, xxi (1908), pp. 81–102; Giorgio Pasquali, *Orazio lirico* (1920); Walter Wili, *Horaz* (1948).

Dramatic Monologue in the Odes of Horace

to Heinze, *occasional verse*, and therefore, by modern standards, clearly an inferior form of poetry.

This, however, is not a necessary concommitant of their dramatic character—where they are dramatic—for, unlike Heinze, I do not regard all the odes as dramatic in form. Since the addressee does not speak, I prefer the term 'dramatic monologue', to which I do not share Heinze's objection. In a few odes it seems to me the monologue is a soliloquy: though the addressee is named, it is not to be supposed that he hears what is said. In an ode which is a soliloquy, communication is of course non-existent. These odes are, in fact, a kind of adaptation of the dramatic convention of the sustained aside, just that sort of inward meditation that Heinze said could not exist in ancient poetry.

Before examining some dramatic monologues, it is as well to remind ourselves that there are at the other end of the scale odes which read, to all intents and purposes, as verse epistles— and odes of course between the two extremes, neither clearly epistolary nor clearly dramatic, whose status is occasionally hard to determine.

The clearest examples of the letter type of ode are found in the fourth book, where Horace's lyric manner shows often the influence of the hexameter epistles which had occupied him between the publication of *Odes* i–iii and *Odes* iv.[1] For example, iv, 9 (*Ne forte credas interitura* . . .), apart from the difference of metre, a rather freer use of imaginative illustration, and perhaps a more contrived word order, reads more like an epistle than an ode. It is in fact good verse rather than poetry.[2] This is the characteristic, almost inevitable feature of the more extreme form of epistolary ode. Our main concern at the moment, however, is to observe that the form of this ode is in no way dramatic. Horace's purpose is to state a case. The first seven stanzas develop the argument that poetry like Horace's will last; though the lyric poets must take second place to Homer, they join with him in preserving the heroic deeds of the past, doomed otherwise to pass into oblivion:

---

[1] How many *Epistles* are genuine letters is something we need not discuss here. Our concern is only with their formal characteristics.

[2] I cannot agree with Fraenkel, p. 423, that iv, 9 'soars from the start into the ether and maintains its high level to the end'.

> uixere fortes ante Agamemnona 25
> multi; sed omnes illacrimabiles
> urgentur ignotique longa
> nocte, carent quia uate sacro.

> *Brave men lived before Agamemnon,*
> *numbers of them; but all, unwept,*
> *unknown, are overwhelmed in long*
> *night, because they lack a holy bard.*

Horace's argument is a little unrealistic (by his time this function had been for centuries discharged more by historians than by poets), and the suspicious reader might suspect *argumentum ad hominem*. He would be right: the final six stanzas are devoted to a fulsome encomium of the politician Lollius, to whom the ode is addressed.[1]

The language is vigorous, the illustrations abundant and effective. Everything, however, is clear-cut and dogmatic. Poetry should not make us feel we are being argued at. The first half has considerable rhetorical merit and the encomium of Lollius also contains some good lines (stanza 11 for example), though the praise of the simple life rings hollow after the impressive build-up that precedes it. The writing, as I said, is statement, phrased in the language of poetry; it does not attempt any of the specially poetic forms of communication. The difference is easily discovered. Let the reader translate this poem, and then translate, say, i, 5 (*Quis multa gracilis te puer in rosa* . . .). He will find the statements of iv, 9 readily rephrasable in English, while the words of i, 5 will stubbornly resist translation—because they achieve that amalgam of sense and words which is characteristic of genuine poetry.

There are better epistolary odes. A good one is i, 6 (*Scriberis Vario fortis* . . .), a letter to Agrippa, Augustus' admiral, telling him, with charm and modesty, that if he wants an epic poem he should apply to the distinguished Varius, not to the trifler Horace. It is perhaps a genuine letter. More often the epistolary form is chosen simply to suggest a practical purpose. Cicero followed a similar convention when he cast his essay on the

---

[1] Fraenkel, pp. 425-6, admits dissatisfaction with the second half: 'If, nevertheless, the eulogy sounds somewhat laboured, this is clearly not the poet's fault', etc.

Dramatic Monologue in the Odes of Horace

perfect orator in the form of a long letter to his friend Brutus. It has been suggested that the convention in Horace's case rests on the actual practice of the members of Epicurean coteries, who seem to have been fond of writing letters to one another offering frank personal advice on problems of conduct.[1]

On the other hand there are odes and epodes which are not just verse epistles, but clearly require some form of dramatic context. For example i, 27 (*Natis in usum laetitiae scyphis . . .*) implies a scene, as well as a speaker, and an audience of a group of people. At a drinking party, which is showing signs of getting out of hand, somebody (it need not be Horace) speaks up to call the guests to order with an appeal to decency. Upon being told to get on with the drinking himself, he neatly diverts the party's attention to a lovesick youth. We see at once how far removed a poem like this is from the argumentative structure of iv, 9. There is a lot of material here that is taken from the long tradition of Greek drinking songs. The traditional material, however, is not just simply given a Roman flavour (by the reference to Falernian for example); it is used to build up a complex little drama. A hint is enough: when Horace refers to the young man as the brother of Megilla from Opus, we are made to feel (as Heinze points out) that Megilla herself is present— and better known, doubtless, to the men than her brother is.

The dramatic structure makes i, 27 more lively than iv, 9, but the poem is not a particularly good one. In the two stanzas devoted to pulling the young man's leg (stanzas 4 and 5) the irony is neatly manipulated and the ascent into real poetry in the final stanza smoothly effected.[2] All the same, there are clear signs that Horace has not resolved the problems involved in making serious poetry out of casual everyday incidents.

[1] See N. W. de Witt, 'Parrhesiastic Poems of Horace', *C.Ph.*, xxx, 1935, pp. 312–19.

[2] A word on a few points of interpretation. (1) The phrase *ingenuo . . . amore* probably means not (as Heinze puts it) 'die eines *ingenuus* würdige Liebe', but 'a mistress who is free'—the contrary, of course, being implied (cf. ii, 4). (2) The words *tutis auribus* (line 18) probably do not mean (as some editors suppose) that the young man is to whisper in the speaker's ear. The ears are those of the whole company, on whose behalf the speaker promises a loyalty to Megilla's brother that is perhaps half meant. Most of the company are his *amici* (see Quinn, p. 80). (3) I am inclined to agree with Pasquali and take *seueri* in line 9 as vocative rather than genitive. It is just possible it could be both. An early experiment, perhaps, in conscious ambiguity: see K. F. Quinn, 'Syntactical ambiguity in Horace and Virgil', *Aumla*, No. 14 (1960), pp. 36–46.

Dramatic Monologue in the Odes of Horace

What interests us in i, 27 is that it is beyond doubt a dramatic monologue. We might point equally well to i, 28 (a much better poem), now generally agreed to be a dramatic monologue.[1] The sixteenth epode is also a dramatic monologue.[2] The seventh epode is another. With these to remind us that the form is a common enough one in Horace, let us now turn to odes whose dramatic form is less evident.

The thirteenth ode of the fourth book divides its critics into two camps. There are the sentimentalists, who find the subject introduced in the opening lines,

> Audiuere, Lyce, di mea uota, di
> audiuere, Lyce: fis anus, et tamen
>   uis formosa uideri
>   ludisque et bibis impudens
>
> et cantu tremulo pota cupidinem   5
>   lentum sollicitas . . .

The gods have answered, Lyce, my entreaty,
amply answered! You're old. And just the same
you want to look a Beauty still,
you flirt and drink unblushingly,

in shaky, tipsy song importune love's   5
unreceptive ear . . .

simply repulsive. Particularly since they take them (wrongly, it will appear) as a brutal attack on Lyce. Heinze dismisses the ode as undiluted abuse (*'ein reines Scheltgedicht'*).[3] In the other camp belong those who do not find Horace's detailed portrait of an ageing flirt necessarily repulsive, and can even admire the realism in the writing. Here belong Wilamowitz[4] and Eduard Fraenkel.[5]

As is understandable, the critics whose judgment is not impaired by initial feelings of dislike for the poem's subject see

---

[1] See Wilkinson's excellent interpretation, pp. 108–14. Wilkinson follows Campbell, p. 229, in describing the ode as a dramatic monologue.
[2] It is so interpreted, fully and intelligently, by Fraenkel, pp. 42–55.
[3] Heinze, p. 452.
[4] U. von Wilamowitz-Moellendorff, *Sappho und Simonides* (1913), pp. 321–2.
[5] Fraenkel, pp. 415–16.

Dramatic Monologue in the Odes of Horace

more in it than undiluted abuse. They are confronted, therefore, with the problem of subordinating what they, too (accepting the traditional interpretation) regard as the brutal attack in the opening lines to the evident tone of what they regard as the poetic core of the ode. 'The jubilant note of the beginning . . .', says Fraenkel (he has Heinze's *'triumphierende Sicherheit'* at the back of his thoughts), 'is not maintained'. For, he continues:

> in the next sentence . . . the pathetic element . . . is predominant. . . . in the subsequent sentences the feeling is deepening and the language becomes impassioned. . . . then the scorn and its wretched victim are almost forgotten, and all that seems to matter is the regret for the lost land of youth.

The reader who is not already committed to liking the poem will suspect special pleading here, an attempt to soft-pedal something unsatisfactory about the poem's construction, or some awkwardness in its emotional development.

We find it, in fact, very hard to argue for the poem's success so long as our interpretation of it is guided implicitly by Heinze's theory (expressed in his second and third points) that the odes are actually directed to their addressees and meant to be heard by them.[1] If we make this assumption explicit, it becomes obvious how ill it suits the poem we have before us. Are we really to imagine the sentimental reminiscence of the fifth and sixth stanzas as meant to be heard by Lyce? Is not the passage from abuse to sentimental reminiscence disconcerting? And what is the occasion anyway? Is Lyce actually doing the things Horace says she does in the first stanza, or are these just generalizations? If the former, how can Horace plausibly be thought of as telling her what she does while she does it? On the other hand it seems we should not reject Heinze's theories outright. To take this

---

[1] Not to mention Heinze's amplification of his third point: that the poet's object is most often to influence the behaviour of the addressee; less often, to refuse a request; occasionally to express a decision taken by the poet, p. 180:
> . . . entweder—und das überwiegt weitaus—will der Dichter des anderen Willen bestimmen, oder, viel seltener, er lehnt eine Forderung ab, die der andere an ihn gestellt hatte; ganz selten der dritte Fall, dass der Dichter positiv seinen Willen äussert . . .

Which could it be here?

poem as a verse epistle like iv, 9 is just as implausible. We should still be confronted with the awkward transition from abuse to reminiscence. And anyway the ode does not sound like argument. There are clear hints, which we cannot afford to ignore, of some kind of dramatic situation.

An examination of the poem must in fact either lead us to the conclusion that it is ill conceived, awkward and unconvincing in its development; or cause us to suspect that we are distorting what despite ourselves we feel to be a fine piece of writing by attempting to interpret it, consciously or unconsciously, in the light of preconceptions that misconstrue the poem's form.

But if we set out from the assumption that the ode is a *dramatic monologue* and adopt the consequences of that assumption, the difficulties and implausibilities disappear. Lyce is not supposed to hear. Even if Horace spoke his thoughts aloud she would be too busy to listen. The dramatic context, in other words, puts beyond dispute the way Horace wants us to take the poem. The monologue is a soliloquy. What he offers us is an inward meditation.

Horace meets at a party a girl he once knew.[1] Some kind of past relationship between them, left for the moment undefined, is suggested by the opening words, but the poem belongs to a group of closely-integrated odes requiring fairly careful exploratory reading before the bits of story, stated and implied, begin to fit into place. The present occasion is perhaps something like the party described by Propertius in iv, 8. Confronted with the spectacle of Lyce's endeavours to entertain the company, Horace's thoughts start to unwind. In a way that is quite natural, as well as in accord with poetic tradition, he begins by addressing the words his thoughts frame to Lyce.

Once we understand that Lyce is not to be thought of as hearing what Horace says, we realize it is not necessary to force upon the opening words a tone that turns out to conflict with the subsequent development of the poem. The lines lose immediately the brutal note critics read into them, to assume instead the frank realism of private thought, innocent of any desire to wound. The repetition is not 'triumphant', but pathetic. We all

---

[1] Heinze's reconstruction of the setting in his commentary, p. 452, is perfectly acceptable.

Dramatic Monologue in the Odes of Horace

know how natural it is to formulate an idea in words, particularly an idea associated with our emotions, and then repeat the formulation, as though it helped our understanding of what we have just come to realize. Horace had asked the gods to make Lyce old (a story starts at once to suggest itself); and now he is confronted with the evidence that his entreaty was answered.

We must be careful to avoid asking irrelevant questions here. All Horace wishes to do is to sketch in briefly a set of circumstances (lover meeting mistress years after an old quarrel), so typical we can accept the situation in a moment and pass to what Horace wants us to concentrate on: the dramatic vignette and the emotions inherent in it. There is another reason why as little as possible is said about the details of the situation. Horace wants to get his readers or listeners working hard and alert in order to make them responsive to the complex poem (for this is a real poem, not a piece of light verse) that he now proceeds to weave around his theme.

So far then the drama has two persons: the speaker (whom, for convenience, we shall call Horace) and Lyce. And the adumbration of a scene: Lyce singing at a party, tipsy. The tone and the situation are further fixed by the words used: *formosa*, which suggests more what we mean by 'a Beauty' than simply beautiful;[1] and *ludis*, which invites us perhaps to think of Lyce as doing some form of dance;[2] but the word is rich and non-specific, implying flirtatious behaviour generally.

The remainder of the second stanza introduces a third person into the drama, the girl Chia:

> ille uirentis et 6
>   doctae psallere Chiae
>   pulchris excubat in genis,

> *It's Chia, though, sapling-supple,*
> *pretty-cheeked, clever instrumentalist,*
> *that Love keeps watch on now.*

---

[1] For the flavour of *formosa*, see the discussion of Catullus Poem 86 in Chap. 3.
[2] Heinze says, p. 452:
ludis meint auch hier vielleicht . . . das Tanzen, vielleicht aber nur übermütiges Gebaren überhaupt.

Dramatic Monologue in the Odes of Horace

The words *doctae psallere* are not simply a statement of Chia's accomplishments; they tell us what she is doing in the scene. The old flirt has a young (*uirentis*) and pretty (*pulchris in genis*) lyre player to accompany her song and dance act. The information about her is not just presented as information, but in a way that sharpens our visualization of her.

The third stanza,

> importunus enim transuolat aridas
> quercus et refugit te, quia luridi   10
>   dentes te, quia rugae
>   turpant et capitis niues,

Past dried-out oaks his glances curtly
slide; they back revolted at the sight
of yellow teeth, wrinkled face,
and the snow-drifts on your head,

continues to build up the drama by the same technique of hints obliquely conveyed.

But this is not simply, or even primarily, a drama: it is a *poem* which assumes dramatic form. Our appreciation of it will be distorted if we neglect its poetic qualities. The realism of the opening lines reaches its climax in line 6. Then suddenly there is a surge of pure poetry,

> ille uirentis et   6
>   doctae psallere Chiae
>   pulchris excubat in genis,

introduced by a reminiscence of a chorus from the *Antigone* of Sophocles (lines 781–4):

> Ἔρως ἀνίκατε μάχαν
> Ἔρως, ὃς ἐν κτήνεσι πίπτεις,
> ὃς ἐν μαλακαῖς παρειαῖς
> νεάνιδος ἐννυχεύεις . . .

The echo is too clear for us to suppose that Horace did not intend it to be heard. And, once heard, it makes the ambiguity built round *cupidinem* neater. In its first context in line 5 the

Dramatic Monologue in the Odes of Horace

primary meaning is 'sexual desire'. In the next sentence *cupido* becomes for a moment *Cupido*, the god of love. The personification, which softens the original harsh statement, is elicted by *excubat*; but it is brought out more fully and better sustained if we catch the echo and remember that Sophocles' words come at the beginning of a choral ode addressed to Eros. Cupid symbolizes of course Lyce's audience, the *iuuenes feruidi* of line 26, who, repelled by her appearance, concentrate their attention (or that part of it most fitly symbolized by *Cupido*) on pretty young Chia.

In stanza 3 we wheel round again from pure poetry and the fanciful to stark realism with the terrible words *quia luridi dentes te, quia rugae turpant*, the redoubled blow mitigated by a concluding touch of fancy, *capitis niues*, in order to keep the two elements, realism and poetry, blended. Since our present concern necessarily accentuates the intellectually analysable aspects of the ode, it is important to keep reminding ourselves how the basis of reportage is transformed by the words Horace uses into serious poetry.

We come now to stanze 4:

> nec Coae referunt iam tibi purpurae
> nec cari lapides tempora quae semel
>   notis condita fastis   15
>   inclusit uolucris dies,

> *Fine, brilliant silks cannot restore to you, no more*
> *than costly stones, the days that time in flight*
> *upon the public record of your past*
> *has lodged for good and all.*

As is often the case in Horace, the central stanza marks a turning-point. From here until the end of stanza 6 the dramatic scene becomes less important. If we remember that this is soliloquy in a scene, the sequence of thought is clear enough. We may say the stark realism of the present scene begins to dissolve into a flashback, though the scene of the flashback is, of course, only in the speaker's thoughts. The 'brilliant silks' and the 'costly stones' that Lyce is wearing in the scene actually before the speaker's eyes serve only to emphasize to him that she is now

Dramatic Monologue in the Odes of Horace

an old woman. That realization sets him thinking about the past conquests of this celebrated beauty. The solemn complexity of the relative clause shows *notis condita fastis* is not intended to wound.[1] It is the dignified statement, economical because oblique, of an important detail: Lyce was a famous beauty who in her time had ensnared many more than Horace. Fraenkel, missing the dramatic force of the stanza ('. . . the words of the fourth stanza make it all but impossible to refer them exclusively, or even primarily, to Lyce, for what is described here is our common lot'), reduces it to a truism.[2] But *Coae purpurae* and *cari lapides* are visual details and *notis condita fastis* does not describe the common lot, but only the lot of Lyce and those few who achieve the success she had enjoyed.

As we look at Lyce now, we see no sign of the power to attract men (*uenus*) she once possessed:[3]

> quo fugit uenus, heu, quoue color? decens
> quo motus? quid habes illius, illius,
>   quae spirabat amores?
>   quae me surpuerat mihi . . .   20

> *Where's vanished allure? Where, ye gods, complexion*
> *fresh and seemly bearing? What is left of her, of her*
> *that was the soul of love?*
> *She ensnared me fast before I knew . . .*

The upsurge of sentimentality, which grated in earlier readings of the poem so long as it was assumed the speaker had set out to taunt Lyce, becomes convincing and moving when we realize he is to be thought of instead as slowly recovering from the shock that he felt on seeing the change the years had wrought. This was a woman you fell in love with before you even realized what was happening.[4] The effortless attraction she once exerted is contrasted implicitly with her unavailing efforts in the scene before

---

[1] Relative clauses are not necessarily a bad thing in poetry. Unlike the incidental, otiose relative clauses criticized in our study of iv, 12 (Chapter 1), this clause sustains the full weight of the train of thought.

[2] Fraenkel, pp. 415–16.

[3] Here *uenus* means much more than 'charm'. Cf. the discussion of Catullus Poem 86 in Chapter 3.

[4] Compare *surpuerat* with Cicero, *Brut.* 76: *a Naeuio uel sumpsisti multa, si fateris, uel, si negas, surripuisti*. Cf. also Catullus Poem 86, 6:
    tum omnibus una omnis *surripuit* Veneres.

Dramatic Monologue in the Odes of Horace

Horace's eyes, to which our thoughts are led back discreetly by the words *decens quo motus?* that spring to his mind as he watches her song and dance, rendered gauche and stridently provocative (*cupidinem lentum sollicitas*) by the passage of the years.

Stanza 6 opens with the speaker's thoughts led a step further in a bridge passage (part of the last question in the Latin):

> . . . felix post Cinaram notaque et artium   21
> gratarum facies. . . .

She, Cinara's successor, reigned, famous for her beauty and all the social graces.

There was only one woman who exerted greater power over him than Lyce, and that was Cinara. The word *felix* almost means 'successful': it implies (particularly with lines 14–16 still in our thoughts) the triumphant possession of a man by his mistress. A contrast in Horace's feelings for the two women is implied: looking back, he thinks of Cinara as the one women he really loved; and of Lyce as the *donna fatale* who drew him to her despite himself (*quae me surpuerat mihi*), who took him from Cinara (*felix post Cinaram*). It is important to understand the two elements in the speaker's feelings as the remainder of the story starts to fall into place. Horace loved Lyce reluctantly, and eventually they quarrelled, Horace calling on the gods to avenge him.[1] But the attachment, while it lasted, brought a kind of happiness sufficient to elicit now his ungrudging acknowledgment of Lyce's past beauty.

Cinara's name touches off a series of contrasts between the two women:

> sed Cinarae breuis
> annos fata dederunt,
> seruatura diu parem
>
> cornicis uetulae temporibus Lycen.   25

But, while fate abbreviated Cinara's years, it plotted Lyce's preservation, rival

in longevity to ancient female crow.

[1] Compare the situation in Catullus Poem 76.

Dramatic Monologue in the Odes of Horace

Cinara died young, whereas the gods, as though in answer to Horace's curse (in prose we have to say 'as though'; poetry, speaking with greater economy and intensity, can state it as a fact), decided long ago[1] to preserve this little withered crow of a woman (*uetulae* is both pathetic and damning), in order to expose her to the ridicule of a generation of young men, eager enough for love but whose hearts are not touched by Lyce's fumbling clutch:

>   possent ut iuuenes uisere feruidi   26
>   multo non sine risu
>   dilapsam in cineres facem.

> *so that fiery youngsters could observe*
> *the incendiary, mirth unchecked,*
> *now crumbled in the ashes of her self.*

The circle of the speaker's thoughts is complete, the actual dramatic scene once more before our eyes, *iuuenes feruidi* picking up *cupidinem* in line 5. Sliding then finally from the actual scene, the young men's contemptuous laughter still in our ears, to the transmutation of that scene into poetry, the poem ends with extraordinary power. The torch of love is a common tag in classical poetry, but here is a torch that has been used to touch off fire after fire of passion, till it is utterly consumed. The young men grouped around Lyce's quenched flame burn indeed (*iuuenes feruidi*), but it is Chia, not Lyce, who sets their lust alight. A fresh, accurate image stiffens a fabric of clichés one might have thought worn threadbare.

It can hardly be doubted we have made a better poem of iv, 13. As a dramatic soliloquy it is coherent where before it was disjointed, clear-cut where before it was woolly. The ode is a kind of sequel to Catullus' Poem 86 (*Quintia formosa est multis* . . .).[2] The verbal echoes (the keyword *formosa*, the richly ambiguous *uenus*, the striking *surpuerat* that recalls Catullus' phrase without reproducing it) even suggest a conscious sequel. Lyce, unlike Quintia, once possessed, as well as looks, the real

---

[1] Note the precise statement of the future participle *seruatura* tied to the past tense *dederunt*.

[2] To which his contemptuous *candida rectaque sit, Satires* i, 2, 123, is pretty certainly an allusion. (See Chapter 3 for a discussion of Catullus' poem.)

Dramatic Monologue in the Odes of Horace

secret of seduction. But, now that the looks have decayed, the seductive power, too, has vanished (*quo fugit uenus* . . .?).

Each poem has its own personal relevance. Catullus had Lesbia to make it plain to him what Quintia lacked. Horace's insight into Lyce's degradation rests on memories of his own involuntary infatuation. That is the hypothesis that gives his poem shape: a woman anyone would have fallen in love with once, seen years afterwards through a victim's eyes. Whether it really happened to Horace hardly matters. What he feels and records is a typical experience.

The attitudes of the two poets, too, are different. Catullus states and analyses a problem that seemed fresh, important and hard to state economically in simple telling words that carried a convincing personal ring. Horace is a man of fifty, twenty years older, probably, than Catullus.[1] He has behind him upwards of forty years of poetic tradition unavailable to Catullus. What drew him to write *Audiuere, Lyce* was not a problem of expression. There is no note of battling with a mystery in *quo fugit uenus*? The ode presents a situation—not to analyse it, but to capture its inherent pathos. Horace's feeling is for people and the situations in which life's merciless irony involves them: a complex, unprotesting, understanding compassion.

The fourteenth ode of the second book (*Eheu fugaces, Postume* . . .), a very famous poem, is by most regarded as a verse epistle, a kind of gloomy sermon.[2] It is usually prized by Horace's less critical admirers for its philosophical sentiments and the gloomy tone is taken to represent Horace's considered personal outlook on life. Others, more discerning, have complained that the sermon is shallow and commonplace.

The most forthright among recent critics is Mr. Collinge. He takes up an old theory, put in different ways at different times, by Hartmann, Tyrrell and others: that—to borrow words once used by Mr. P. G. Wodehouse in an essay on Shakespeare —'while his stuff sounds all right, it generally doesn't mean

---

[1] In iv, 1 Horace speaks of himself as 'about fifty' (*circa lustra decem*). Since both odes contain reminiscences of the mysterious Cinara, they probably belong to the same period.

[2] Heinze, p. 216: '. . . in dieser Klage, die doch indirekt gleichfalls Paränese ist'.

Dramatic Monologue in the Odes of Horace

anything'.¹ The nineteenth-century version of the theory was that the odes were exercises in metre. More recently the theory has been lent fresh life by Professor Howald, who argues that Horace, like the French symbolists, subordinated meaning to verbal poetry.² For Collinge, the odes are 'very largely exercises in form, to the exclusion of content' (p. viii). II, 14 he finds a sorry string of moral clichés:³

> ii. 14 (*Eheu fugaces*) almost looks like a *cento* of Horatian commonplaces—the inexorable flight of time, the tearless nether gods, the universality of death, the uselessness of attempts to evade it. No particular pattern emerges for sixteen verses, apart from a shift at *v.* 9 from the second to the universalizing first person plural. The four stanzas simply say that death has no regard for (1) character, (2) offerings, (3) status, (4) evasive action.

Of course he is right—so long as we take it for granted the ode is a verse epistle; or, as Collinge calls it, 'an open letter to a Roman gentleman'. But that means ignoring clear hints in the poem of dramatic form. As for being a sermon, the ode can only be regarded as an attempt at constructive moralizing (as many, less roundly condemnatory than Collinge, would allow) by ignoring the palpable clue which Horace provides, as we shall see, to warn the reader that he is philosophically uncommitted to the moralizing; and interested instead, as in iv, 13, in the situation in which the monologue is spoken, and which it evokes.

The scene implied is a rather different sort of dinner party from those in i, 27 or iv, 13. The reader is once again called upon to fill in the semi-extraneous details for himself, and each reader will naturally fill them in differently.⁴ A speaker (whom

[1] P. G. Wodehouse, 'An outline of Shakespeare', in *Louder and Funnier* (2nd edn. 1933), p. 120.
[2] Ernst Howald, *Das Wesen der lateinischen Dichtung* (1948).
[3] Collinge, pp. 87–8.
[4] This economy of detail is essential to the poetic quality of dramatic monologue. A remark of Ezra Pound is of interest here:
> To me the short so-called dramatic lyric—at any rate the sort of thing I do—is the poetic part of a drama the rest of which (to me the prose part) is left to the reader's imagination or implied or set in a short note. I catch the character I happen to be interested in at the moment he interests me, usually a moment

Dramatic Monologue in the Odes of Horace

we should be ingenuous in taking to be Horace himself) breaks in on a conversation to address his host, Postumus, with a gloomy earnestness that comes (we may suspect, taking up a hint in the last stanza) as much from what he has imbibed of his host's liquor as from what he has imbibed of Epicurean philosophy. The poem begins with a striking repetition of the name of the man spoken to—a device that in itself should warn us of the dramatic flavour in what follows (compare the similar repetition at the beginning of iv, 13):

> Eheu fugaces, Postume, Postume,
> labuntur anni nec pietas moram
>   rugis et instanti senectae
>   adferet indomitaeque morti.

I tell you, Postumus, year after year is slipping headlong off. Decent living will not hold the rout or stay the onward thrust of wrinkly age, of death, that never lost a fight.

What the speaker says is commonplace enough—naturally, considering the circumstances. The theme is human mortality, introduced by the reflection 'you're getting old and there's nothing you can do about it'. From the point of view of intellectual content, the starting point is the same as in iv, 13. Horace, however, is not concerned with preaching; but, as in iv, 13, with weaving poetry around a dramatic vignette taken from everyday life in contemporary Roman society. Here, as there, it is important from the outset to grasp the dual character of the ode: it is part drama, part poetry. The scene is real life, but the words the speaker uses are non-realistic. Alcaics after all do not suggest conversational realism.

It should be observed that the commonplace is introduced with an urgency which often disappears in translation. For *fugax* means more than 'fleeting'—the word favoured by translators of this ode. The passage of the years is smooth, surreptitious

---

of song, self-analysis, or sudden understanding or revelation. And the rest of the play would bore me and presumably the reader.
(From a letter to W. C. Williams, 21 October 1908, *Letters 1907–1941* ed. D. D. Paige [English edn. 1951], p. 36.)

enough (*labuntur*); but they are *running away* from us. It is the word used of a fugitive slave or—more to the point here—the soldier who deserts his post in battle.[1] The military metaphor, suggested by *fugax*, is continued by *instanti* ('pressing the attack') and *indomitae* ('never defeated').

The dramatic scene and the speaker's earnest tone established, Horace is content to elaborate his theme in two stanzas of pure poetry. The dinner party recedes from the foreground and a flood of imagery takes its place:

> non si trecenis quotquot eunt dies, 5
> amice, places illacrimabilem
>   Plutona tauris, qui ter amplum
>   Geryonen Tityonque tristi
>
> compescit unda, scilicet omnibus,
> quicumque terrae munere uescimur, 10
>   enauiganda, siue reges
>   siue inopes erimus coloni.

> *Not if each day that comes by three hundred oxen slain* 5
> *you sued for terms with Pluto. He's not prone to tears,*
> *my friend, whose prisoners three times giant Geryones*
> *and Tityos by Hell's gloomy*
>
> *waters are confined. The same, you realize, that all*
> *whom this earth's produce feeds* 10
> *must take passage over, whether king or*
> *hard-up yokel we embark.*

Stanza 2 draws upon the evocative power of a mythological hell. Stanza 3 develops a further moral commonplace ('death comes to rich and poor alike'), sustained by evoking a familiar Homeric tag—*quicumque terrae munere uescimur* calls to mind Homeric lines such as *Iliad* vi, 142:

εἰ δέ τίς ἐσσι βροτῶν, οἳ ἀρούρης καρπὸν ἔδουσιν.

---

[1] The same image is found in *Odes* iii, 30, 4–5:
> innumerabilis
> annorum series et fuga temporum.

Stanza 4,

>frustra cruento Marte carebimus
>fractisque rauci fluctibus Hadriae,
>>frustra per autumnos nocentem 15
>>corporibus metuemus Austrum,

>*Pointless to shun the battle's slaughter*
>*and the hoarse Adriatic's jagged swell.*
>*Pointless in autumn-time to fear the pestilential* 15
>*southerly blast will turn our bodies sick,*

carries the sequence of ideas forward a step: 'it's no good trying to avoid death.' But its main purpose is again to make poetry out of a commonplace. This central section of the poem alternates between imagery taken from the real world (stanzas 3 and 4) and imagery based on the hell of mythology (stanzas 2 and 5).

Now we come back to the picture of hell and some of its more celebrated victims:

>>uisendus ater flumine languido
>>Cocytos errans et Danai genus
>>>infame damnatusque longi
>>>Sisyphus Aeolides laboris. 20

>*You must look on Hell's black streams, sluggishly*
>*meandering, on Danaus' ill-reputed brood,*
>*on Sisyphus, Aeolus' son, condemned*
>*to long hard labour.*

All this is not moralizing rhetoric aimed at giving renewed emphasis to statement, but poetry woven round a familiar idea. The reader insensitive to poetry will naturally feel his time is being wasted.

The line of meaning remains relatively unimportant until we get to stanza 6:

>>linquenda tellus et domus et placens 21
>>uxor, neque harum quas colis arborum
>>>te praeter inuisas cupressos
>>>ulla breuem dominum sequetur.

Dramatic Monologue in the Odes of Horace

*You must quit the earth, your house, your wife
that pleases you. Of these trees you tend the hated
cypresses alone will keep company with
their short-lived owner.*

The opening line of the stanza brings us quickly back to the present scene: the house of the speaker's host, his wife. The abrupt return to reality is accompanied, in the case of the lettered reader for whom Horace wrote, by a sudden feeling of recognition. The statement:

> linquenda tellus et domus et placens
> uxor

leans heavily on a well-known passage in Lucretius. It is, moreover, I feel sure, a passage we are meant to recognize in Horace's recasting of it. For Horace has a special reason for wanting the original recalled. Lucretius' words (iii, 894–6) are:

> iam iam non domus accipiet te laeta, neque uxor
> optima nec dulces occurrent oscula nati
> praeripere et tacita pectus dulcedine tangent.

Gray's imitation of them is so close it may serve in place of a translation:

> *For them no more the blazing hearth shall burn,
> Or busy housewife ply her evening care:
> No children run to lisp their sire's return,
> Or climb his knees the envied kiss to share.*[1]

What is the context of these lines in Lucretius? They are given as typical of the talk of men at dinner parties when among their cups they start to lament the brevity of human life:

---

[1] 'Elegy in a Country Churchyard', stanza 6. Gray's 'Elegy' is of course itself a dramatic monologue. It resembles ii, 14 in offering a series of commonplaces about mortality, but in form is closer to *Odes* iii, 13 (see Chapter 3), presenting the private unwinding of the speaker's thoughts.

Dramatic Monologue in the Odes of Horace

Hoc etiam faciunt ubi discubuere tenentque
pocula saepe homines et inumbrant ora coronis,
ex animo ut dicant 'breuis hic est fructus homullis;
iam fuerit neque post umquam reuocare licebit.'[1]

*Often men do this, too, when they're reclined at table,
cup in hand, faces shaded by the garlands that they wear:
the words heart-felt, 'Short is poor man's pleasure here,'
they say; 'soon it's gone, with no possibility of recall.'*

Horace, we should repeat, is writing for an audience that knows its Lucretius. An audience that can be relied on to catch the echo of a familiar quotation. And, more than that, to recall the context of a familiar quotation. Now, in Lucretius, as we have seen, the original of Horace's

> linquenda tellus et domus et placens   21
> uxor

is ironical. His words exemplify conventional talk at parties, talk that reflects a sentimental preoccupation with death regarded by Lucretius as foolish. When we realize this, and remember that Horace is close enough in time and philosophical outlook (as expressed non-dramatically in the satires and epistles) to be called, loosely, a disciple of Lucretius, it seems unlikely that well-known words of Lucretius spoken with palpable irony should be reflected by Horace (the original words only slightly modified) in a line meant to be taken at its face value. We must surely refuse to accuse Horace of such careless use of allusion.

What he is up to is actually fairly clear. The Lucretian echo is intended to provide a carefully worked-out clue to the form of the ode. Horace is conscious, perhaps, of the novelty of his dramatic technique, and anxious not to be misunderstood in the way that centuries of critics have misunderstood him. The whole ode, in other words, is woven out of the conventional talk of men at parties. But, in the transference from satiric-didactic style to serious poetry, the focus is sharpened by substituting for the generalized *saepe homines* the monologue of a particular

---

[1] Lucretius iii, 912–5. The order of the lines in this passage of Lucretius is disputed. Some editors follow Postgate in putting 912–18 immediately before 894–9.

Dramatic Monologue in the Odes of Horace

man in a particular scene, voicing however just the sentiments Lucretius says men do voice on such occasions.[1]

The dramatic context is discreetly underlined at this point by the demonstrative pronoun *harum* in the phrase immediately following:

> neque harum quas colis arborum 22
> te praeter inuisas cupressos
> ulla breuem dominum sequetur.

What trees are these? If we add them to the *placens uxor*, we are led, I think, to the right answer: not a rural scene, but a scene in a wealthy Roman's house in the city. The speaker is looking out from the *triclinium* into his host's formal garden in the *peristylium*.

There is just sufficient adumbration of scene, in fact, to enable Horace to utilize in the final stanza the hints built in earlier:

> absumet heres Caecuba dignior 25
> seruata centum clauibus et mero
> tinget pauimentum superbo,
> pontificum potiore cenis!

> *Your heir will down the chateau wines you guard*
> *with hundred keys—and more rightly, though he splash*
> *tiled floor disdainfully with vintages you'd not trade*
> *for a banquet with the pontiffs!*

The *pauimentum* is the paved floor of the dining-room where the party is taking place. The dramatic character of the poem underlined, it ends by modulating into a different key. A deliberately flippant note contrasts with and corrects the weight of the imagery of the central section of the poem. The big talk is brought into perspective by reminding us of the comparatively trivial occasion: a speaker waxing eloquent, and rounding off

[1] Gray's echo of Lucretius' words, being remote in time and outlook (and the recasting in another language), is much less specifically allusive. Rather as 'animated bust' later in the poem recalls Virgil's *spirantia aera* (*Aeneid* vi, 847) in a spirit of literary evocation. (The phrase, incidentally, has puzzled modern critics with little Latin: see F. W. Bateson, *English Poetry: A Critical Introduction* [1950], p. 182.)

Dramatic Monologue in the Odes of Horace

his eloquence with a broad hint to his host to be more liberal with the wine.

This ode is a particularly good example of the way interpretation is led astray so long as we focus our attention on the line of meaning, treating the poem as a series of statements accepted at their face value instead of a poem, concerned primarily with things transcending statement. Some words of Professor I. A. Richards are apposite here:[1]

> Whenever we hear or read any not too nonsensical opinion, a tendency so strong and so automatic that it must have been formed along with our earliest speech-habits, leads us to consider *what seems to be said* rather than the *mental operations* of the person who said it. If the speaker is a recognised and obvious liar this tendency is, of course, arrested. We do then neglect what he has said and turn our attention instead to the motives or mechanisms that have caused him to say it. But ordinarily we at once try to consider the objects his words seem to stand for and not the mental goings-on that led him to use the words. We say that we 'follow his thought' and mean, not that we have traced what happened in his mind, but merely that we have gone through a train of thinking that seems to end where he ended. We are in fact so anxious to discover whether we agree or not with what is being said that we overlook the mind that says it, unless some very special circumstance calls us back.

Richards is describing a wrong frame of mind in which to approach poetry, though it is the one usual among editors of Horace. It is a frame of mind less usual among the Greeks and Romans than with us, even in the statements of everyday life, let alone the statements poetry makes. Perhaps they had more liars. Even today the normal reaction of a Greek or Italian to something said is more likely to be 'Why does he say that?' than 'What's that he says?' We may recall, too, the regular practice of Homer's characters who take it for granted that the story told is dictated by circumstances rather than by respect for fact.

At any rate, Horace's concern in his dramatic monologues is

[1] I. A. Richards, *Practical Criticism* (1929), pp. 6–7.

Dramatic Monologue in the Odes of Horace

not to tell his readers something. We are two removes from simple statement. First, Horace wishes to present us with a speaker and a situation. It is not, perhaps, so much the *mental operations* of the speaker that interest him as his emotions. Or rather the emotions the reader recognizes as lying behind what is said. Second, he wishes to make a poem out of this. Consequently, though the emotions are meant to be recognized as those of a real person and the situation as typical of those that involve real people, the statements made are more often poetic statements than realistic speech.

Two examples are naturally not enough to explore the use Horace makes of dramatic monologue. It seemed best, however, to study two poems with some care, leaving the reader to examine others for himself guided by our method of dealing with these two. Let the reader remember it is not claimed that the two examples studied constitute a case for dramatic monologue in Horace's odes. That case rests on the more obvious examples mentioned at the beginning of the chapter. The Odes to Lyce and to Postumus are presented as examples of odes where recognition of their dramatic form is less easy, but essential to our appreciation of the poetry.

We may conclude with a short list of poems the dramatic structure of which seems to me quite certain. There are a number of types. In some the interest is primarily in situation. I, 28 (*Te maris et terrae numeroque carentis harenae* . . .), ii, 3 (*Aequam memento rebus in arduis* . . .),[1] ii, 14 (*Eheu fugaces, Postume* . . .), iii, 10 (*Extremum Tanain si biberes, Lyce* . . .), iii, 19 (*Quantum distet ab Inacho* . . .) and *Epodes* 7 (*Quo, quo scelesti ruitis?* . . .), 13 (*Horrida tempestas caelum contraxit et imbres* . . .) and 16 (*Altera iam teritur bellis ciuilibus aetas* . . .) are of this type. In others interest is concentrated on the thought process of the speaker, the unwinding of his thoughts in a scene. Of these it is even truer to say that the unity is psychological rather than logical or philosophical. I, 9 (*Vides ut alta stet niue candidum* . . .) is perhaps the most interesting example. An old man's thoughts

---

[1] ii, 3 also leans on Lucretius. The setting is similar to ii, 14, but outdoors, a picnic instead of a dinner-party. There are obvious echoes of Lucretius ii, 14–34, and v, 1392–6. What is perhaps truly Epicurean about ii, 3 and ii, 14 is less their 'philosophy' (which is shallow and often inconsistent with Epicurean teaching) than the way they allow Horace to play the serene spectator of life, as Lucretius enjoins, ii, 7–10.

Dramatic Monologue in the Odes of Horace

take him from the scene before him, a winter's day in the country, through a clearly marked psychological sequence to a boy and girl flirting with one another in a corner at a dinner-party in town. I, 5 (*Quis multa gracilis te puer in rosa* . . .), iii, 13 (*O fons Bandusiae* . . .)[1] and iv, 13 (*Audiuere, Lyce* . . .) are other examples of studies in thought sequence. In some the audience may be assumed to hear the monologue; others are better regarded as soliloquies. We saw how this was true of iv, 13. It is true also of i, 5, ii, 13 and iii, 13. III, 9 (*Donec gratus eram tibi* . . .) is an isolated example of a duologue. The conversation sketches in a situation (boy and girl sparring with one another in words, anxious for a reconciliation, but reluctant to admit it) but no scene—the interest lies purely in the clash of personalities.

The list is not offered as exhaustive, but it should be long enough to provide the reader with ample evidence of the necessity for grasping Horace's dramatic technique.[2]

---

[1] See the discussion of this ode in Chapter 3.

[2] The reader unfamiliar with the way modern poets have exploited the dramatic monologue may find it helpful to consult Robert Langbaum, *The Poetry of Experience: the Dramatic Monologue in Modern Literary Tradition* (1957). E.g., his theory (Chapter ii) of a tension in dramatic monologue between our sympathy with the speaker and the moral judgment we might form of the speaker were he simply described.

5

Tacitus' Narrative Technique

WE talk too much perhaps of Tacitus' *style*. The way the man wrote is allowed to detract attention from what he wrote, from the intellectual calibre of the historian, the newness and the greatness of his historiographical achievement. His style very likely struck his contemporaries as less bizarre than it does the modern student, for whom Latin prose is the prose of Cicero. We need reminding that Tacitus began his *Annals* something like a hundred and fifty years after the murder of Cicero; that nearly two hundred years separate early Cicero from late Tacitus.

The figures become more meaningful if we glance at periods closer to us, where our sense of historical perspective is more instinctive. Just over a hundred and fifty years separate Gibbon's *Decline and Fall*, the first volume of which appeared in the year of the American Declaration of Independence and the last a year before the outbreak of the French Revolution (1776–88), from G. M. Trevelyan's *English Social History*, which appeared in the year of the Allied victory at Alamein (1942); not quite two hundred years lie between Voltaire's *Histoire de Charles XII* (1731) and Rabelais' *La vie inestimable de Gargantua* (1534).

Literary languages develop, of course, at varying speeds. But, style apart, considering only the current literary language at the disposal of each writer, we may fairly put the linguistic gap that separates Tacitus from Cicero at something greater than the very appreciable gap the reader feels himself step across in

Tacitus' Narrative Technique

passing from Gibbon to Trevelyan; it appears insignificant beside the abyss that yawns between Rabelais and Voltaire.

For in many respects his style represents a sharpening and an intensification of the literary Latin of his time, assiduously disciplined and individualized. Like his contemporaries—the younger Pliny for example—he is restrained only by the normal tendencies toward conservatism of a healthy literary language. Moreover, the usual style of the time tended to favour classical models other than Cicero. Above all Sallust—whose outlook as much as his way of writing must have appealed strongly to writers who had endured the reign of Domitian. Tacitus himself was deeply influenced by Virgil. Little in their admiration for the writers of the past pulled these men back in the direction of Cicero. Literary Latin was still a living idiom: there was none of that spiritless impulse to ape the past that condemned the stylists of the later second century, Fronto and Aulus Gellius, to reviving a classical Latin as artificially reactionary in their hands as the classical Greek of their contemporary, the Syrian Lucian. With Fronto and Gellius style has become an end in itself. Tacitus has something to say.

But if the bizarreness of Tacitus' style is sometimes exaggerated, its individuality and distinction are beyond dispute. Yet, though the matter has been a good deal discussed in recent years, the analysis of Tacitus' style continues in the main to be conducted along the lines laid down by Boetticher in 1830. We still do little more than make lists of examples illustrating the three headings Boetticher used to sum up Tacitus: *varietas, brevitas, poeticus color*.[1] The three headings provide indeed a very satisfactory summary appraisal. But they encourage a method that is not really illuminating: the generalizations are supported by a profusion of detail, odd words, epigrammatic phrases and minutiae of syntax; divorced, however, from their context, the details can hardly produce any real feeling for how Tacitus wrote.[2]

---

[1] W. Boetticher, *Lexicon Taciteum, sive de Stilo C. Cornelii Taciti* (1830). The section 'De stili Tacitei varietate, brevitate et poetico colore' occupies pp. lxvi–cii of the 'Prolegomena'. It comprises exclusively words and phrases, classified according to an elaborate system, without reference to context.

[2] This is substantially the method of Sir Ronald Syme in his chapter on 'The style of the *Annales*', *Tacitus* (1958). Rigorous examination of detail is a method that has been used fruitfully for the investigation of Latin syntax by Einar Löfstedt,

Tacitus' Narrative Technique

Moreover, detailed analysis of vocabulary and syntax without reference to context encourages a further error of method: the isolation of form from content. It is a commonplace of modern literary criticism that in a serious work of literature, in any piece of writing where the act of writing is not mere drudgery expended on a mass of fact presenting no problems of communication, a constant process of interaction takes place between 'form' and 'content'.[1] What the writer begins by wishing to say, the idea he starts with, is shaped by the battle for effective expression of that idea. Often the idea emerges only with the words that present themselves as the writer struggles. What is finally said is often an odd mixture of what he began by wanting to say and what it seems finally best, or least unsatisfactory, to say.

Take Tacitus' well-known epigrammatic appraisal of the Emperor Galba, that he was 'equal to being emperor, if he hadn't been emperor' (*capax imperii, nisi imperasset, Histories* i, 49). Tacitus started perhaps with the idea that Galba was a disappointment. He seemed to possess the talents needed, but his rule proved a short-lived fiasco. A failure's credentials are apt to look unimpressive after the event. The crisp, businesslike *capax imperii* gets round this difficulty. So far we have nothing more than efficient collaboration between content and form, between idea and expression. The second half of the phrase shows their interaction: *nisi imperasset* suggests so much more than it can be said explicitly to convey. First of all, the feeling of anticlimax: Galba, of whom so much had been so long expected, became emperor at the age of seventy-one—and lasted a bit over six months. With that, the suggestion, somehow implied by the unreal past conditional clause, that the anticlimax needn't have occurred: Galba was not ambitious for office, had previously refused it. It is almost as though the fact that he had ruled and failed were an unimportant, irrelevant detail. Next, the feeling of unresolved illogicality, of something wrong: how could a man with such talents turn out to be such a

[1] See Miss Walker's short chapter, 'The relation between style and subject-matter', *The* Annals *of Tacitus* (1952), pp. 158–61.

who has influenced Syme. But Löfstedt's method, while ideal for presenting the actual facts of syntactical usage and exposing the superficiality of normative grammar, is of limited value in building up an overall picture of what a writer is like.

Tacitus' Narrative Technique

fool? Finally, and most penetrating, the intuition that Galba did not simply turn out to be a fool. It was being emperor that made him a fool: when power came into his hands, he could not grasp it. The words make us feel the ludicrousness of the situation, and at the same time how the old man's long record of modest distinction somehow stands disgraced by the disastrous final episode. We first smile, then ponder. It cannot be said that Tacitus had all these ideas before him and then looked for words to convey them. Rather the actual process of looking for the best words itself contributed to the insight of the final appraisal. Tacitus uses words as a poet does, to *suggest* a cohering intuition of life's complexities, rather than as a rational, analytic historian. Lists of words and idioms will not get us far toward grasping the secret of his style.

There have, of course, been attempts to relate the works that have come down to us to the methods of the craftsman who produced them. Professor Mendell has a useful chapter on 'Technique of Composition',[1] Miss Walker some penetrating remarks, based on Jung's distinction between 'sensational' and 'intuitive' types, which draw our attention to the fact that Tacitus' mind seizes more readily the significance of men's actions than the details of what they do.[2] Both offer us more than words and phrases in isolation; but their purpose is still to support generalization by example. They give us ideas about Tacitus and list, and partly quote, the evidence. It is not really the business of either to do justice to the literary artist. So that Miss Walker leaves us feeling Tacitus is negligent of his facts (an important point for those who are interested in the *Annals* as history) without perhaps fully realizing the need to correct that impression by an adequate demonstration of his poetic gift for impressionistic evocation of an historical situation.

A fresh approach may be useful, if only as an escape from the impasse into which existing methods quickly lead. The method I propose is more usual in dealing with poetry than prose. It consists in the integrated study of a continuous passage of some length—observing the writer at work, rather than trying to sum him up after he has left us from notes we made during our interview with him. The method involves a consideration of a

---

[1] Clarence W. Mendell, *Tacitus the Man and his Work* (1957).
[2] Walker, op. cit., pp. 189ff.

different kind of detail. Not abstracted details drawn from the *Annals* as a whole, but details that hang together because they all belong to a single passage kept continuously before us. Instead of describing the writer's tools, as Syme does, or accounting for his choice of tools, as Miss Walker attempts to do, let us watch the man using his tools on a particular job. This is the familiar method of practical criticism. The sensible practical critic does not claim it is a substitute for other methods of getting in contact with a writer, or even necessarily the best method. Applied, however, to a writer like Tacitus, who has hitherto been subjected to analytical methods that disregard context or confine themselves to drastically limited, isolated contexts, a method founded on the careful consideration of a broader context, one wide enough to permit some real insight into Tacitus' intentions and his techniques for carrying them out, may throw fresh and needed light on a complex talent.

The fourteenth book of the *Annals* begins with an extended account of Nero's murder of his mother. Pausing only to mark a new year by the formal statement of its consuls, Tacitus announces the theme that will occupy something like a fifth of the book:

Gaio Vipstano C. Fonteio consulibus diu meditatum scelus non ultra Nero distulit.

In the year of the consulship of Gaius Vipstanus and Gaius Fonteius, Nero postponed no longer a crime he had long been meditating.

The deterioration in the relations between the emperor and his mother following the murder of Britannicus had formed the subject of several chapters in the earlier part of the previous book. We were told the point was reached where Nero became impatient to do away with her (*interficiendae matris auidus*, xiii, 20, 14). That was nearly four years before (A.D. 55); since then we have heard no more. Now the subject is abruptly reintroduced. It is as though Tacitus' impatience to begin his account of the murder were intended to parallel Nero's impatience to commit it. We learn that the emperor's mistress Poppaea is urging him on—'a woman', Tacitus observed in a thumbnail sketch of her when recording the beginning of the

Tacitus' Narrative Technique

liaison, 'who had everything, except an honest mind' (*huic mulieri cuncta alia fuere, praeter honestum animum*, xiii, 45, 6–7). Agrippina stands in the way, we are now told, of Poppaea's ambition to marry Nero. Careful preparations for a staged accident in the Bay of Naples are related with some fulness. The attempt failed; Agrippina got ashore, and made her way to the villa that had been placed at her disposal nearby.

Tacitus continues:

> interim uulgato Agrippinae periculo, quasi casu euenisset, ut quisque acceperat, decurrere ad litus. hi molium obiectus, hi proximas scaphas scandere; alii quantum corpus sinebat uadere in mare; quidam manus protendere; questibus, uotis, clamore diuersa rogitantium aut incerta respondentium omnis ora compleri; adfluere ingens multitudo cum luminibus, atque ubi incolumem esse pernotuit, ut ad gratandum sese expedire, donec aspectu armati et minitantis agminis disiecti sunt.
>
> Anicetus uillam statione circumdat refractaque ianua obuios seruorum abripit, donec ad foris cubiculi ueniret; cui pauci adstabant, ceteris terrore inrumpentium exterritis.
>
> cubiculo modicum lumen inerat et ancillarum una, magis ac magis anxia Agrippina quod nemo a filio ac ne Agerinus quidem: aliam fore laetae rei faciem; nunc solitudinem ac repentinos strepitus et extremi mali indicia. abeunte dehinc ancilla 'tu quoque me deseris' prolocuta,
>
> respicit Anicetum trierarcho Herculeio et Obarito centurione classiario comitatum: ac, si ad uisendum uenisset, refotam nuntiaret; sin facinus patraturus, nihil se de filio credere, non imperatum parricidium. circumsistunt lectum percussores et prior trierarchus fusti caput eius adflixit. iam in mortem centurioni ferrum destringenti protendens uterum 'uentrem feri!' exclamauit multisque uulneribus confecta est.
>
> haec consensu produntur. aspexeritne matrem exanimem Nero et formam corporis eius laudauerit, sunt qui tradiderint, sunt qui abnuant. cremata est nocte eadem conuiuali lecto et exequiis uilibus; neque, dum Nero rerum potiebatur, congesta aut clausa humus. mox domesticorum cura leuem tumulum accepit, uiam Miseni propter et uillam Caesaris dictatoris quae subiectos sinus editissima prospectat. . . .

Tacitus' Narrative Technique

By now it was common knowledge that Agrippina's life had been in danger, though it was presumed she had met with an accident. Everyone on learning the news made quickly for the beach. There were men climbing on to breakwaters, scrambling into the first boats to hand, wading out into the sea as far as they were physically able, raising hands to heaven. Lamentations, prayers, shouted questions, each asking something different, vague answers shouted back filled the whole beach. A great crowd of people carrying lights gradually drifted together. When the news sank in that she was safe, a movement started to go and congratulate her, but it was thrown into confusion at the sight of soldiers, armed and grim-faced, marching.

Anicetus surrounded the villa with a guard and smashed open the main door, seizing any slaves he met on his way to the bedchamber. A few men guarded the entrance, the rest having fled panic-stricken before the invaders.

In the bedroom, which was moderately lighted, a single slave-girl remained with Agrippina, who was becoming increasingly nervous because no one had come to her from her son, not even Agerinus: the thing looked bad, and now nobody to be seen, sudden uproar, it spelled the worst. Then the slave-girl started to go. 'You too are forsaking me,' Agrippina burst out, and, as she did so,

she turned around and saw Anicetus, accompanied by a naval commander, Herculeius, and a sergeant-major of marines, Obaritus. 'If,' she said to Anicetus, 'this is a call you are making, you may say I am better. If you are about to perpetrate a crime, I cannot believe my son has ordered his mother's murder.' The assassins stood on either side of the bed. The naval commander was the first to strike: a crushing blow on the head with a club. While the sergeant-major was preparing to dispatch her with drawn sword, she thrust forward her womb towards him with the cry, 'Strike the belly!' There was a succession of blows, and then all was over.

Up to this point there is general agreement about the facts. Some have gone on to relate that Nero viewed the body of his dead mother, and praised its beauty. Others reject the story. She was given a mean funeral the same night and cremated on a dining-room couch. As long as Nero reigned no stone was placed over the grave, nor was the earth raised in a mound.

Tacitus' Narrative Technique

Afterwards a few household slaves saw to it that she was given a small mound beside the Misenum road not far from the villa of Caesar the dictator, which stands on a great height looking out over the curving coastline below. . . .

We need hardly remind ourselves that not all Tacitus is like this. Nor is it an isolated purple passage. It is the climactic episode of a carefully executed piece of writing, occupying a dozen chapters. We may fairly regard the whole as representative (though longer than usual) of the sustained narrative writing which in Tacitus alternates with the curt, annalistic sections of his work, intended to keep us up to date with the progress of events of secondary importance to his main purpose. While, ideally, we should consider Tacitus' account of the murder of Agrippina in its entirety, our present task is reduced to manageable proportions if we concentrate on the episode just quoted. It is, moreover, an episode which enables us to judge Tacitus' narrative powers by modern standards. The murder of individuals by authority in the middle of the night is something we feel we know about; even though it is something that we, like the majority of Tacitus' contemporaries, have not in all probability ourselves witnessed or participated in.

Our first impression is surely one of wonder at the skill with which Tacitus elicits our emotional response. For, told other ways, Agrippina's murder need not affect us so. We need only turn to the account given by Tacitus' contemporary, the younger Pliny, of a crime that bears some resemblance to Nero's to see this. After relating the story of a Vestal Virgin found guilty of adultery at the whim of Domitian and condemned to be buried alive, Pliny concludes his narrative:[1]

> missi statim pontifices, qui defodiendam necandamque curarent. illa nunc ad Vestam, nunc ad ceteros deos manus tendens multa, sed hoc frequentissime clamitabat: 'me Caesar incestam putat, qua sacra faciente uicit, triumphauit?' blandiens haec an irridens, ex fiducia sui an ex contemptu principis dixerit, dubium est. dixit, donec ad supplicium, nescio an innocens, certe tamquam innocens ducta est. quin etiam,

---
[1] Pliny, *Epistles* iv, 11.

cum in illud subterraneum cubiculum demitteretur, haesissetque descendenti stola, uertit se ac recollegit, cumque ei carnifex manum daret, auersata est et resiluit foedumque contagium quasi plane a casto puroque corpore nouissima sanctitate reiecit omnibusque numeris pudoris

'πολλὴν πρόνοιαν ἔσχεν εὐσχήμων πεσεῖν'.

The priests were despatched at once to put into effect the sentence of death by burial alive. Arms raised she prayed to Vesta, and to the other gods as well. One phrase, however, kept recurring: 'Does Caesar think that I am unchaste,' she cried, 'I who discharged my sacred office at the time of his victory, his triumph?' Whether the words were intended as flattery or as mockery, whether they were prompted by a consciousness of her own innocence or by contempt for the emperor, it is hard to say. She continued until she was led to her death—if not innocent, at least giving every appearance of innocence. Indeed, while she was being taken down to that subterranean chamber, her dress caught during the descent and she turned to free it. The executioner reached out his hand, but she started back, her gaze averted, obviously by a final gesture of sanctity to preserve her chaste and pure body from contact with something vile. In all respects her modesty 'was most attentive honourably to fall'.

Apart from the fussiness of Pliny's account, it is the moralizing tone that offends. One of Tacitus' greatest achievements as an historical artist is to avoid the stridently moralizing note that is characteristic of the Roman prose tradition. Events move us more powerfully if they appear to speak for themselves. Tacitus is not, of course, a neutral reporter. The words 'a crime that he had long been meditating' open his account. The murder completed, he passes to an analysis of Nero's reactions with judgment plainly pronounced (xiv, 10, 1–2):

sed a Caesare perfecto demum scelere magnitudo eius intellecta est.

Now that he had at last gone through with his crime, Nero realized the magnitude of it.

Tactitus' Narrative Technique

The moral impact of Tacitus' story is unerring and the more telling because the blows fall discreetly: simply *scelus*, no exclamatory adjective. Consider the objectifying effect of transferring the moral judgment to *magnitudo*, which looks impersonal and final. In his account of the murder itself, Tacitus scrupulously avoids even this degree of judgment, reserving his words of restrained comment for before and after.

He can even manipulate the tradition that the dying person must say something of significance, and adapt it to his way of writing history. Agrippina's first words to her assassins are completely convincing: the halting formal dignity of her opening (*si ad uisendum uenisset, refotam nuntiaret; sin facinus patraturus* . . .) is followed by a pathetic, illogical collapse into basic words and syntax (*nihil se de filio credere, non imperatum parricidium*). They help us to accept the grim plausibility of her final cry '*uentrem feri!*' At first, though, we want to reverse the order of the key words in the sentence: 'She thrust her belly forward with the cry, "Strike the womb!"' seems the natural order, and Tacitus' order oddly strained. Then we realize we are foisting on Tacitus the moral anecdote he has taken pains to avoid—and accusing him of a gauche attempt at elegant variation. Aware of the artificiality of the moralizing tradition, Tacitus is anxious, I think, not to attribute dying words to Agrippina that are overtly and theatrically symbolic. If we like, we can take them as expressing only the final vanity of a beautiful woman—the wish to avoid disfigurement, even in death. Most of us would like her to mean more than that; but Agrippina gains in tragic stature if her mind is not open, as Pliny would make it, for our casual inspection. At the same time Tacitus endeavours to ensure, by preceding her words with his own brief, specific commentary, that their symbolic significance is immediately apparent. Tradition has been cleverly adjusted to new standards of historical subtlety, perhaps a shade too cleverly: for once we may be left with the feeling Tacitus has tried too hard. Pliny's Cornelia on the other hand *is* theatrical, in her behaviour as well as her words. Or rather her behaviour, in itself plausible, has a theatrical flavour imparted to it by the way Pliny writes. And there is too much explanation of motive, too much fuss over incidental detail (e.g., '. . . *while she was being taken down* to that subterranean chamber, her dress caught *during the descent* . . .'), too much eagerness not to appear on Cornelia's side—all this drains the scene of its dramatic force, as well as its moral force. Tacitus' Agrippina is by no means the innocent victim of her mad son's moral irresponsibility, but he has the taste and dramatic sense not to fuss about guilt and innocence at moments when these cease to count.

Yet Tacitus is not above using the paraphernalia of the moralist unadapted when it suits his purpose. The lines immediately following the passage we have selected (Ch. 9, 2)—the anecdote of the slave who kills himself at his mistress's funeral, Agrippina's remark when told her son would one day kill her ('Let him kill me, so long as he is emperor')—are typical moralist's stuff. Though the remark opportunely reminds us of Agrippina's ambitions, and the anecdote of her power to inspire personal loyalty, we wonder for the moment why Tacitus allows these jottings to spoil a conclusion led up to with such force. We quickly see their purpose. It is to slacken the tension for a while, to provide a few lines of easy reading between the dramatic climax and Tacitus' carefully drawn picture in the next chapter of Nero passing the remainder of the night with his conscience.

But the superiority of Tacitus over Pliny is not simply superiority of a writer with sure dramatic instinct over the retailer of moralizing anecdote. Obviously we are dealing, too, with a more accomplished literary craftsman. The murder of Agrippina is so much more vivid. So vivid in fact we should be likely, recalling it with the text not before us, to describe it as a detailed account. Actually we shall be nearer the truth if we say Tacitus distributes his detail better. He marks the steps in his narrative precisely and offers us at each step a deft selection of detail, enabling us to build up for ourselves a sharp mental picture of action in progress. Pliny, on the other hand, is led by his moralizing purpose to squander detail on a single step. It might be argued that it would have been hard for Pliny, in a letter to a friend, to create the atmosphere of a story, told with an urgent high seriousness, that speaks for itself. I expect there is some truth in this. Our purpose here, however, is not to compare Pliny and Tacitus; but to make use of a quick look at Pliny in order to understand better the way Tacitus lays out his story.

Tacitus' Narrative Technique

So, if looking at Pliny causes us to think of Tacitus' narrative as *detailed*, that is an impression a second quick comparison must correct.

Let us glance at a few lines from Suetonius' account of the death of Nero, taking it up at the point where Nero decides after all not to drown himself:[1]

> sed reuocato rursus impetu, aliquid secretioris latebrae ad colligendum animum desiderauit; et, offerente Phaonte liberto suburbanum suum inter Salariam et Nomentanam uiam circa quartum miliarium, ut erat, nudo pede atque tunicatus, paenulam obsoleti coloris superinduit; adopertoque capite et ante faciem obtento sudario, equum inscendit, quattuor solis comitantibus, inter quos et Sporus erat. statimque tremore terrae et fulgure aduerso pauefactus, audiit ex proximis castris clamorem militum, et sibi aduersa et Galbae prospera ominantium, etiam ex obuiis uiatoribus quendam dicentem 'hi Neronem persequuntur', alium sciscitantem 'ecquid in urbe noui de Nerone?' equo autem odore abiecti in uia cadaueris consternato, detecta facie agnitus est a quodam missicio praetoriano et salutatus.

He checked his impulse, however, and expressed a desire for some reasonably safe hiding-place to collect his thoughts. The freedman Phaon offered him a house he had near the city between the Salt road and the road to Nomentum, close to the four-mile post. Nero mounted a horse as he was, barefooted and dressed in a tunic, pausing only to throw over it an old discoloured travelling cloak and to cover his head and tie a kerchief over his face. Four men including Sporus were his only companions. As they set out, Nero was thrown into terror by an earthquake and a flash of lightning in his path. From a camp close at hand he could hear the cries of soldiers calling down curses on himself while wishing good luck to Galba. He heard, too, one of the people they met on the road say: 'They're after Nero.' Another he heard asking eagerly: 'What's the news from Rome about Nero?' At one point his horse took fright at the stench of a corpse lying on the road. Nero's face became uncovered, a discharged guardsman recognized him and saluted him.

[1] Suetonius, *Nero*, 48.

Tacitus' Narrative Technique

Here is detail, abundant and precise. First of all their destination: the house's position clearly fixed and its owner named. Then Nero's appearance: barefooted, wearing a *tunica* with a *paenula* over it (and not just a *paenula*, but an old, discoloured one), head covered, his face concealed by a kerchief. Four companions, one of them nameable. And so on. No ancient historian is quite like Suetonius with his passion for small details, though the ingenuous framework into which the details are fitted suggests often they are given for picturesque effect rather than noted down in a spirit of scientific curiosity.[1]

It is clear, then, that, if Tacitus' narrative impresses us as clear-cut, that impression is not the result of an abundance of detail. Indeed, the moment we look for detail we realize how imprecise his vivid scenes are. (On the other hand, though Suetonius tells us so much, we have a lot of the time no clear impression of scene, no describable mental image of the action.) Take the opening lines of our Tacitus passage. The place is not defined, even if by the time Tacitus has finished with his first scene, we feel the image of it sharply imprinted on our minds. Nor are the participants singled out. What, for example, does *ut quisque acceperat* mean? When we start looking for detail we realize Tacitus' economy: all that is needed to build up the picture, nothing to detract from its clarity, nothing to satisfy idle curiosity.

Sir Ronald Syme and Miss Walker ascribe this characteristic of Tacitus to the dictates of what he calls 'the grand manner' and she 'the influence of epic'.[2] Undoubtedly there is something in this. We may compare the impreciseness of Virgil in the *Aeneid*—and contrast it with the preciseness of Catullus in his *Marriage of Peleus and Thetis*. Miss Walker, however, sees more deeply perhaps into the matter when she makes her distinction between sensational and intuitive types. Both writers

---

[1] Einar Löfstedt has made brief, but interesting comparisons between the treatment by Suetonius and Tacitus of comparable events in 'On the style of Tacitus', *J.R.S.*, xxxviii (1948), pp. 1–8.

[2] Syme, op. cit., p. 342:
What Tacitus avoids can be no less instructive. The grand manner is hostile to the anecdote, it deprecates sordid or humorous items, and refuses the precise detail of scandalous revelations.
Walker, op. cit., p. 154:
There is in his work little of the realistic, even homely detail found in Plutarch and Suetonius.

Tacitus' Narrative Technique

assume Tacitus sacrifices dramatic vividness for stylistic nobility. Our comparison, I think, suggests the opposite conclusion.

Now that we have seen some of the things that Tacitus' narrative is not—not moralizing anecdote, not the story told with all recoverable detail indiscriminately recorded—we shall be able, perhaps, to look at the passage we have selected with eyes better prepared to catch its distinctive features. Observe first the fundamental structure of Tacitus' narrative. Our passage, the final act of the tragedy, falls into four clearly marked-off scenes and a concluding epilogue. For convenience I have printed the four scenes and epilogue as separate paragraphs, though in one case this means making a paragraph division in the middle of a sentence (between Scenes 3 and 4). The four paragraphs represent four steps in the narrative. In the first three the décor changes: on the beach; at the villa, but outside the bedroom; in the bedroom. But the four scenes are sharply distinguished, as well, by the style of writing; they arouse emotional responses in the reader that one might better compare to four movements of a musical composition than to four scenes of a play.

For most of the scene on the beach confusion predominates. Confusion is a state of mind natural enough in an Italian crowd in the circumstances, and it might seem at first that Tacitus has relaxed his usual standards of economy in description. In fact he is not describing, but using words to create atmosphere. The facts related are, as we have seen, quite vague: no precise statement of where we are, or what people are doing what. Then the tempo slows slightly. Instead of confusion and excitement, a more orderly movement (*adfluere ingens multitudo cum luminibus*) as the crowd starts to come together, no longer dimly lit in our mental image by the clear night sky,[1] but splashed with the flickering light of a bunching mass of torches. Then the news 'She is safe!' permeates the crowd; and with it there is a swing away from anxious purposefulness to a new joyous purposefulness: 'Let's go to her!' And then a fresh confusion as the crowd is thrown into disorder by marching troops, whose appearance immediately dispels relief and leaves the crowd feeling as apprehensive for Agrippina (but for a new reason),

[1] Tacitus commences his account of the night with the remark: *noctem sideribus inlustrem et placido mari quietam . . . dii praebuere* (Chapter 5, *init.*).

Tacitus' Narrative Technique

and as helpless, as at the beginning of the scene. To a crowd in these unhappy times the arrival of the emperor's soldiers is never reassuring. This is not an accident, they sense, but something sinister. The words *donec aspectu armati et minitantis agminis disiecti sunt* ring out harshly at the end of a long pattern of easily moving clauses. The mood of the opening scene has veered four times in twice as many lines.

The crowd scene has served its purpose: without apparently commenting himself on the situation at all, beyond the single word *minitantis* ('grim-faced'), Tacitus has us keyed up, prepared for the most overt brutality, above all on Agrippina's side to an extent difficult to secure by any rational assertion of her claim on our pity. This achieved, Tacitus abruptly switches the scene to the villa, to soldiers breaking down the door and sweeping through the house, thrusting aside all who try to stop them. The mood of this scene is clear and sharp: ruthless, purposeful activity. The terror it produces is underlined in the concluding words of the section (*ceteris terrore inrumpentium exterritis*). And then the scene again changes abruptly. We are inside the bedroom. The mood now is one of inactivity and uneasy disquiet. *We* have been told what is happening in the house. Agrippina and the maid are left to guess.

Without warning, in the middle of a sentence in fact, Scenes 2 and 3 now blend, the main actors of Scene 2 joining those of Scene 3 for the death scene. It is the technique of parallel narrative which we find in Virgil.[1] The artistry with which the blending of scenes is contrived is truly theatrical. The maid makes to go away; Agrippina's gaze follows her to the door—and falls on Anicetus standing there with his thugs. Her nerve gone, she blurts out the first things that come into her head, clutching desperately, as we saw, at her royal dignity, and then letting it slip from her grasp. The assassins say nothing.

The first half of the death scene is an instructive example of how the lightest touch can state precisely. Agrippina speaks only to Anicetus, an abominable creature, but her son's minister and on a different footing from his companions. A fussy writer would draw our attention to this pathetic assertion of her rank; Tacitus leaves it to the singular verbs *uenisset, nuntiaret* and

[1] For parallel narrative in Virgil, see the discussion of the death of Polites (*Aeneid* ii, 526–32) in Chapter 8.

Tacitus' Narrative Technique

patraturus to make the point unobtrusively, but three times. It is part of his technique to appear only to recover events, not to describe them, taking care that the events selected and the fashion of reporting them cause us to realize for ourselves what others would feel it necessary to tell us. For, as I said, events never speak for themselves. They need a sensitive observer to perceive their significance, and a discreet reporter to relate them in such a way that their significance appears so self-evident we are not conscious of the hand of the artist, selecting and arranging the detail. We are on the contrary so impressed by the way our reporter scrupulously avoids comment on what he is relating that we may fail to realize that he can be as concerned as the moralist with a moral purpose, though more adroit in achieving it.

In like manner it is made clear Anicetus takes no hand in the murder himself: the single word *prior* makes the point with just sufficient emphasis. Moreover, we realize when we come to *prior* that *percussores* just before is not a loose summing-up of all three, but a firm stamping of their true character upon Herculeius and Obaritus, who were introduced with what we see now to be an ironically careful underlining of their status as respectable members of the armed forces.

There is a similar economical sureness of touch in Agrippina's dying words 'Strike the belly!' She uses the second person singular, *uentrem feri*, not *feriat*, or even *ferite*; all pretence at dignity wrenched aside, she turns directly to the assailant about to raise his sword.

But more important than these details is the tempo of the four scenes. It is dictated primarily by the events related. But it is underlined by Tacitus' exploitation of the resources of the Latin verb. In the first scene, the main verbs are all historic infinitives (*decurrere, scandere, uadere, protendere, compleri, adfluere, expedire*). The historic infinitive, more than the imperfect indicative, suggests action in progress: it is often conveniently translated by the periphrasis 'began to . . .', our normal English mechanism for dealing with past action which begins and then *goes on*; though of course the Latin historic infinitive denotes only the process of going on. The effect here is of many things *going on* at once. No definite, clear-cut action until we come to the brutal *disiecti sunt*, which throws the whole scene on the beach

Tacitus' Narrative Technique

into a fresh confusion before abandoning it in order to turn our attention to the villa. The words *disiecti sunt* belong, in grammar, not to a principal clause, but to a subordinate clause. Their position, however, and their significance lend the clause all the emphasis of a main statement. The emphatic *donec* clause with its verb in the perfect indicative and concluding a complex narrative sentence is another stylistic mannerism borrowed by Tacitus from Virgil.[1]

The second scene begins with two historic presents, *circumdat* and *abripit*—the classical historian's device since Herodotus for highlighting the crucial stages in a narrative, or those most intrinsically dramatic. The use Tacitus makes of an alternation between aoristic perfect (events simply recorded) and historic present (events vividly described) closely follows Virgilian practice.[2] The *donec* clause this time has its verb in the subjunctive (*ueniret*) because the emphasis here is on the purpose lying behind action and not, as in *disiecti sunt*, in the finality of the event itself. Tacitus, however, does not overplay his historic presents; he wishes to keep the device in reserve for what is to come. The atmosphere of urgent purposeful action established, he reverts to description and imperfects (*adstabant, inerat*), followed by a short passage purporting to note down the thoughts running through Agrippina's mind.

In the death scene the arrangement of the verbs is planned with equal care. The rapid tempo of action created at the beginning of the second scene and then held in suspense is abruptly re-established by a single historic present, *respicit*; and then held in suspense again while the scene is briefly sketched and Agrippina's heightened agitation obliquely conveyed. Then another historic present (*circumsistunt*) sets the action in progress afresh. We might expect Tacitus now to continue to use that tense. He abandons it, however, for the aoristic perfect.

---

[1] Virgil normally combines this use of *donec* with an historic present or aoristic perfect in the principal clause, but the combination of historic infinitive in principal clause and aoristic perfect in *donec* clause is found in *Aeneid* x, 298–302:
> quae talia postquam
> effatus Tarchon, socii *consurgere* tonsis
> spumantisque rates aruis *inferre* Latinis,
> donec rostra tenent siccum et *sedere* carinae
> omnes innocuae.

[2] For a discussion of the variation in the *Aeneid* between aoristic perfect and historic present, see Chapter 8, under sub-heading 'The narrative sentence: tenses'.

Tacitus' Narrative Technique

The difference between the two tenses is a subtle one. The historic present strikes the graphic, more excited note. But what the tense gains in vividness it loses in finality. The action is described as though it were before our eyes; but the fact that the action is over and done with, belongs now irrevocably to the past, is neglected. It is as though with *circumsistunt* Tacitus permitted himself one final graphic touch; and then, for the most terrible events of the whole episode (*fusti caput eius adflixit, 'uentrem feri!' exclamauit,* and *multisque uulneribus confecta est*) resumed the sober pose of historian recording the past. We seem to move away from the scene at its climax, and the narrative concludes with an unemotional, ungraphic euphemism: *confecta est*.

The tenses of the epilogue are of less concern to us, though we should note the distinction implied between the perfect subjunctive *tradiderint* and the present subjunctive *abnuant*. There are writers who over the years have recorded Nero's final infamy, but there are still people who reject the story. If the two verbs had both been perfect subjunctive, it would have been as though the accounts were equally divided. By shifting to the present, Tacitus manages somehow to discredit by implication the unhistorical, irrational attitude of those who refuse to accept what the past has told them. It is a good example of *varietas* that is not just mechanical variation; it enables Tacitus to influence his reader a little towards a view he could hardly hope him to accept if plainly stated.

The narrative of the epilogue is quiet and unemphatic. Agrippina's hurried, sordid funeral is tersely noted, Nero's petty refusal to grant her a proper grave reported and contrasted with the devotion of slaves. Each of these events has a moral point, and the discretion with which the points are made is admirable. The simple words *nocte eadem* imply indecent haste while contriving to appear perfectly neutral. Observe, too, how Nero's own ignoble, violent death is quietly kept from our thoughts lest it weaken our pity for Agrippina and our revulsion at her son's refusal to allow her a proper grave: instead of 'not until after Nero's death', or even 'not while Nero was alive', the unemotional 'not so long as Nero was in power' (*dum Nero rerum potiebatur*).

But the main purpose of the epilogue is not narrative. The

details given have partly, as we have seen, a moral objective. At the same time, by establishing in us the feeling that he is rounding off his account with a statement of incidentals, Tacitus leads us naturally to words whose purpose seems merely to fix precisely the position of Agrippina's grave.

The phrase beginning *uiam Miseni propter* looks as innocently precise as the similar-sounding phrase we saw in Suetonius. But it ends with a word that startles us: 'close to the villa of Caesar the *dictator*'. Not '*uillam diui Iuli*', according to the complimentary official phraseology. But why Caesar the dictator? Syme has noted that Tacitus generally avoids the precise terminology of government, preferring words that do not look too technical.[1] Here, however, the formula *Caesar dictator* is irreproachably exact historically, though it ignores the current cult of the Julian house.[2] Tacitus' reason for preferring the unusual if exact term to the usual honorific one is clear enough. It reduces, as it were, to human stature the whole dynasty of which Nero was the last representative. Once again, while maintaining his pose of the impartial recorder of fact, *sine ira et studio*, Tacitus manipulates seemingly neutral words, so that they speak to the sensitive reader more eloquently than open comment. As the curtain comes down on the tragedy of Agrippina, the participants in the drama are unobtrusively stripped of their sham divinity.

At the same time, by leading our thoughts back to the beginning of the dynasty (a century and a half from the time of writing instead of a mere sixty years), Tacitus creates in us momentarily the feeling that these are things all over and done with. The scenes of horror recede, their place taken by the tableau con-

[1] Syme, op. cit., pp. 343–4:
The terminology of the Roman administration was awkward or monotonous. Tactitus varies or evades it. For 'proconsul' he can revive the archaic 'praetor'; he will go to any lengths or contortions rather than denominate the governor of an imperial province by the exact title; and the convenient but prosaic neologism 'praeses' slips in only twice. Again, 'praefectus praetorio' is successfully avoided.

[2] Actually Tacitus scrupulously records the official formula *diuus Iulius* half a dozen times in the *Annals*—on the lips of others, in speeches or edicts. The words *dictator Caesar* (in that order) occur three times in the *Annals*, all in more or less technical contexts. It would appear from Gerber and Greef's *Lexicon Taciteum* (1903), which however omits our present passage, that the only comparable use of the phrase *Caesar dictator* in the *Annals* is in ii, 41, 4, in a reference to the gardens, *quos Caesar dictator populo Romano legauerat*.

Tacitus' Narrative Technique

jured up by the concluding words of the sentence. The words are casually introduced by a relative pronoun,

> ... uillam Caesaris dictatoris quae subiectos sinus editissima prospectat ...

> ... *the villa of Caesar the dictator, which stands on a great height looking out over the curving coastline below* ...

but they provide the only precise description of scene to be found in the passage we have been considering. And they contain the only trace of emphasis or emotion that Tacitus permits himself. The effect of the two words *editissima prospectat* (to which sound and rhythm contribute much) is indescribable. We are left with a scene of peace and seclusion, uncontaminated now by any contact with the Julio-Claudian line, of whose mad exploits Tacitus made himself the historian.[1]

[1] The words *editissima prospectat*, as explained earlier, are not the end of the whole story of Agrippina, but they mark the end of the narrative section. After a few details, Tacitus passes to the analysis of Nero's conscience.

6

Propertius, Horace, and the Poet's Role

The Importance of Propertius

PROPERTIUS is an exciting poet—and a depressing one. His verse is notoriously difficult; but it is not that alone, or even that primarily, which produces this divided attitude in us. His difficulty, however, is symptomatic. Often it seems due to mere slovenliness. But often, too, Propertius' Latin is difficult because he is the only Roman poet to experiment consistently with the non-rational possibilities of language.

We find complexity of statement in other Roman poets, layers of symbolism, interweavings of ambiguities; but the basis is rational statement. Even though it proves often a poor guide to the rich experience the poem has to offer, there is a firm line of meaning to which the despairing or the insensitive may cling. Propertius' techniques look odder therefore in Latin than they might look if he were writing in English or French. A Propertian sentence may be clear enough, but just not mean what is says; or it may be wilfully irrational; or its rational content may be almost negligible.

A word more on this aspect of Propertius before we tackle his attitude to love. Here are short examples of each of these three types of para-rational statement. Take, to begin with, the opening line of the first elegy:

The Importance of Propertius

Cynthia prima suis miserum me cepit ocellis.

Cynthia first captured piteous me with her eyes.

It is in the first place an example of Propertius' habit of running two statements into one: Cynthia was the first to make me her prisoner; she did it with her eyes. Then the stress falls equally on *cepit* and on *prima*: Cynthia was not the first woman in Propertius' life, but the first who mattered—not the first *he* pursued, but the first who captured *him*.[1] The subject of the book is not to be innocent love, but the degradation of the poet from his position of male supremacy by his subjugation to a *donna fatale*. That is the sense in which he is 'to be pitied' (*miserum*). Finally, by *ocellis* we find two lines later he means, not so much that Cynthia had beautiful eyes, but that she gave him a look that withered his own donjuanesque glance of appraisal. The meaning the sentence ultimately acquires can hardly be inferred from what the words appear to state. The whole story of the affair is adumbrated in the opening line; but to minds accustomed to rational techniques of communication it seems intolerable to begin a collection of poems with an introductory poem, the first line of which requires a commentary before its correct meaning can be extracted.

As an example of wilfully irrational statement we may take, from later in the same elegy, the famous lines:

> at uos, deductae quibus est fallacia lunae
> et labor in magicis sacra piare focis,   20
> en agedum dominae mentem conuertite nostrae,
> et facite illa meo palleat ore magis!

But you, with your show of bringing down the moon,
and your industry of magic fires and powers appeased:
now's your chance, transform my mistress' attitude to me,
see to it her cheeks' pallor outdoes mine!

Housman declared the first couplet might mean any one of three things—and then proceeded to demonstrate that in the

[1] K. P. Schulze, *Römische Elegiker* (5th edn. 1910), p. 168 (quoted by Enk, p. 4) was apparently the first to see this: 'Die wahre Leidenschaft der Liebe lernte er erst durch Cynthia kennen.'

context none of the meanings was possible because all involved flagrant disregard of logic.[1] He made the mistake of assuming Propertius is attempting precise statement about a rational state of mind. The poet's object in fact is to convey the irrational anxiety of the lover—desperate either to free himself from the passion he realizes is degrading him, or at any rate to find a way of getting the girl to relent and love him in return. Intellectually he knows that witches cannot bring down the moon from the sky; and intellectually he is probably just as sceptical about their power to instil and expel passionate love. But his is one of those predicaments where men resort to the aid of forces they don't in their sane moments believe in. The lines are designed to convey, and convey excellently, the conflict between residual intellectual irony and an irrational impulse to try anything.

Finally in this note on three types of Propertian statement let us take the opening lines of Elegy i, 7:

> Dum tibi Cadmeae dicuntur, Pontice, Thebae
>   armaque fraternae tristia militiae,
> atque, ita sim felix, primo contendis Homero,
>   (sint modo fata tuis mollia carminibus:)
> nos, ut consuemus, nostros agitamus amores,   5
>   atque aliquid duram quaerimus in dominam;
> nec tantum ingenio quantum seruire dolori
>   cogor et aetatis tempora dura queri.

You, Ponticus, tell your story of Cadmus' Thebes,
of brother joined with brother in war's grim service,
matched yourself in duel, as I'll swear, with the real Homer
(though fate, I hope, will treat your verse unmartially);
while I, it is my way, with my love am occupied,   5
preparing offensive upon a cruel mistress.
My labours must be on love's pain expended, not poet's fertile
fancy, at a cruel stage in life my protest voiced.

[1] *J.Ph.*, xvi (1888), p. 25. Housman's words are quoted and the passage very fully discussed and rightly interpreted by D. R. S. Bailey, *C.Q.*, xliii (1949), p. 22, though Propertius (a 'poet with whom logical consistency is notoriously not a strong point') perhaps deserves more credit for capturing a very human inconsistency.

The Importance of Propertius

The lines make sense. Ponticus is told that, while he is engaged on an epic poem about the Seven against Thebes, Propertius is as usual writing love poetry and unhappy. But it can hardly be said that the object of the eight lines is to tell Ponticus, or us, that. The antithesis is too well worn to call for such full statement. The object, as Mlle Guillemin has seen,[1] is to provide a simple framework of statement to support a series of clichés, the sense of which is ironically reversed. It turns mainly on the implication of fresh connotations for *mollis* and *durus*, epithets that in contemporary literary criticism were used to sum up elegiac and epic poetry respectively. Here *durus*—the word Ponticus might use approvingly of one of his epic heroes—is used of Propertius' mistress, implying her attitude is unreasonable or uncivilized, one appropriate to war, not peace. And while the epic hero expects to face *aetatis tempora dura*, the lover doesn't. On the other hand, the fates are asked to be *mollia* to Ponticus' poem. Then there are the implications of *contendis*. The duel he describes between Eteocles and Polynices involves Ponticus in a different kind of duel with Homer, whom Propertius calls *primus Homerus*—a way of implying Ponticus is a second Homer. To round the idea off, Propertius prays that fate will treat Ponticus' poem, despite the martial hardness of his theme and his literary battle with Homer, in the soft, affectionate way one hopes to be treated by one's mistress. It is all very clever, the sort of word-play coterie poets find amusing. Only here and there is there any bite in the cleverness. Take the line

armaque fraternae tristia militiae,

of brother joined with brother in war's grim service.

First, the sense is adequate: it *is* a grim fight that makes brother confront brother. Then the form: the two epithets also confront one another at the caesura, locking the line together (*fraternae* belongs to the noun in the second half of the line, *tristia* to *arma*). What really saves the poem, though, is perhaps the touch of pathos in *ita sim felix*—a casual enough formula of

[1] A. Guillemin, 'Sur les origines de l'élégie latine', *R.E.L.*, xvii (1939), pp. 282–292.

Propertius, Horace, and the Poet's Role

asseveration apparently ('so help me!'), until we see from the following lines how poor are Propertius' prospects of *felicitas*.

Clearly any value the passages we have looked at possess as poetry derives from qualities that have no straightforward connection with the actual statements made. But our misgivings about Propertius are provoked by something more fundamental in his poetry than a special technique of using language to create a mood or evoke a complex situation. Language is only one aspect contributing to an initial impression which, I think, all sensitive readers receive. It may be summed up, perhaps, as a feeling that here is a mind worth grappling with. It is this probably more than anything else that has drawn so many scholars to worry over Propertius' verses in an effort to pummel sense out of them—and then caused them to lay them aside disappointed or exasperated, denied either the simple pleasure they can get from a logical skimming of Tibullus or the deeper satisfaction Virgil generously bestows on his diligent admirers. Hence no doubt, with the resultant corruption of the manuscript tradition, the eighty-odd editions of Propertius that have seen the light of day: echoing M. Schuster's despairing cry, *quot editores, tot Propertii*, we must agree with Dr. Bailey that Propertius' critics can still find more profitable things to do.[1]

There is no reluctance, then, to grapple with the mind of Propertius. The results are not impressive. The student of Propertius has at his disposal a very serviceable commentary on the first book; for the remainder, quite unserviceable ones. He will find scholars in profusion eager to tell him the meaning of a word, a line, a couplet, up to half a dozen lines; few to tell him the meaning of a poem. It is distressing to discover how little insight into his poetry Propertius has surrendered to the scholarly inquisition that has racked him so long. The things worth reading on the poetry are quickly listed. They amount, apart from a handful of short articles, to two monographs, one German, one Italian, and a short study in French of Propertius' use of mythology.[2] Yet Propertius is of capital significance to

---

[1] D. R. S. Bailey, 'Some recent experiments in Propertian criticism', *P.C. Ph.S.*, No. 182 (1952-3), p. 20. The quip, which heads Schuster's introduction to his Teubner text, is taken from Phillimore.

[2] Erich Reitzenstein's rewarding *Wirklichkeitsbild und Gefühlsentwicklung bei Properz*, *Ph.* Supplementband, xxix, 2 (1936), follows the best German tradition of sober, systematic structural study of Roman poetry inaugurated by Richard

The Importance of Propertius

the literary historian. He represents the real point of failure in a line of poetic tradition of the first importance, beginning with Catullus and continuing through Horace and Virgil. Reaching Propertius, the line fractures. When we turn to Ovid, we see that the contact Roman poetry had established with the worth-while levels of intellectual and social life has been lost.

It is not Ovid who is the renegade. In the few years separating Ovid from the older elegists the failure has occurred. Ovid, realizing it, nonchalantly abdicates the moral stature Catullus, Horace and Virgil had won for poetry, in order to assume, with panache and a terse verbal elegance, the role of entertainer to which the poet had been relegated by Roman society before the advent of Catullus and the *poetae novi*. No Roman writer writes neater Latin than Ovid. He exploits to the full the possibilities of tension between clean sobriety of statement and a line of sense that is based on a deadly accuracy of observation, bubbling sometimes with risqué innuendo, sometimes the purest fun. His advice, for example, to the dumpy girl, that she should avoid standing up in the presence of her prospective lover,[1]

si breuis es sedeas, ne stans uideare sedere,

If you're short sit, in case standing you look seated,

---

[1] Ovid, *Ars* iii, 263.

Heinze in his monumental *Vergils epische Technik*. Luigi Alfonsi's *L'elegia di Properzio* (1945), is short, difficult and ill laid out, but a real attempt to deal with the poetry of Propertius. (An indication of how rare this kind of study is is provided by the fact that Schuster, in the short bibliographical apparatus which he added to the Teubner edition of the text, regularly gives page references to Alfonsi's remarks on individual elegies.) Pierre Boyancé's 'Properce' in *L'influence grecque sur la poésie latine de Catulle à Ovide*, Fondation Hardt, *Entretiens sur l'antiquité classique*, ii (1956), pp. 169–220, provides a stimulating introduction to Propertian use of mythology. One might add a recent useful systematic monograph on Propertian vocabulary: Hermann Tränkle, *Die Sprachkunst des Properz und die Tradition der lateinischen Dichtersprache*, *Hermes*, Einzelschr. 15 (1960). It contains much useful information on vocabulary and syntactical and stylistic detail, but less than the title promises. The chapters on Propertius in the standard handbooks have little to contribute. Gilbert Highet, *Poets in a Landscape* (1957), contains some showy generalizations. G. Luck, *The Latin Love Elegy* (1959), has two chapters on Propertius: the first short and superficial; the second, which deals with Propertius' relationship to Callimachus, is solider; but less worth reading than I. Lonie's 'Propertius and the Alexandrians', *Aumla*, No. 11, 1959, pp. 17–34.

might figure as an example in a manual on Latin prose composition—though that would mean neglecting three properties of the statement beside its pure, simple syntax. First, it is verse. Second, it is screamingly funny. Third, it has just a hint of that feeling for the *pathos* inherent in a situation that can cause Ovid in the *Metamorphoses* to rise to a level approaching poetry. But poetry that sets out to explore, unravel, record the problems of human experience (instead of achieving these things incidentally, through sheer genius) Ovid never writes. His role is strictly to entertain.

Nor can we really blame Tibullus, the placid second-rater without the calibre to sense the dangerous inadequacies of the genre he has adopted but cannot revitalize. Tibullus *has* the qualities Quintilian and a host of pedants since have attributed to him.[1] He *is* clear-cut (*tersus*), though only in framing a sentence, not in handling a theme. He *is* elegant, in that he has a pure Latin style, its limpidity untroubled either by Propertian toughness of thought or by Ovidian ingenuity of expression. He shows moreover a true peasant's feeling for the Italian countryside—its simple tradition of contented routine and joyous, pious relaxation; not its beauty or its mystery. Save the ability to write good Latin, it is his only real claim to consideration. Had he lived in an age where the general level of poetic achievement was higher, Tibullus might, by relying on others, have written verse that justified the comparisons sometimes made with Collins, Longfellow and similar minor poets of moderate distinction. As one of a group of second-raters, he might have learnt to use verse to say things worth saying; things which, if not fresh or penetrating, revealed at any rate some power of observation or some refinement of sensibility or imagination. As it is, the poverty of his talent is exposed. We are never given the impression Tibullus *cares* for Delia (or the others); or is capable of analysing his thoughts about her; or that love represents for him more than a casual brutish sensuality. The fresh, startling achievements of Catullus, Horace and Propertius somehow passed him by, to leave him versifying at the prevailing level of mediocrity that they transcended. And

---

[1] Quintilian, x, 1, 93:
Elegia quoque Graecos prouocamus, cuius mihi tersus atque elegans maxime uidetur auctor Tibullus.

The Importance of Propertius

at that level he rambles on inexcusably, despite the efforts of his more pretentious admirers to excuse him.[1]

The true responsibility for the failure lies with Propertius, the one poet who at the critical moment could have been expected to prove himself adequate to the emergency. For he realized the crisis. We see him in elegy after elegy, impatient with the shoddiness of a tradition he cannot find adequate ways of strengthening, essaying theme after theme, slap-dash in his handling of them because the poet in him tells him he is wasting his time. To us the failure seems almost wilful. It is as though Propertius were unwilling, rather than unable (we have such clear evidence of ability), to follow the lead of Horace.

For Horace, affecting occasionally to be in love himself but not expecting us to take him seriously, was turning poetry into a kind of urbane commentary—succinct, sensitive, humane, gently humorous—on contemporary life. It sounds perhaps a frivolous end for poetry to serve. An example will show the penetrating, sober comment Horace's whimsy can convey. *Odes* i, 8 is a poem about a young Roman whom Horace calls Sybaris—intending by the name to suggest the conventional judgment that he is behaving like a sissy. Sybaris has fallen in love with a girl called Lydia, and has been cutting parades he should attend as a member of a sort of cadet training corps.[2] Horace reproaches the girl with 'ruining' Sybaris, putting on a fine show of stout support for convention. To show the harm she is doing, he lists the various forms of physical training that Sybaris is now neglecting, despite his former manly enthusiasm for them:

---

[1] It is fashionable to compare Tibullus' habit of wandering through the clichés, relevant or irrelevant to his theme, to a symphony. The comparison, originally made by F. Marx in his article on Tibullus in *R.E.* (1894), was taken over by M. Ponchont, *Tibulle* (1924), and by M. Schuster, *Tibull-Studien* (1930). A more thoroughgoing rehabilitation has recently been attempted by Gilbert Highet, who finds evidence of a man who wrote 'in grave psychological trouble', op. cit., p. 164:

> The style of Tibullus's poems is a clue to the secret of his life. They are not disorderly, half-crazed, disorganized: they are neither frenetic nor psychotic. But they are weak, filled with anticipations of death, confessions of spiritual invalidism, fascinated examinations of his own moral impotence.

[2] Sybaris, like the *robustus acri militia puer* of *Odes* iii, 2, is either already a member of Augustus' *militia equestris*, or a member of the revived *Lusus Troiae*. On the former, see Pasquali, pp. 667–71; on the latter, R. D. Williams, *Aeneid* v (1960), p. 146.

Propertius, Horace, and the Poet's Role

> Lydia, dic, per omnis
> hoc deos uere, Sybarin cur properes amando
>   perdere, cur apricum
> oderit campum, patiens pulueris atque solis,
>
>   cur neque militaris   5
> inter aequalis equitet, Gallica nec lupatis
>   temperet ora frenis?
> cur timet flauum Tiberim tangere? cur oliuum
>
>   sanguine uiperino
> cautius uitat neque iam liuida gestat armis   10
>   bracchia, saepe disco,
> saepe trans finem iaculo nobilis expedito?

Tell me, Lydia, in name of all
you hold sacred, why you're hurtling Sybaris to ruin
with your loving. Why's he now no time
for track and open air, though he could take the sun and dust?

Why, when there's an exercise   5
for youngsters of his age, is he not here, checking mount
with jagged Gallic bridle?
What's his fear of touching yellow Tiber water? Why shun,

like bottled viper's venom,
his rub-down oil, display no more arms black and blue   10
with bruises—he who broke
record after record with javelin cast and discus throw?

Somehow, despite the irreproachably conventional tone of disapproval, Horace's recital of the manly sports contrives to make them sound singularly unattractive. The reader begins to realize why Horace has called his young man Sybaris: his association with Lydia has turned an impressive young athlete into a sissy. When he cuts parades now, it isn't, we feel, just to spend the time with Lydia: he has allowed himself to get so soft he finds repulsive the dust, dirt and bruises of athletics. In Horace's words we hear the echo of Sybaris' expression of distaste. And, with Horace on his side, we find it hard to blame him. His behaviour, though of course we must pretend to treat it as scandalous, begins to elicit our tolerant approval.

The Importance of Porpertius

So far we have little more than banter and a discreetly suggested conflict between the attitude overtly adopted and that covertly suggested. The last four lines carry the poem up to new levels of poetry and social comment. The modulation into a more solemn key is marked by an allusive periphrasis that is not just embellishment, but intended to conjure up memories of Homer's Thetis, prostrate with grief because her son must die so young:

> quid latet, ut marinae
> filium dicunt Thetidis sub lacrimosa Troiae
>   funera, ne uirilis   15
> cultus in caedem et Lycias proriperet cateruas?

Why lurk in cover, as did
sea-goddess Thetis' son, they say, when Troy's awful
doom impended, afraid acting like
a man would plunge him into slaughtering Phrygian squadrons?

Achilles, the bravest of all the Greeks who fought at Troy, according to an old story disguised himself as a girl, in order to avoid being sent to the war. While keeping out of the way of the military authorities (to re-phrase a heroic situation in terms appropriate to Sybaris) he made love to the daughter of the king with whom he was staying, and she bore him his son Neoptolemus. However, as we all know, he turned out all right in the end by the most conventional standards of manliness, dying bravely for his country. Need we then worry too much about Sybaris? Won't he turn out all right, too, given time?

It is an intelligent many-sided comment, full of common sense and uncommonly sensitive humanity. But it is only the second stage in our judgment of Sybaris. During the first stage, Horace concentrated on him. By a loaded re-statement of the charge against him, he won him our indulgence. The next stage was to introduce the parallel of Achilles, and imply that no real harm will come of Sybaris' seeming lapse into effeminacy. The third stage is to suggest guarded, positive approval of Sybaris. This officially heretical attitude is made to occur to us by Horace's discreet manipulation of the ambiguity in *uirilis cultus*. The meaning drawn to the surface by the Achilles story is 'manly dress'. But the more general and more obvious

Propertius, Horace, and the Poet's Role

meaning of the words, 'manly behaviour', is also appropriate. If Achilles had behaved like a man, he would have gone off to the war at once.[1] The Sybaris story and the Achilles legend now interlock, to prepare for a penetrating final judgment.

By conventional standards it must be admitted both failed to 'behave like men'. They evaded military service. They became sissies. (Horace here implies a neat reinterpretation of the symbolism that inspired the old story of Achilles dressing as a girl, and shows how we may reconcile it with the other story that he fell in love with Deidamia.) Achilles really didn't *want* to go to war, Horace leaves little room for doubt. We begin to guess Sybaris has no appetite either to see active service. Once again the suggestion is disgraceful to the worshippers of the manly cult, for whom the only explanation for reluctance is cowardice; and once again Achilles exculpates Sybaris. Who can believe Achilles was a coward? Look again at that concluding clause:

> . . . ne uirilis   15
> cultus in caedem et Lycias proriperet cateruas . . .

> . . . *afraid acting like*
> *a man would plunge him into slaughtering Phrygian squadrons* . . .

isn't it killing perhaps, just as much as being killed, that he hung back from? The words invite each interpretation equally.

Horace's final comment now emerges: it is directed against the shallowness of the conventional concept of acting like a man. Why should any normal young man, whose sense of values has not been blunted by the manly cult, *like* war if war brings only death and sorrow (*lacrimosa funera*), be willing to get involved in the brutality of war, give up for that, before he absolutely must, the company of a girl he loves, the happy, civilized life that being with her brings?

Propertius, however, continues to cling to love poetry in the Catullan manner, or rather to that stylization and near-caricature of it that elegy represents.[2] Yet the point had been reached in

---

[1] The ambiguity is discussed by Heinze, p. 47.
[2] The explanation can hardly lie in the supposed rivalry between Propertius and Horace, about which much has been written and much supposed. Propertius has been assumed to be the victim of Horace's bad-tempered remarks about a

The Crisis in Roman Love Poetry

Roman love poetry where, short of a complete revision of the presuppositions upon which it was based, the role of the passionate poet-lover had really become untenable. We must now consider why this was so.

The Crisis in Roman Love Poetry

Propertius began experimenting with love Poetry something like thirty years after Catullus had established the short personal love poem in Latin as a literary form entitled to proper recognition. The form was a slight one and it needed a serious purpose to give it weight. The formula for securing this is clear enough. If the poet is to speak in his own person, or through a *persona* that he assumes (the passionate lover, for example), and claim our recognition of what he writes as worth-while poetry, he must, in addition to showing us he can write, convince us as well that he, or the *persona* he creates, is worthy of our respect. The slightness of the form, the compressed craftsmanship and the resultant demands upon the reader all necessitate worth-while content. In this type of poem, the poet is not the anonymous artist, but a person engaged in a special kind of conversation with the reader. While what he says need not be fresh or profound, it must not sound trite or silly. We shall not have the patience to study and savour the refinement and complexity of the poem's structure unless we can as well take the poet seriously as a person.

The short love poem must in fact display either emotional or intellectual strength. We may see the poet involved in an emotional problem that commands our interest. Or we may simply feel the poet to be a person whose intellectual calibre makes the expression of his thoughts arresting.

The astonishing thing is that Roman personal poetry could provide both requisites from the start. The formula, however, was too rigid. The Roman personal poets stuck too much to love. In itself that was apt to become boring. Propertius' embarrassment at the inevitable repetitiousness of personal

---

Roman Callimachus, *E.* ii, 2, 99–101, and (with less probability) to be the bore of *S.* i, 9. On the other hand, the opening elegies of Propertius' third book contain clear echoes of Horace's odes, which are usually taken as intended by Propertius as a compliment to Horace. For a recent review of this very speculative controversy, see N. O. Terzaghi, *R.A.L.*, xiv (1959), pp. 179–201.

love poetry is clear. What was more fatal to Roman love poetry, however, was the influence of contemporary ideas about love, a prevailing intellectual climate that made the perpetuation of poetry in the Catullan tradition at a serious poetic level eventually impossible.

The love poems of Catullus make us feel something is being taken seriously we could take seriously ourselves. We may have at the back of our minds a suspicion that something rather tawdry is being treated as though it were something rather sublime and tragic. But we do not find it difficult to believe that we might ourselves talk this way—and we should be proud to find ourselves capable of saying the things Catullus said. When occasionally his poetry acquires hints of tragic rhetoric, we may regret the verse has not stayed as tight and as light as we find it in his finest poems (compare the poignant, graceful Poem 8 with the more rhetorical Poem 76). But the attitudes struck, while we might feel shy of striking them ourselves, do not stand in the way of our appreciation of the poetry.

Even if we suspect that the problem of making poetry came to concern Catullus more than love for Lesbia, we are prepared to go along with him. Consider the elegiac fragments devoted to the linguistic exploration of his relationship with Lesbia: they are terse, dignified, stimulating; there is nothing maudlin, no otiose repetition, no falsely strident notes. At most an occasional self-righteous touch offends. We forget the real Lesbia in the heat of the linguistic, poetic battle with concepts that to the poet are fresh, and therefore hard for him to frame, exhilarating and worth framing.

We cannot feel this way about the love poetry Propertius wrote thirty years later. Even when he is closest to the Catullan tradition (in that opening elegy of hopeless love, for example), he remains disconcertingly blasé. He is so ready to show himself casually realistic about Cynthia. She is beautiful, talented, but falling in love with her produced no illusions. And none were shattered when she started to play fast and loose with him. Just as there is none of the freshness of idyllic love (think of Poems 5 or 7 of Catullus), there is little of Catullus' agonized protestation at the conflict between heart and head. Propertius *accepts* the reality of powerful physical attachment, its irrational nature, its unpleasantness, the havoc it can cause in a man's

The Crisis in Roman Love Poetry

life despite his intellectual awareness of what is happening. The heart-head conflict is not for Propertius the terrible revelation it was for Catullus, but a common experience to be endured. We might almost say that where Catullus left off in the *odi et amo* poems, Propertius starts. His opening elegy, as Professor A. W. Allen has shown,[1] is a brilliantly tense statement of this mood of powerless awareness.

We may, if we choose, call Catullus a romantic—provided it does not make us suppose his verse resembles English or French Romantic verse.[2] More precisely, he lends the events of real life an unrealistic stature which we may term either romantic or tragic. He plays up his initial ingenuousness, gives free rein to his initial illusions in order to magnify the impact of disillusionment. It is a process we find it easy to be indulgent about if the poetry that emerges avoids sloppiness. We do not have to pretend to ourselves that love really works this way. Somehow, so long as a poet's ideas about love, or about any other aspect of human behaviour, are not patently ridiculous (to the point that their absurdity forces itself upon us), or actually repulsive to us, we do not have to believe in the poet's ideas ourselves. Often we allow our sense of the past to intercede in the poet's favour. If his ideas draw the poet on, and their power to stimulate him is matched by his ability as a poetic craftsman, this can be enough. We read some poets for their wisdom, but really not so many.

But the poet himself finds it much harder to suspend disbelief in the ideas that lie behind his verse. They must have some valid relationship—not necessarily one of identity—to the intellectual climate of his time. But ideas on certain subjects—love is one of them—can alter radically from one generation to the next. When that happens it becomes just not possible to base serious poetry on a set of concepts that have lost all valid relationship with contemporary beliefs. It is this that separates Propertius from Catullus.

[1] A. W. Allen, 'Elegy and the classical attitude toward love: Prop. I, 1', *Y.Cl.S.*, xi (1950), pp. 255–77. The readiness with which commentators confess their incomprehension of this introductory poem does not lead one to hope they can help much in understanding the lover it introduces: Butler and Barber, p. 153:
> The precise significance of this elegy and the circumstances of its composition are debatable.

Enk, p. 2: 'Quid haec elegia sibi velit, non ita facile dictu.'

[2] I find E. M. Blaiklock's *The Romanticism of Catullus* (1959) overstated.

Propertius, Horace, and the Poet's Role

The music-lover can listen to Mozart and forget the existence of Beethoven, Wagner and Stravinsky. The serious contemporary composer cannot ignore the existence of post-Mozartian music. Most of us might feel pleased with ourselves if we could produce a tolerable pastiche of Mozart; but creative writing in a dead idiom is impossible. The attempt is doomed to artificiality and sterility. In somewhat the same way, while readers may continue to enjoy poetry that is the product of worn-out ideas, it ceases to be possible for poets to make good poetry out of them. Yet that is what, too often, the poets of Augustan Rome tried to do.

The artificiality and sterility of much of Augustan elegy (almost all Tibullus, but a fair bit of Propertius and Ovid, too) are, it seems to me, as simply explained as this. Its mediocrity is due much less to lack of talent (all three surviving elegists are remarkably talented in their way) than to a failure to find effective ways of renovating ideas about love that could no longer be maintained in any valid relationship to a changed intellectual climate. I don't mean of course that Roman literature had reached a point where love poetry was impossible. I do mean a point had been reached where love poetry could be saved only by a radical revision of the poets' attitude to love.

The Catullan tradition of love poetry was dealt a crippling blow, almost at its outset, by Lucretius' treatise on sexual love, which forms the last section of the fourth book of the *De rerum natura*. It is one of those curious accidents that sometimes influence a whole literary tradition. For there is no reason to suppose Lucretius wished to attack Catullus. His aim was a strictly scientific one, unrelated to contemporary literature. Likely enough, Lucretius was not even acquainted with the poetry of Catullus, for his poem seems earlier in date. The effect upon poetry was none the less profound.

Lucretius makes three main points about love. The first is that love is a form of madness. Here he is in accord with well-established literary as well as philosophical tradition,[1] though ancient love poets, understandably, are not all prepared to be self-confessed lunatics. His second point was that love is sordid as well as foolish. His third, that love is transitory—a passion

---

[1] As Allen, art. cit., shows very fully. Allen seems to me, however, to neglect the significance of Lucretius' other points.

The Crisis in Roman Love Poetry

that is promiscuous as well as capricious, unrelated to real affection. Together, the three points represent pretty much the view of love which we find in the comedies of Plautus and Terence. But in comedy love's absurdities are looked at through rose-tinted spectacles; Lucretius treats them with the withering contempt of one struggling to stand aloof from human weaknesses.

It is obvious how each of Lucretius' points challenged an important aspect of the Catullan tradition. The first reduces the whole exhilarating experience of love to a form of madness. The second, the sordidness of love, assails the Catullan concept of idealized, ennobling love. The third, the transitoriness of love, undermines Catullus' attempt to build on lovers' protestations of lasting love in order to create the concept of a bond that can go on drawing strength from affection and understanding.[1]

But need what a philosopher has to say about love affect what the poet wants to say? It is, after all, not surprising if the two kinds of authority disagree. Catullus himself does not seem to have been seriously disturbed by Lucretius' attack on love, though clearly he knew the *De rerum natura* and was in other ways influenced by it. We find, for example, a fair number of Lucretian echoes in his poetry, especially in Poem 64—ideas as well as details of diction, ways of looking at things as well as ways of putting things. The rational tone of the Lesbia epigrams, Catullus' persistent analysis of his ideal of love owe a good deal, probably, to the Lucretian technique of doggedly argumentative analysis. When it came to love, however, he had apparently enough confidence in the worth-whileness of his ideal and the new kind of poetry he was creating to dismiss Lucretius from consideration.[2] His successors clearly could not.

The impact of Lucretius' ideas upon Roman poetic tradition

---

[1] For the Catullan tradition, see Quinn, Chapter V, 'The Catullan experience', and F. O. Copley, 'Emotional conflict and its significance in the Lesbia-poems of Catullus', *A.J.Ph.*, lxx (1949), pp. 22–40.

[2] For an impressive list of passages where Catullus appears to have used Lucretian imagery and diction, see Friedrich's commentary (1908), pp. 396–7. As for ideas, Friedrich suggests, p. 395, that Catullus took the theme of the gods turning their backs on human degradation (Poem 64) from Lucretius:

C. nimmt die Lehre des Lucrez an, dass die Götter ganz abgesondert von den Menschen leben; aber er erklärt es anders: durch ihren Frevel haben die Menschen diesen Zustand herbeigeführt.

Propertius, Horace, and the Poet's Role

results, I think, not so much from his contribution to the spread of the Epicurean philosophy in Rome during the period of the civil wars, as from the great prestige of Lucretius as a poet. It was not simply that Lucretius lent strength to ideas about love which became so prevalent in thinking society that it was necessary for poetry to attempt some valid relationship to these ideas. There was the additional and perhaps more important factor that the ideas were those of a very great poet whom the Augustan poets respected as a craftsman. Had they been those of a strictly academic philosopher, the poets would have been brought less into contact with them. It is easier to ignore the ideas of a writer we find repulsive or alien than those of a writer to whom our artistic sympathies draw us strongly.

The next quarter century shows Roman personal love poets groping for a valid relationship to new ideas about the nature and importance of their subject. Once we understand the poetic as well as the intellectual prestige of Lucretius throughout this period, the coarseness of Horace's treatment of love in his early work is seen in a truer light. We may believe that Horace was not the man, anyway, for passionate, idolizing love. His work reflects throughout too conservative an attitude to the place of women in society for him to have found attractive the Catullan ideal of lasting companionship with a woman, transcending passion. But we do not feel he is the man either for gratuitous coarseness. The fact is, I think, that his natural sympathies are initially overstated in his verse because they seemed underpinned by the moral authority of a poet whom Horace, along with Virgil, placed, both as thinker and as artist, in the very front rank. Hence the second satire of Horace's first book and its exhortation to casual promiscuity. To those Victorian scholars who could bring themselves to read it at all,[1] the second satire seemed only to disgrace the name of a poet they held in affection, not realizing that Horace must have intended it as at any rate *intellectually* respectable. For it is a strict restatement, with the sans-gêne appropriate to the comic-satiric tradition, of Lucretius' more theoretical and more caustic *prise de position*.

Hence, too, to some extent the, to us, apparently unforgivable grossness of the Canidia epodes—they are much worse than the

---

[1] James Gow (1901), ended his commentary on this satire at line 24 with the words: 'The last 110 lines of this Satire are not read.'

The Crisis in Roman Love Poetry

Canidia satire. Horace is just too much the young man eager to devour, and regurgitate, the more easily digestible portions of the new enlightenment. His adherence in his early work to the Epicurean line on love is quite servile. Even in the *Journey to Brundisium* satire (with i, 9, *The Bore*, the most urbane and civilized in either book) the sole reference to love (lines 82–5) not only conforms to the Lucretian precept that one should seek casual satisfaction, but contains a clear echo of the master's words (iv, 1030–6) on erotic dreams. All this aggressive indecency contrasts sharply with the Catullan treatment of love. Catullus' more casual poems are packed with violently indecent abuse—most of it light-heartedly tossed off, hardly meant to offend and certainly not meant to be taken literally. But his love poetry scrupulously avoids indecency of language or suggestion.[1]

Yet Horace's coarseness is not really excused by Lucretius. What Lucretius says about the physiology of sex follows naturally and strictly upon a scientific argument. The physical details form a necessary part of a demonstration of the physical basis of many aspects of human behaviour. Inevitably the scientific presentation of the facts removes a good deal of the glamour. Lucretius does not, to be sure, restrain his ironical contempt for those who glamorize love, though it is an exaggeration of Romantic criticism to call this section of his poem —as many do, citing Jerome's story of the love philtre—a violent or bitter attack.[2] Whatever his personal feelings there is no superfluous indecency in what Lucretius says.

This aspect of Horace's Epicureanism probably owes more to Philodemus, the refugee intellectual, poetaster and literary critic whose ideas clearly had an important influence on Roman poetry. As a love poet Philodemus is a strict Epicurean. He writes in Greek, but about life in Italy. His short poems stress the sordid, transitory folly of love. They are realistic, brisk, matter-of-fact. He plays the part of the *désabusé* sensualist—the

---

[1] The final agonized *identidem omnium ilia rumpens* of Poem 11 is made to sound almost solemn by its emotional context. In the concluding *glubit magnanimi Remi nepotes* of Poem 58, about which commentators contrive to imply all manner of unspeakable things, *glubit* probably only means 'strips'—of their clothes (= ἐκδιδύσκει, *A.P.* v, 309) and then of their bank balance as the contemporary examples from Varro, etc., in *T.L.L.* indicate. The famous lines of Poem 16 clearly do not refer to Catullus' serious love poetry: see Quinn, p. 79.

[2] See, e.g., Cyril Bailey's commentary, Vol. iii (1947), pp. 1302–3.

Propertius, Horace, and the Poet's Role

role Horace allots him in *Satires* i, 2, 102–4, lines that are to be taken, the echo of Catullus Poem 86 (*candida rectaque sit*) suggests, as a contemptuous reference to the Catullan tradition.[1] We may welcome Philodemus' realism after the conventional, literary imagery of his elder contemporary Meleager—though Meleager is the better poet. And he shows a flair for dramatic form. These are aspects of his work from which Horace could profit. But his coarsening influence on Horace's attitude to love —in his earlier poems—can only be deplored.

We have Virgil to thank, I think, not for changing Horace's attitude, for it remains strictly Epicurean, but for refining his treatment of love. Virgil's own treatment in the *Eclogues* is gently ironical. However idyllic the life of his shepherds and shepherdesses may be, their love affairs bring them little lasting happiness. The second Eclogue, for example, is filled with a whimsical irony that must have shown Horace how it was possible to retain Epicurean beliefs almost intact and yet avoid the coarseness of Philodemus and his own early poems. On a more serious level, Virgil's Dido is looked at through essentially Epicurean eyes. The spectacle of her moral disintegration and eventual suicide is a moving one; but Virgil shows her as a foolish woman degraded by passion. And Aeneas sheds his folly only just in time.

The Elegiac Compromise

In his search for a solution to the crisis, Horace's ideas about the treatment of love in poetry undergo a considerable development. Their intellectual basis is Lucretian scientific scepticism, originally coarsened by a tradition of gross sensuality easiest seen in Philodemus but probably common among Hellenistic poets, and then refined by contact with Virgil's sensitive humanity. His progress towards a valid relationship to contemporary thought is accompanied by a rise in standards of craftsmanship. The odes are very much better poetry than the epodes and satires.[2]

---

[1] See, e.g., *A.P.* v, 126 or 46—or most of the Philodemus epigrams in the fifth book. For Catullus Poem 86 see Chapter 3.

[2] See K. F. Quinn, 'Two crises in Horace's poetical career', *Aumla*, No. 5 (1956), pp. 34–43.

The Elegiac Compromise

At the same time his opposition hardened to attempts by the Roman poets working around him to salvage what seemed to him outworn ideas. The earliest odes of Horace and the earliest elegies of Propertius both date, as nearly as we can tell, from the years immediately following the battle of Actium (31 B.C.).[1] It is instructive therefore at this point in our discussion to turn from Horace and the Lucretian tradition to the efforts of Propertius to find a way out of the crisis that threatened the Catullan tradition.[2]

What attempt does elegy make to accommodate itself to new ideas? Clearly the prestige Lucretius enjoyed with the generation that followed him, as a poet as well as a philosopher, made serious personal love poetry to the Catullan formula—a lasting, affectionate relationship with one woman—difficult to write when all remembered how Lucretius had branded love as sordid, transitory folly. It remained possible, of course, to write of other people believing in eternal love, and there were possibilities which the poet who could observe the foibles of others either with contempt or with tolerant irony might exploit. We have seen this is Horace's solution. But personal poetry stating, or at any rate implying, this belief for the poet himself was another matter. Elegy attempts, in fact, a number of solutions, Propertius himself more than one. But all are aimed at preserving, somehow, the poet's role of the passionate lover.

We must not make Propertius' efforts to find a viable role for the personal love poet sound too systematic; for his ideas, particularly in Book II, betray a good deal of confusion. The

[1] Horace is usually supposed to have started work on the odes in 30 B.C. See, e.g., L. P. Wilkinson, 'The earliest odes of Horace', *Hermes*, lxxxiv (1956), pp. 495–9. As for Propertius, October 28 B.C. is usually given (e.g., by Butler and Barber) as the *terminus ad quem* for Book I. The *terminus a quo* varies in accordance with conjectures about the date of the poet's birth, a much argued point: guesses vary between 45 and 55 B.C.

[2] The position of Cornelius Gallus in the tradition remains an enigma. Virgil's references to him in the *Eclogues* suggest he wrote personal love poetry in the Catullan tradition. On the other hand, if he utilized in his elegies the romantic stories that Parthenius prepared for him, it seems likely the elegies were more Hellenistic in inspiration: an elaborately told *mythos* with a short personal lead-in. Propertius i, 20, and Horace *Odes* iii, 27, are perhaps vestiges of this otherwise vanished type of poem the existence of which Rostagni has posited for Hellenistic elegy in 'L'influenza greca sulle origini dell'elegia erotica latina' in *L'influence grecque sur la poésie latine de Catulle à Ovide*, Fondation Hardt, *Entretiens sur l'antiquité classique* Vol. ii (1956), pp. 59–90. (See the discussion of *Odes* iii, 27, in Chapter 9.)

first elegy of the first book, however, announces an attitude to love that is fairly well maintained throughout that book. Propertius, like Catullus, is desperately in love, at grips with a passion that marks him off from other men. But Catullus' idealism has gone. Propertius (I mean, of course, Propertius in the role he casts for himself in Book I) is perfectly aware of the folly of love and the degradation of the 'enslavement' (*seruitium*) that passionate love involves—a conventional, vague metaphor for us, but a vital, meaningful one for a Roman.[1] Yet the avowal is offset by the poet's insistence upon the extraordinary intensity of his love for Cynthia. He begins by telling us, as we saw, that she is the first woman to make him her, and love's, prisoner. He goes on to tell us of the havoc this causes in his life—he now lives *nullo consilio* (line 6), the victim of a madness from which all year there has been no respite (line 7). He rages against women of this type, hitherto unexperienced, who don't yield to the man's whim:

> tum mihi constantis deiecit lumina fastus 3
> et caput impositis pressit Amor pedibus.
>
> *Then she cast down my gaze—coolly appraising hitherto—*
> *and Love planted both feet upon my head.*

He can see no solution (lines 17–18), though he would resort to witchcraft if only that would make her relent; or to surgery (lines 27–8); or our modern remedy, the long sea voyage (lines 29–30)—if any of these would free him of his passion. Meanwhile his passion tortures him all night long and leaves him no peace (lines 33–4). In the last third of the poem he contrasts his ill fortune with the good fortune of his friends, who are able to love without falling in love. He hopes they will be able to remain, as he has not, within the limits of safety (line 32), as prescribed by Lucretius when he advised the wise man to stick to casual attachments.

Here then is love poetry of a new and impressively vigorous

---

[1] To the elegiac poets the enslavement of love meant, for example, not so much physical suffering, as the mental anguish of not being able to act, and in particular *speak*, like free men. Cf. Propertius' words in this opening elegy:
sit modo *libertas* quae uelit ira loqui. 28

The Elegiac Compromise

kind. Its strength resides in a rigorous analysis of the poet's conflicting emotions. Intense love is shown to be not simple but complex. The trouble is it is difficult to maintain this emotional fervour. Protracted unrequited love begins quickly to sound ridiculous. And once Cynthia returns Propertius' love, the emotional conflict naturally ceases. The poet cannot protest he wants to free himself from a successful love affair with the anguish he could reasonably display so long as his mistress cruelly rejected his advances. So that, once we get beyond the introductory poem, the nature of the degradation alters. The emotional conflict is revived by making Cynthia beautiful admittedly, but possessed of so sharp a tongue that the poet is rightly afraid to wake her when he comes home late (i, 3); or by introducing the theme of jealousy (i, 8).[1]

The difficulty is to find situations that are fresh and can yet be taken seriously; which will sound like Lucretian realism and yet not make the role of passionate lover appear so ridiculous that poetic exploration of it becomes absurd. Soon we find Propertius resorting to devices such as telling a friend who looks like falling in love as deeply as Propertius has done of the anguish that lies in store for him (i, 9):

> necdum etiam palles, uero nec tangeris igni:
>   haec est uenturi prima fauilla mali.
> tum magis Armenias cupies accedere tigris
>   et magis infernae uincula nosse rotae, 20
> quam pueri totiens arcum sentire medullis
>   et nihil iratae posse negare tuae.
> nullus amor cuiquam facilis ita praebuit alas,
>   ut non alterna presserit ille manu.

You've not the pallor yet, not felt the real fire inflicted.
This is just the first spark of all that you'll endure.
Then you'll wish you faced Armenia's tigers rather,
were bound instead to the wheel that turns in hell— 20
not felt the boy archer's concentrated fire deep inside,
able to deny nothing to your mistress's wrath.
No love ever gave a man wings to soar upon
unless, other hand extended, love pinned him down.

[1] See Chapter 9 for a discussion of i, 8.

Propertius, Horace, and the Poet's Role

He even warns a prospective rival (i, 5),

> quid tibi uis, insane? meos sentire furores?   3
> infelix, properas ultima nosse mala,

What do you want? To feel the madness that I feel?
Poor crazed fool, anxious to experience suffering's worst,

because that, too, offers him an opportunity to restate the emotional conflict. The terms Propertius uses to express the violence of his emotional state (*furor, dolor, lacrimae, seruitium,* above all *miser*—a word which implies, incidentally, that the lover has a lot to put up with rather than that he is miserable[1]) are often taken as the exaggerations of a *langage galant.* Propertius means them at their face value. He is playing out the role of the lover in Lucretius who lets himself become the victim of passion's turmoil. Yet we *feel* the anguish of Propertius, and do not despise him for displaying it: such is his ability as a poet. Our recognition of his insight suppresses the reaction that the poet's stance is exaggerated or ridiculous.

When, however, the anguish degenerates into cliché, the atmosphere that makes poetry possible quickly evaporates. When, for example, Propertius says, in an elegy of the second book (ii, 17),

> durius in terris nihil est quod uiuat amante,
> nec, modo si sapias, quod minus esse uelis,   10

No life's harder than the lover's on this earth,
none (if you had sense) you'd not sooner choose,

the neatness of the lines strips off the illusion, on the whole maintained in the first book, that his verse is externalizing

[1] Compare Caesar's use of the word to contrast the conditions his army has had to put up with in the weeks before Pharsalus with the luxurious conditions enjoyed by Pompey's men who none the less had accused Caesar's army of soft living (*B.C.* iii, 96, 2):
   at hi miserrimo ac patientissimo exercitu [dative] Caesaris luxuriem obiciebant, cui semper omnia ad necessarium usum defuissent.
Caesar several times stresses that the morale of his men remained high between Dyrrhachium and Pharsalus. It is therefore clear that he means they had a great deal to put up with in the way of hardships, not that they were miserable or dispirited. On the use of *miser* to describe the lover, see A. W. Allen, art. cit.

The Elegiac Compromise

emotions deeply felt. Propertius himself must quickly have realized the limited validity of the compromise formula exploited in Book I. The compromise was too artificial: however much he tried to vary the dramatic situation, the emotional conflict was too stereotyped to stand repetition in elegy after elegy.

The discredit the passionate elegiac lover was beginning to bring on himself is more evident in the hands of exponents of the genre whose intellectual calibre is less than Propertius'. Some of the more mediocre elegies of Tibullus show the ineptness to which the talented versifier satisfied with manipulating clichés can plunge. Observe how these opening lines of a Tibullan elegy (ii, 4) reiterate Propertius' first elegy, but with all the intellectual and emotional strength that gave Propertius' verse life and dignity gone:

> Sic mihi seruitium uideo dominamque paratam:
>   iam mihi, libertas illa paterna, uale.
> seruitium sed triste datur, teneorque catenis,
>   et numquam misero uincla remittit Amor,
> et, seu quid merui seu quid peccauimus, urit.   5
>   uror, io, remoue, saeua puella, faces!
> o ego ne possim tales sentire dolores,
>   quam mallem in gelidis montibus esse lapis,
> stare uel insanis cautes obnoxia uentis,
>   naufraga quam uasti tunderet unda maris!   10

> *So I see slavery and a mistress ahead:*
> *farewell now to my ancestral freedom.*
> *Harsh slavery instead, held in chains:*
> *Love never releases the wretch from his bonds;*
> *innocent or no of sin or wrong, he burns me.*   5
> *Lo! I burn. O savage girl, remove the brands.*
> *Would I could not feel such pains.*
> *How I'd rather be a stone on icy mountain top,*
> *or rocky crag that's victim of the raging wind,*
> *pounded by the desolate, ship-destroying waves!*   10

Tibullus works through cliché rather than image. Compare his trite evocation of the torch-of-love metaphor with Horace's vital, imaginative adaptation of it in *Odes* iv, 13 (discussed in Chapter 4). And the clichés are undiscriminatingly multiplied, no attempt made to work out their relevance. How is Tibullus a slave? What are his chains? How does he burn? The assertions are not backed up by any sign that they are meant, and therefore fail to carry conviction. We are left feeling Tibullus has no insight into his own supposed predicament and the attitude struck becomes maudlin, instead of moving: the poet, we suspect, is merely acting a part—a silly part he does not himself believe in. Not all Tibullus is as bad as this. He has quite a flair for sentimental pictures of himself and his mistress proving the simple pleasures of a countryside described with an unpretentious realism that contrasts very favourably with Marlowe's conventionally idyllic setting.[1] His mistake is to essay the role of passionate lover. When Tibullus takes up that theme, he loses all touch with reality.

Horace's Assault on Love Elegy

Here we should turn back to Horace. Round about this time the sillier manifestations of the passionate lover in elegiac poetry were beginning to draw his sniping fire. Tibullus was one of his targets. Horace's attitude is expressed in the first of a pair of odes which are of considerable interest, not only for their value as documents in the history of the evolution of literary ideas in Augustan poetry, but also for the urbane deftness with which Horace makes his points. He is less concerned with the badness of this kind of elegiac poetry than with the absurdity of its intellectual basis. Writing still from a strictly Lucretian point of view, mellowed now to a restrained but incisive irony that demonstrates how far the Horace of the twenties B.C. has progressed poetically beyond the Horace of the thirties, he concentrates his fire on what seemed to him the weakest point in the elegiac tradition. He objected less to the way the elegiac poets got worked up about falling in love; it was after all hard to be an Epicurean saint, to remain uncontaminated by the folly of love. What seemed to him really silly was the fuss they

---

[1] Unfortunately he will combine in a single elegy (e.g., i, 1) these happy, convincing rural scenes with artificial statements of passionate anguish couched in language so conventional they carry no conviction at all.

Horace's Assault on Love Elegy

made when their mistresses deserted them. A man *could* be expected to have enough sense to know love does not last, and accept the fact, instead of carrying on, as Tibullus does (in i, 5 for example).

Let us take first *Odes* i, 33, addressed to an Albius generally admitted to be Albius Tibullus:[1]

> Albi, ne doleas plus nimio memor
> immitis Glycerae neu miserabilis
> decantes elegos, cur tibi iunior
>   laesa praeniteat fide.

*Stop lamenting, Albius, your memory's too acute
of Glycera—heartless girl! No more of this string
of elegies sorrow-drenched, surprised the glamour of a
younger man spells treachery to you.*

The irony of Horace's consoling words is transparent enough. Horace had himself demonstrated in his fifteenth Epode the proper attitude for the lover to assume when his mistress deserts him for another man: not tears, but a few words of gentle reproach to the girl and a few blunter words to the man, rounded off with a warning that the girl will desert him, too, before long. These are things that happen—annoying, but you must accept them and you may always derive a little sardonic satisfaction by sitting back and confidently awaiting further developments. If you can take it in that spirit, yours will be the last laugh (*ast ego uicissim risero*).

Bearing in mind what Horace himself had written a decade earlier, or thereabouts, one can understand better that he permits himself a trace of malice in consoling Albius. He makes Glycera desert Albius for a *younger* lover—hardly, one would suppose, an attribute the elegiac poet himself would care to acknowledge in his rival. Horace is perhaps thinking of the fifth elegy of Tibullus' first book, which begins with some very competent writing expressing the poet's bitterness and dejection, and then reveals that he has been deserted for a *richer* lover (*diues*

---

[1] The identification is accepted, e.g., by Georg Luck, op. cit., p. 64. For a discussion of the objections that have been raised, see Albert Brouwers, 'Horace et Albius' in *Etudes horatiennes* (1937), pp. 53–64.

amator), whom he proceeds to abuse. Horace is, in fact, undercutting the stock assumption (made by himself in *Epodes* 15) that only money will prize the girl from her lover's arms.

He continues to console Albius; not by sympathizing, by granting the enormity of his misfortune, but with a series of illustrations aimed at pointing out that what has happened to Albius is a common occurrence. It goes like this: A (beautiful girl) is desperately in love with B (attributes unspecified). B, however, is in process of falling for C (she has a nasty temper). C spurns B's advances. This is, of course, an old story and reference to the *ronde de l'amour* doesn't make a poet an Epicurean. We find the commonplace worked out similarly in the fifth idyll of Moschus. But in a sense what Lucretius did in his treatise on love was to utilize literary commonplaces, the stock material of comedy in particular, in a serious discussion of human behaviour. For him it was not just fun to think of love working that way. This was really the way love worked.[1] And Horace here follows up five lines of apparent banter with three that assume an arresting earnestness:

> sic uisum Veneri, cui placet imparis   10
> formas atque animos sub iuga aenea
> saeuo mittere cum ioco.

Thus has Venus decided, whose pleasure is to despatch shapes and minds ill-matched beneath her yoke of bronze in sardonic jest.

These lines fix the relevance of the A-loves-B-loves-C persiflage to Albius' misfortune. It is not so much the *ronde de l'amour* itself that Horace is thinking of, but the cause of it; the fact that in every affair there is pretty soon *l'un qui baise et l'autre qui tend*

---

[1] Once again Propertius is a good enough poet to try to face up to reality. He admits (ii, 8, 8, in an elegy written within a year or two of Horace's ode) that the lover has always to reckon with competition:

> uinceris aut uincis, haec in amore rota est.

His answer would probably have been (at any rate as long as he maintained the passionate-lover pose of Book I) that he despised the *lentus amator*, the lover who held his emotions in check, as Horace pretended to do. Cf. i, 6, 12:

> a pereat, si quis lentus amare potest!

Horace's Assault on Love Elegy

la joue. Venus keeps throwing together couples who find themselves irresistibly attracted. But these liaisons that seemed indissoluble at their inception quickly prove to have yoked together people quite unsuited to one another, physically as well as temperamentally (*imparis formas atque animos*).

There is a sudden seriousness here in Horace's words betraying the firm conviction that underlies his attitude to the human comedy. He moves quickly away from it in a final teasing stanza,

> ipsum me melior cum peteret Venus,
> grata detinuit compede Myrtale
> libertina, fretis acrior Hadriae   15
> curuantis Calabros sinus,[1]

Take myself: when better loving was to hand, my Myrtale
imprisoned me (and I blessed my chains)—she the slave
originally, a girl more tempestuous than
the Adriatic's Calabria-fretting waves,

that both lightens the tone by its confession of Horace's own (past!) folly and softens the irony by abandoning the satirist's impersonal stance. Finally, in the last phrase the whole situation is moved away from, in a way that is characteristically Horatian, into an image whose poetic quality lessens argumentative tension.[2]

A parting thrust at the conventions of elegy should not be missed. The reference to 'chains' (*compede*) picks up the trite imagery Tibullus uses as a substitute for emotional analysis. 'All right,' says Horace in effect, 'call infatuation a chain,

---

[1] The 'better girl' was pursuing Horace, but he allowed himself to be ensnared instead by Myrtale, who now shows signs of impatience with her conquest. I.e., while the main purpose of the final stanza is to support the statement in the previous stanza that the wrong people fall in love with one another, it serves as well as a further illustration of the *ronde de l'amour*.

[2] The philosophical content of this ode and its function as a piece of literary criticism are well summarized by Heinze, p. 139:

> Dem Horaz ist die Liebe eine unberechenbare, an äussere oder innere Gleichartigkeit nicht gebundene Leidenschaft, für deren Entstehen oder Vergehen kein Mensch verantwortlich ist und mit deren Launen der Verständige sich unschwer abfinden wird; für den Elegiker ist die Liebe jedesmal als ewig gedachte Liebe das eine grosse Anliegen, und die 'Untreue' der Geliebten unbegreifliche und unverzeihliche Verworfenheit, die das Lebensglück des Verratenen zerstört.

Propertius, Horace, and the Poet's Role

what's wrong with chains? Personally I found my enslavement rather enjoyable (*grata*), despite the dance the girl led me.' Though it is Tibullus, the easier victim, who is under attack, Propertius, too, must have found criticism like this hard to take. No sneer at 'tepid lovers'[1] can really parry Horace's exposure of the unreality of the presuppositions made by elegiac love poetry of the kind written by Tibullus and by Propertius in his earlier manner, or defend its lack of emotional restraint.

In Horace's ode to Valgius (ii, 9), a minor elegiac poet, the point stressed is really a more damaging one: it is the boring repetitiousness of poetry that keeps harping on the same narrow, gloomy theme. For it can be argued that a particular elegy, though unreal in its assumptions and violent in its expression of emotion, is none the less good writing. The objection that, however good the individual pieces, they are too much alike and too numerous is aimed at the thematic poverty which is the real root of Propertius' difficulties in finding a solution to the crisis.

The ode to Valgius, a better poem incidentally than the ode to Albius, makes its point with the subtle reticence of Horace's maturest manner:

> Non semper imbres nubibus hispidos
> manant in agros aut mare Caspium
>   uexant inaequales procellae
>   usque, nec Armeniis in oris,
>
> amice Valgi, stat glacies iners   5
> mensis per omnis aut Aquilonibus
>   querqueta Gargani laborant
>   et foliis uiduantur orni.

> *Not for ever do the clouds pour their rain*
> *on dishevelled fields, or disturbing winds*
> *the Caspian sea continuously*
> *importune. Nor is it the whole year*

---

[1] See Propertius i, 6, 12 (quoted above). Cf. iii, 8, 20, and ii, 15, 29–30:
    errat, qui finem uesani quaerit amoris:
      uerus amor nullum nouit habere modum.
These are signs the battle is on, but it is tricky to answer Horace back directly.

Horace's Assault on Love Elegy

round, friend Valgius, that the inert ice   5
lies firm in Armenia, or that in Apulia
the oak forests suffer the north wind's oppression,
and the ash are bereft of leaves.

It opens with a series of images as geographically remote as they appear to be remote from Horace's theme. The images, moreover, are unfolded in Horace's best sinewy, graphic style. The cultivated fields drenched with rain; the stormy Caspian (two scenes full of movement); the stiff, frozen steppes of Armenia; and (movement again) the forests of Apulia, struggling with the northerly which strips the ash of their leaves. But however good the writing, however comprehensive the images geographically, the cumulative picture they paint of nature is a distorted one. The world is not *always* like this. Though each image is good, their unrelenting succession creates a mood of gloom which begins to sound just a shade ridiculous.

With Horace's point no more than sensed, our attention is turned to Valgius and the way he laments in tearful verse (*flebilibus modis*) the loss of his beloved Mystes. Taken by itself, isolated from its context in the poem, the third stanza looks almost like neutral statement:

    tu semper urges flebilibus modis
      Mysten ademptum, nec tibi Vespero   10
        surgente decedunt amores
          nec rapidum fugiente solem.

You for ever assail with lugubrious verse
Mystes' loss. Neither with the brightening of the
evening star are you quit of love, nor at his
retreat before the hastening sun.

Only *urges* suggests a faint note of disapproval.[1] In the context of the poem Horace's point, though discreetly made, is apparent. Those two first stanzas, still at the back of our minds, delicately imply the unnaturalness of grief that lasts from morn till night; the juxtaposition *non semper: tu semper* underlines the link.

[1] See Heinze's excellent note on *urges*.

Propertius, Horace, and the Poet's Role

Without insisting further, Horace passes now to a series of *exempla* from mythology:

> at non ter aeuo functus amabilem
> plorauit omnis Antilochum senex
>   annos, nec impubem parentes   15
>   Troilon aut Phrygiae sorores
>
> fleuere semper.

> *Yet he who completed three times a mortal span*
> *did not grieve for Antilochus whom he loved*
> *all his ageing years; nor was Troilus, though*   15
> *so young, by Phrygian father, mother, sisters*
>
> *for ever wept.*

The *exempla* are the more effective because (as in i, 8) their relevance is left unstated. Nestor had lost his son Antilochus. Priam and Hecuba, too, had lost a son in battle and their daughters a brother. How can Valgius' separation from his beloved compare with bereavements such as these? Yet they did not weep for ever. I suspect two kinds of ironical relevance in the lines in addition to their argumentative function. First, Valgius' elegies were very likely filled with the apparatus of mythology in what we may suppose to have been the manner of Cornelius Gallus.[1] It is as though Horace were saying: 'The imagery of mythology, not that of the real world, is what you understand; so for a time I'll speak your language.' Second, I suspect that Mystes, unlike Antilochus and Troilus, had been 'snatched away' (*ademptum* leaves the issue very open), not by death, but by our old friend the rich admirer—*diues amator*. In other words, both the theme and manner of Valgius' elegies may have followed that of Propertius' elaborate version of the rape of Hylas (i, 20). This kind of love poetry is so much a matter of stock themes, the suggestion seems at least plausible. The poem assumes a heartless tone surely if we suppose Mystes is really dead, and Horace's advice in lines 17–18, *desine mollium tandem querelarum* (instead of, say, *tristium . . . querelarum*),

[1] See Note on p. 149.

Horace's Assault on Love Elegy

needlessly insensitive.[1] If we are right, lines 13-17 effect a twofold argument *a fortiori*: Nestor, etc., did not weep, even though they lost a son (or a brother), not just someone they were in love with; nor did they weep, even though it was death that caused the separation, not just a transfer of affection.

Now comes the specific exhortation to abandon love elegy:

> desine mollium
> tandem querelarum, et potius noua
>   cantemus Augusti tropaea
>   Caesaris et rigidum Niphaten,   20
>
> Medumque flumen gentibus additum
> uictis minores uoluere uertices,
>   intraque praescriptum Gelonos
>   exiguis equitare campis.

> *Cease at length this effete*
> *lament, and rather let us sing*
> *the news of August Caesar's victory*
> *trophies; or of Niphates (dour mountain)*   20
>
> *and Medus river numbered with the conquered,*
> *(carrying their heads a little lower now);*
> *or Gelonian horsemen on the tiny fields*
> *edict has prescribed.*

The recommendation to turn instead to patriotic poetry looks unsympathetic and not perhaps what we should expect from Horace who did so little of this sort of thing (until the fourth book). The lines may only reflect the urgent need for a poet just good enough to write encomia of the new régime (so that Horace and Virgil could be left in peace). Perhaps in a poem where hints are so lightly formulated we may suspect as well that the hint to Valgius is that one stock theme is as good as another. In any case, the reason why Horace now proceeds to develop the theme in the way he does is clear: through a series of illustrations he brings us back to the real, geographical

---

[1] Admittedly Horace wants a contrast between love poetry, regularly described as *mollis*, and epic, for which the epithet is *durus*.

world in which the poem began, away from the unreal, artificial world of Valgius' poetry.

The Search for Fresh Solutions

Tibullus, and Valgius it seems, needed Horace's gracefully barbed reminder that they were losing their sense of emotional and artistic proportion. Propertius perhaps did not. There are signs that the unreality, and therefore the superficiality, of personal love elegy became early in the piece uncomfortably clear to him. His second book contains a variety of experiments aimed at discovering new ways of writing about love without jettisoning altogether the role of the victim of irresistible infatuation.

To the literary historian looking back, the paths that could lead the elegiac poets out of the swamp up into high, hard ground and clear air stand out. They are numerous enough, but in the main follow two routes: if the poets wished still to write of love, either their theme or the manner of its treatment demanded drastic revision. The *theme* could be revised, as Horace had revised it, by a realistic acceptance of new scientific ideas about love, though such a theoretical basis was hard to reconcile with the role of the passionate poet-lover; or by introducing, or reviving, a fresh complex of fantasy not as yet discredited: the neatest solution here is the creation of the Don Juan *persona*, a new kind of perpetual lover, exploited so successfully later by Ovid, who built, of course, upon Hellenistic traditions of cynical sensuality.

The *manner* of elegiac poetry could be revised by abandoning its seriousness—and turning poetry into a kind of elegant entertainment, as Ovid was forced to do in order to make his Don Juan *persona* palatable and something like credible. Or by shifting the emphasis of seriousness from the theme to the manner of handling it, strengthening by artistic or intellectual complexity shallow or conventional ideas.

Propertius tries most of these solutions. The result is the chopping and changing in the poet's role that we find in his second book, a natural source of bewilderment to critics who assume the poems to be autobiographical or expect them at any rate to create a consistent fiction. We find donjuanesque bravado (e.g., ii, 22a, *Scis here mi multas pariter placuisse puellas* . . .)—

The Search for Fresh Solutions

though on the whole Propertius experiments little with this solution—mixed up with asseverations of lifelong love in the old manner (e.g., ii, 13b, *Quandocumque igitur nostros mors claudet ocellos* . . .). Both these elegies are pieces of some distinction, a fact which increases our confusion.

Professor Allen[1] has argued, plausibly and with ingenuity, that we are mistaken in expecting consistency from Propertius, because the Roman notion of sincerity was a rhetorical one. All the Romans expected from a work of art, says Allen, was internal consistency. So long as individual poems are inwardly coherent and individually convincing, they may vary in their attitudes, just as the speeches a lawyer makes for different clients may cause him to assume different *personae*. Allen's thesis is a useful corrective to the tendency to take everything a Roman poet says *au pied de la lettre*. It helps, too, I think, to explain how a genre-writer like Tibullus, in passing from one ostensibly passionate elegy to another, can switch even the sex of his beloved. Such an explanation becomes harder to accept, however, with a poet of Propertius' intellectual calibre. I think we shall understand better the chopping and changing in his second book if we regard the book as containing a series of experiments aimed at establishing new formulae that would enable elegiac love poetry to be taken seriously as poetry.

Most of the experiments and the most interesting poems involve a shift in the manner of treatment of the theme rather than in the theme itself. On its resumption in Book II the liaison generates less fire. If, as seems a possible assumption, the introductory elegy to Maecenas can be taken as representing the poet's considered attitude to his work, it is clear that, although formal allegiance to the Catullan tradition persists, a new elegance emerges in handling it which betrays the shift in emphasis. Propertius still maintains (ii, 1, 3–4):

> non haec Calliope, non haec mihi cantat Apollo.
> ingenium nobis ipsa puella facit;

> *It's not the Muse dictates my song, nor bardic god.*
> *The girl I love alone can grant the power to write;*

[1] A. W. Allen, ' "Sincerity" and the Roman elegists', *C.Ph.*, xlv (1950), pp. 145–60.

Propertius, Horace, and the Poet's Role

but observe how the elegy continues:

> siue illam Cois fulgentem incedere cogis, 5
> hac totum e Coa ueste uolumen erit;
> seu uidi ad frontem sparsos errare capillos,
> gaudet laudatis ire superba comis;
> siue lyrae carmen digitis percussit eburnis,
> miramur, facilis ut premat arte manus; 10
> seu cum poscentis somnum declinat ocellos,
> inuenio causas mille poeta nouas;
> seu nuda erepto mecum luctatur amictu,
> tum uero longas condimus Iliadas.

> *Imagine her approach in shining silk of Cos:* 5
> *one Coan gown becomes a full-length roll of verse.*
> *Have I seen a wisp of hair wander down her brow?*
> *Happy she departs, proud I praised her coiffure so.*
> *From lyre, perhaps, her ivory fingers strike a chord?*
> *How I praise the artistic lightness of her touch!* 10
> *Does her gaze droop, eyes clamour sleep?*
> *A thousand promptings the poet in me finds.*
> *Does she with me stark stripped for action wrestle?*
> *Iliads entire become the work in progress then.*

The Catullan anguish is still formally present (ii, 3):

> Qui nullam tibi dicebas iam posse nocere,
> haesisti, cecidit spiritus ille tuus!
> uix unum potes, infelix, requiescere mensem,
> et turpis de te iam liber alter erit.
> quaerebam, sicca si posset piscis harena 5
> nec solitus ponto uiuere toruus aper;
> aut ego si possem studiis uigilare seueris:
> differtur, numquam tollitur ullus amor.

> *Are you the man said none could hurt you now?*
> *And here you're trapped, prostrate, dispirited!*
> *A month of quiet at most and now a second book*
> *is under way, poor fool, to damn your reputation with.*
> *Could fish live landed high and dry? Or savage boar* 5

The Search for Fresh Solutions

*endure an ocean habitat? Or I spend night awake
for pleasures scholars seek? I made experiments and found
you can suspend love's business, never end it.*

But it is only a step from here to Ovid. All that separates the poets now is the tenderness of tone and the poetic sensitivity apparent in Propertius' verse. A degree of seriousness is preserved which is lacking in Ovid's glib bravura. It is the difference, perhaps, between Herrick and Byron.

The liaison is thought of as continuing indefinitely. Some of the elegies in Book II read almost like chapters from a modern novel. We have poems made out of visits by lover to mistress when she is alone first thing in the morning (ii, 29b, *Mane erat, et uolui, si sola quiesceret illa* . . .), or when she is giving a party (ii, 6, *Non ita complebant Ephyraeae Laidos aedis* . . .). If he is late one day because he has been to the opening of a new temple (ii, 31) that, too, is made the subject of a poem. The poems, of course, are little concerned with telling a story. Only the most paltry fabric of fact can be woven out of the scattered threads the episodes provide. Propertius' lack of concern for story is shown by his repeated use of a simple device for varying the circumstances: an absence (impending or actual) from Rome that separates the lovers temporarily. Nor is any particular effort made to ensure that what story there is should seem coherent or consistent. The impression we get is indeed not unlike the rather disjointed impression produced when one skims quickly through a novel, skipping chunks: a sort of loose framework of story from which stand out episodes of some interest for their own sake.

The trend is continued in Book III. The very fine poem on his mistress's birthday (iii, 10), for example; or the elegy containing the poet's reflections on the contents of a lost letter from his mistress (iii, 23). The themes of these two poems show the pretence that the poet is the slave of love is wearing thin. Another sign is the progressive disappearance of Cynthia's name. It has been constantly on the poet's lips in the first book, much less so in the second. In the third it occurs only in the renunciation poems. Propertius is now impatient to abandon love poetry altogether for other themes which will occupy him almost exclusively in his fourth book, but cannot concern us here.

Propertius, Horace, and the Poet's Role

A last word about the renunciation poems. In iii, 21 Propertius embarks at last on the sea voyage the possibility of which we saw him contemplate in the opening elegy—he hoped it might free him of his passion. It is a piece of urbane writing, with very little really to say about love. The other two (iii, 24 and 25) are quite remarkable for their bitterness. The violence with which he denounces his own stupidity and the brutality with which he attacks Cynthia alike seem out of all proportion to the emotional level of the liaison in Book III. It is apparent that Propertius wants to dispose of Cynthia and love-poetry for good and all. And that, like Conan Doyle, who threw his hero Sherlock Holmes over an alpine precipice in order to get rid of him, Propertius is determined on a rupture that will leave him in peace for other things in life altogether. Like Holmes, Cynthia shows in Book IV a tendency to come back from the dead; but on the whole iii, 24 and iii, 25 are the end of her.

Propertius attempted one other solution to the elegiac problem before abandoning love poetry for the aetiological themes of Book IV. It is a solution that involves a much more extreme shift in the ratio of emphasis between theme and manner of treatment. The result is a group of very successful, highly intellectual poems, structurally much too complex to permit any useful discussion of them in general terms. Detailed discussion is something we must postpone until the next chapter. They involve, however, little alteration in the poet's role, though in other respects they represent perhaps the only poetically successful solution to the impasse with which Propertius was faced.

7

Propertius and the Poetry of the Intellect

A HANDFUL of Propertius' love elegies stand apart. The three we shall discuss in this chapter form a group, to which one or two others, less distinctive individually, will be seen to attach themselves once we have put our finger on the special qualities of these three.

The first thing to notice perhaps is that the customary emotional conflict, the head-heart antithesis, which in the previous chapter we ascribed to Propertius' attempt to fortify Catullan idealism against Lucretian realism, now fades into the background. Propertius' intellectual vigour—the most characteristic and the most fundamental attribute of his poetry, a quality of the man himself, not something he owes to traditional influences—is nowhere sharper. The passionate note, however, is muted. The poet is in love—naturally, since these are love elegies. We are to assume even that he is deeply in love. But it becomes no more than an initial presupposition. There is no vibrant, tense opposition, grimly accepted, between head and heart, between reason and passion. Instead we have a cool detachment.

This is no longer poetry built around incidents in the poet's affair with his mistress according to the recipe given in the opening poem of Book II. It is not poetry of the passions at all. Its success does not depend on its power to convince us of the poet's emotional involvement, but on the quality of the

Propertius and the Poetry of the Intellect

poet's thinking as actually demonstrated and recorded in the poem. Not his capacity for philosophical thinking, of course; but for poetic thinking. In a very real way the emphasis is not on what the poem is about or the emotions that produced it; it is on the poem itself as a piece of imaginative argument, a delicately complex, poetic development of an idea. We may perhaps call this 'the poetry of the intellect', bearing in mind that each term is essential to the definition: not thinking which happens to have poetry for its vehicle, but thinking the whole manner of which is poetic. The two elements fuse and jointly they produce Propertius' most important contribution, perhaps, to the development of the short personal poem in Latin.

The Power of Love (ii, 12)

Our trio all come from Book II. Let us turn first to Elegy ii, 12. The poem is so tightly constructed we should make an effort to get some grasp of the whole before grappling with details:

> Quicumque ille fuit, puerum qui pinxit amorem,
>   nonne putas miras hunc habuisse manus?
> is primum uidit sine sensu uiuere amantis,
>   et leuibus curis magna perire bona,
> idem non frustra uentosas addidit alas,   5
>   fecit et humano corde uolare deum:
> scilicet alterna quoniam iactamur in unda,
>   nostraque non ullis permanet aura locis.
> et merito hamatis manus est armata sagittis,
>   et pharetra ex umero Cnosia utroque iacet: 10
> ante ferit quoniam tuti quam cernimus hostem,
>   nec quisquam ex illo uulnere sanus abit.
> in me tela manent, manet et puerilis imago:
>   sed certe pennas perdidit ille suas;
> euolat heu nostro quoniam de pectore nusquam,   15
>   assiduusque meo sanguine bella gerit.
> quid tibi iucundum est siccis habitare medullis?
>   si pudor est, alio traice tela tua!
> intactos isto satius temptare ueneno:
>   non ego, sed tenuis uapulat umbra mea.   20

The Power of Love (ii, 12)

quam si perdideris, quis erit qui talia cantet,
  (haec mea Musa leuis gloria magna tua est),
qui caput et digitos et lumina nigra puellae
  et canat ut soleant molliter ire pedes?

I

Whoever first love as a child portrayed,
think you not he had a cunning hand?
He first saw how lovers senseless live,
by trivial dealing profitless distraught.

Pertinent, too, the windy wings he added then,   5
devising a god that flits within man's heart.
(Plainly conflicting ways the eddy tosses us;
ours is a breeze whose set does not abide.)

Likewise just the barbed tip that arms his hand,
the Cretan quiver from each shoulder hanging.   10
(Against foe that unseen strikes no staying safe:
none whom he hits makes off unmaimed.)

II

In me the boyish guise, the pointed arrow holds,
but those wings of his love's lost somehow:
from my heart he never flies away; in my   15
veins I feel love's unrelenting war.

III

Why dwell in dried-out bones? What pleasure there?
Have you no shame? Aim your shafts another place—
against the unafflicted the poison better turned;
not me but my wasted shadow they assail.   20

That destroyed, who will be your singer then?
(My frivolous Muse has brought you much renown.)
And who'll my black-eyed mistress sing, head and toe,
when she walks, how her steps do melting go?

    The elegy is justly praised, though with the reticence that is characteristic of commentators on Propertius when they turn from textual criticism to appreciation. Postgate called it a 'finished little poem' and concluded the section on **Propertius'**

Propertius and the Poetry of the Intellect

literary style in his formidable Introduction by claiming the pleasure (as he put it) of appending Elton's translation.[1] Butler and Barber thought it 'charming', though they complain of confusion in the imagery. The evident intellectual strength of the elegy, its provocative tightness of argumentation have continued to exercise a fascination on scholars, not always revealed by their words of faint praise. Dr. Bailey devotes to it five pages of his *Propertiana*—no other poem except the opening elegy of the collection gets more.

Yet obviously it is only formally a love poem. No recital of the poet's adventures or emotions is attempted. We are asked to take it for granted that the poet is in love, so that he can involve us in an intellectual argument. His thought needs unravelling with more care than we at first realize; more, certainly, than his commentators (so prone to fall to wrestling with details of exegesis) have elected to expend.

The elegy is a meditation on the nature of love. Propertius begins with a firm stride forward into his subject, as though he had just been struck by the appositeness of the conventional Hellenistic representation of love as a child—the child we in English call Cupid:

> Quicumque ille fuit, puerum qui pinxit amorem,
> nonne putas miras hunc habuisse manus?

> *Whoever first love as a child portrayed,*
> *think you not he had a cunning hand?*

The syntactical limpidity conceals considerable compactness of argument. Like the opening line of Elegy i, 1 which we discussed in the previous chapter, these lines illustrate Propertius' habit of beginning with a statement that is easily enough translated, but unintelligible until we read well on into the poem.

The Greeks represented love in more than one human shape. First there was the goddess Aphrodite. Later came the youth Eros, the handsome, purposeful young athlete, winged and armed with bow and arrows. We meet him in Latin as the virile Cupid of the Cupid and Psyche episode in Apuleius' *Metamorphoses*. Last came the *child* Eros who shoots his arrows aimlessly,

---
[1] J. P. Postgate, *Select Elegies of Propertius* (2nd edn. 1884), p. lxxxviii.

The Power of Love (ii, 12)

or for fun;[1] in literature he first becomes common in Hellenistic poetry, though in art we find Eros depicted as a winged child (apparently unarmed) as early as Macron's vase-painting of the rape of Helen. (Another version, that Aphrodite had not one but several sons, is familiar to us from Roman painting, notably the child Cupids that adorned the house of the Vettii at Pompeii.)

A feeling that the child Eros is a later, less true, artistic convention perhaps underlies Propertius' opening couplet. At any rate the emphasis falls on *puerum*: the artist's stroke of genius did not lie in portraying love as a human figure, but in making the portrait that of a *child*. Propertius' reason follows in the next couplet:

> is primum uidit sine sensu uiuere amantis, 3
> et leuibus curis magna perire bona.

> *He first saw how lovers senseless live,*
> *by trivial dealing profitless distraught.*

The child Cupid symbolizes the childishness of lovers, who live irrationally (*sine sensu*) and put their lover's whims before the really important things in life. Line 4, which reflects of course the opposition common in Latin poetry since Plautus between the hardheadedness of the practical man of business and the softheadedness of the infatuated lover,[2] is delicately double-edged. The statement the line makes, while not innocently asserted, is not simply ironical either; it acknowledges that a good deal can be said for the practical view-point, while hardly trying to win our acceptance of it.

Propertius now singles out two more ways in which the artist's child Cupid may be regarded as a just symbol. To each he allots a four-line stanza.[3] But before we turn to these, we must consider some of the implications already raised in the opening stanza. Does Propertius really believe in this child Cupid? We shall discover it is necessary for us to be clear about

---

[1] See H. J. Rose, *A Handbook of Greek Mythology* (1928), p. 123.

[2] Cf., e.g., Plautus, *Trin.*, 230, where Lysiteles deliberates:
'amorin med an rei opsequi potiu' par sit?'

[3] It is convenient in discussing Propertius to divide a poem into *stanzas*. The term is justified by Propertius' habit of developing his argument in blocks, usually of four, six, or eight lines. The only metrical unit in an elegy is, of course, the couplet.

Propertius and the Poetry of the Intellect

our answer to this question in order to follow the argument of the poem. We may feel pretty sure that he does not believe in Cupid in any strict sense. Indeed actual belief in Cupid (unlike belief in Venus) is, I think, not seriously implied by any Roman writer. But we may suppose Propertius feigns belief as a literary convention, expecting us to join him in the pretence for the duration of the poem. This is the normal state of affairs in Hellenistic poetry. It is the position adopted, for example, by Meleager in several epigrams, some of which are quoted as lying behind Propertius' poem.[1] And in adopting it, various degrees of seriousness are possible.

At this point we should distinguish Cupid and Cupid the child. I think we may regard it as clear that Propertius does not express even conventional belief in Cupid *the child*, considering him purely as an artist's fiction. The probing intellectual strength of the succeeding argument is surely inconsistent with any pretence of taking the artist's fiction as true. It might be argued that Propertius believes, however (genuinely, or as a poetic convention), in Cupid the god, while regarding the artist's representation of the god as a child as inspired artistic convention.[2] The reader who finds this improbable should be warned that it is the usual view of the commentators. They reach this opinion observing that the poet turns to address love in the final section of the poem. They assume it is only Cupid that Propertius can be addressing and that it is Cupid, therefore, that he has in mind throughout the poem.

Butler and Barber are clear-headed enough to see that the poem's argument then becomes seriously muddled; but they fail to observe the muddle results from a wrong initial assumption about what the poet means. Before we go further with the poem, we must, I think, consider carefully the meaning, or meanings, of *amorem* in the opening line—a question usually begged by the commentators, who print the word with a capital letter, taking it for granted that *Amorem* must mean Cupid. But if they are wrong, what then does Propertius mean by *amorem*? We may seem in danger of becoming involved

---

[1] E.g., *A.P.* v, 198 and 215.

[2] It appears as well to have been a convention of the rhetorical schools in the early Empire: see the quotations from Cornutus and Quintilian in the commentators. This makes real belief in Love the child even less likely.

The Power of Love (ii, 12)

in a tiresome semantic discussion when we should be getting ahead with our reading of the poem. There is no escape. We are faced with a question we shall have to raise before we have finished the poem, unless we are prepared to lay it aside without understanding Propertius' argument.

The Latin word *amor* can be said to have three main meanings which it will be convenient to tabulate, though we must warn ourselves against expecting, either in general usage or in Propertius' argument, the sort of clear-cut demarcation between them that tabulation suggests.

First comes what we may call 'the thing Love', love in its most limited, least imaginative sense. Let us call it a thing rather than an abstraction in order not to trick ourselves into attributing to Propertius, or to any ancient Roman, too modern a slickness in dealing with abstractions. There is something we call love and which the Romans call *amor*. Let us call 'love the thing' *amor* Sense 1.

Sense 2 we may call 'the power Love'—that force which to the Roman (and to us as well often enough, I suppose) seems sometimes inside, sometimes outside, us, driving the lover to 'fall in love' (Sense 1). The Greeks readily personified this power as a god in human form. The Romans, except when they were pretending to be Greeks, characteristically stopped short of full anthropomorphism, as Erich Burck has pointed out.[1] Though Plautus frequently talks of what we might call the power of Love, he hardly ever thinks of a clear-cut divinity. As a result this *amor* Sense 2 constantly merges into *amor* Sense 1.[2]

Finally (for our present purposes) let us isolate *amor* Sense 3: the god Cupid. (We are not called upon to consider Propertius' belief or unbelief in Aphrodite since she is excluded linguistically: *amor* is not used of her.)

In normal contexts one of these three meanings will preponderate, sometimes with overtones led in by another of the meanings. While the meanings naturally most often merge, they are occasionally opposed—usually for effect, as when Apuleius talks of Psyche 'falling in love with Love' (*in Amoris incidit amorem*, M. v, 23).

---

[1] Erich Burck, 'Amor bei Plautus und Properz' in *Commentationes in honorem Edwin Linkomies* (1954), pp. 32–60, especially 33–4.
[2] E.g., in Lysiteles' monologue (*Trin.*, 223–75), studied by Burck, art. cit.

Propertius and the Poetry of the Intellect

With this classification at hand, let us see if we can clarify the thought-structure of Propertius' elegy. Which of our three meanings does *amorem* bear in his opening line? Or is more than one sense present? As we saw, editors of Propertius usually plump for Sense 3 alone. Yet this gets us into difficulties at once: quite apart from the confusion complained of by Butler and Barber, we notice a fresh source of confusion, one that seriously compromises the poem's success. It is that each of the three features of the artist's Cupid singled out for comment (the fact that he is represented as a child, the fact that he has wings, the fact that he is armed with bow and arrows) is tested, not by reference to some kind of *amor* Sense 3, but by reference to the lover.

If Propertius' object were really to discuss *amor* Sense 3, this would surely be an unnecessarily confusing procedure. If, however, his object is to discuss the nature of *amor* Sense 1 plus Sense 2 (as I believe is evident when one reads the poem with care), the procedure becomes not only readily intelligible, but inevitable. In this case *amor* Sense 3 is treated strictly as a fiction, a piece of symbolism that helps us to understand the complex nature of the only real *amor*, which is what the lover experiences, some amalgam of Sense 1 and Sense 2.

Let us now test the correctness of our assumptions about what Propertius is trying to say by resuming our consideration of what he says. It will be seen that, once we have straightened out the main line of argument, the details (many of which have perplexed editors) fall pretty readily into place.

The first stanza, as we saw, was pointed at the childlike aimlessness of the lover. The second expresses Propertius' approval of Cupid's wings as a just symbol of the lover's fickleness:

> idem non frustra uentosas addidit alas,   5
>   fecit et humano corde uolare deum:
> scilicet alterna quoniam iactamur in unda,
>   nostraque non ullis permanet aura locis.

Pertinent, too, the windy wings he added then,
devising a god that flits within man's heart.
(Plainly conflicting ways the eddy tosses us;
ours is a breeze whose set does not abide.)

The Power of Love (ii, 12)

The gap between symbol and lover's abstract attribute is bridged by the verbal ambiguity of *uentosas*. The primary reference is to Cupid's wings, 'filled with wind', completing the visual image. The secondary meaning, 'fickle, impetuously inconsistent', applies to the lover—since the wings only exist as a symbol of the lover's conduct, there is no reason why they shouldn't have symbolic attributes.[1] The lover is 'fickle' in two ways: he keeps falling in and out of love; and the object of his love keeps changing.

A lot of needless fuss is made over the second line of Stanza 2. Some commentators, not observing how Propertius in the second half of each of the three opening stanzas steps back from his symbol, *amor* Sense 3, to his real subject, the non-visual *amor* Senses 1–2, have complained of the difficulty of visualizing the second half of this line and wanted to amend it.[2] Propertius' statement is of course again extremely compact. Restated fully in conventional philosophical prose the line might read: 'The artist represented the thing that the lover feels deep within himself (*amor* Sense 1) as a god with wings, to be thought of as flying about there.' The compression is achieved partly by a complicated nexus of emphasis, partly by Latin's ability to get on without a definite or an indefinite article: *fecit uolare deum* = (*a*) 'made-to-fly *a* god' and (*b*) 'made the god *fly*'. Then *uolare* links in a fresh pattern with *humano corde*: 'in man's heart he made it fly'—not meaning, of course, that he actually drew Cupid inside a man's heart, but that, in giving his fiction wings, he expected us to imagine it there, using its wings.

The line in fact illustrates admirably the way in which the method appropriate to poetry and that appropriate to philosophical discussion differ. If Propertius had attempted to say what he meant in accordance with the conventions appropriate to philosophical discussion, poetry would have become impossible. In the first place his statement would have become flatly

---

[1] For the first sense, editors quote Virgil *Aeneid* xii, 848, *uentosasque addidit alas*, rightly described by Butler and Barber, p. 210 (in an implied correction of Postgate's 'from Virgil') as 'probably an imitation of Propertius'. For the second sense they could quote Virgil *Aeneid* xi, 708, *iam nosces uentosa ferat cui gloria fraudem*.

[2] Bailey, for example, p. 85:
The vulgate in 6 could only mean that the artist painted Love flying about inside the human heart. To say nothing of the pictorial difficulties, what then becomes of the allegory?

Propertius and the Poetry of the Intellect

verbose. As well as that, he would have abandoned poetry's power to tease the responsive reader into collaboration through striking, compact, many-sided statement: put in prose, the thing has so many obvious loopholes we are tempted to pursue these, instead of feeling we have been presented with a concretization of something elusive.[1]

The imagery abruptly changes in the second half of the stanza. Now we are asked to picture a boat tossed by the waves. To those critics who assume the poem is about Cupid, Propertius appears guilty of negligently mixing his metaphors. But once we grasp his technique of using Cupid merely as a starting point, from which to obtain the visual embodiment of an unseen thing, or power, the objection loses its force. Indeed the switch in metaphor is Propertius' warning perhaps that he wants us to consider the artist's picture of Cupid only at the beginning of each stanza, as something to be kept detached from the poem's real subject—the nature of *amor* Senses 1–2. And to illustrate that impalpable entity, two images are better than one. Or rather, the god's wings *symbolize* an aspect of love that can be more graphically *pictured* as a small boat, buffeted, from one direction after another, by a choppy sea and a veering wind; just as the lover (according to the Lucretian tradition) keeps falling violently and helplessly in love with different women.[2] The new image allows the introduction of an effective ambiguity: *aura* is the breeze that keeps changing; but the word is also used by the Roman poets to represent the mysterious breath of fascination that emanates from an attractive woman.[3]

---

[1] In addition to the complexities I have mentioned, I strongly suspect the presence of another: that *humano corde* is descriptive ablative with *deum*, *as well as* locative ablative without preposition. So that in addition to its primary meaning —the one considered here—the line means as well: the artist contrived a divinity that veers about, human in temperament though a god. Though this reading of the line is summarily dismissed by Bailey, it seems to accord well with the intellectual complexity of Propertius' statement.

[2] I accept Bailey's rendering of *alterna in unda*, 'on one wave (of love) after another' (*C.Q.*, li [1947], p. 89). The sea imagery is conventional: see the full list of parallels in Burck, art. cit., p. 50.

[3] For *aura* in this sense cf. Horace, *Odes* ii, 8, 24, and i, 5, 11 (used in a comparable ambiguity). The idea is found again in iv, 13, 19. The *aura* seems to have been regarded as a subtle, intoxicating emanation, such as divinities traditionally emitted—an attempt to describe in physical terms what we would regard as an attribute of personality. See Propertius ii, 29, 15–18, and (probably) Catullus Poem 11, 11–14.

The Power of Love (ii, 12)

With this sense, private to the lover, supported by the emphatic *nostra*, the line becomes a fresh statement of the lover's fickleness.

Stanza 3 brings us back to Cupid for a third symbol, this time his bow and arrows:

> et merito hamatis manus est armata sagittis,
>   et pharetra ex umero Cnosia utroque iacet: 10
> ante ferit quoniam tuti quam cernimus hostem,
>   nec quisquam ex illo uulnere sanus abit.

> *Likewise just the barbed tip that arms his hand,*
> *the Cretan quiver from each shoulder hanging.*
> *(Against foe that unseen strikes no staying safe:*
> *none whom he hits makes off unmaimed.)*

As before, two lines are devoted to describing the symbol and two to the poet's comment on its justness. The onslaught of love is violent, unexpected, apparently haphazard. These are the attributes Virgil has in mind in his simile in *Aeneid* iv, 69-73, where Dido is likened to the victim of the herdsman whose random shot lodges in a deer. Though he knows nothing of it, his shaft inflicts a fatal wound (*haeret lateri letalis harundo*). The child Cupid, too, shoots at random, before we can sense the danger; his arrows are barbed and, once lodged, cannot be shaken free.

The symbolic picture complete, a short second section (it comprises a single stanza) follows, and with it comes a sudden increase in seriousness. Whereas in the first section the threefold symbolism seen by Propertius in the artist's representation of Cupid was tested by referring it to lovers in general (the plurals *iactamur, cernimus, nostra* strike us as true plurals), it is now tested by reference to Propertius himself. His case is typical in two respects: his behaviour is childish; he feels the pain of love's wound. But not typical on the third count: the love he feels is not passing, or shifting, but permanent and for one woman. It is, of course, Propertius' favourite role. But the point is worth making and it is neatly made with just the right hint of pathos and melancholy in the first half of stanza 4:

> in me tela manent, manet et puerilis imago: 13
>   sed certe pennas perdidit ille suas.

Propertius and the Poetry of the Intellect

*In me the boyish guise, the pointed arrow holds,
but those wings of his love's lost somehow.*

The repetition is partly for the sake of pathos, partly to detach the ambiguous *in me tela manent* ('in me the arrows hold fast', and 'in my case the symbol of the arrows holds good') from the unambiguous *manet et puerilis imago*.

The next two lines,

> euolat heu nostro quoniam de pectore nusquam,   15
> assiduusque meo sanguine bella gerit,
>
> *from my heart he never flies away; in my
> veins I feel love's unrelenting war,*

involve the confusion of imagery that Butler and Barber complain of (p. 210):

> Charming as the poem is, there is some confusion in the imagery, since Love is at once the archer shooting from without, and the tormentor dwelling in the lover's heart.

Their complaint springs from the usual mistake about the poem's structure. The subject of these lines is not Cupid (*amor* Sense 3), the usual fiction, but *amor* Senses 1–2, the reality which is the subject of the poem. Restated with philosophical fullness and precision, Propertius' argument might run: 'Of the three attributes of this conventional symbolic representation of love, two can serve as imaginative or poetic descriptions of love as I experience it. Love makes me behave childishly. It makes me behave as though I had received a physical wound. But the love I experience never takes wing, to leave me in peace or to turn its attention elsewhere.' The argument is not easy to follow, partly because of the ironic intent of lines 14 and 15; partly because of Propertius' trick of jettisoning symbol for more graphic image—as he did in lines 7–8, but now in a harder context and in mid-couplet, so that we may think for a moment he is gauchely mixing metaphors.

Propertius' thought may be hard to follow, but it is not confused, even if he does not mean what we are most liable at first to assume he means. We must have the patience to wrestle with

The Power of Love (ii, 12)

his compressed poetic thinking. The poem is not a facile piece of allegorizing, but a painstaking attempt to scrutinize the validity of a conventional symbol. Its argument is characteristic of the Roman distrust of allegory; from that its toughness and integrity largely derive. In a poem which aims at honest, searching examination of a problem (in contrast to the superficial, purely formal, purely 'literary' imagery, say, of ii, 13a), Propertius cannot bring himself to take Cupid very seriously. Nor can he enter into the spirit of the fiction with the lighthearted suppleness of a Hellenistic Greek like Meleager. Love really *is* for Propertius what it was for Plautus, the woolly amalgam of Senses 1 and 2. There can be no doubting the reality of *love the thing*, Sense 1; any lover knows the difference between being in love and not being in love. And for a Roman Sense 1 merges easily into Sense 2, *love the power*, though the two add up to something imprecise, not something to be visualized, at the level of sober belief, in anthropomorphic terms.

It is in fact because love is so real and yet so imprecise that the poem's thinking achieves the level of seriousness that it does. To the more flexible mind of a Greek or a modern, Propertius' position is apt to appear both confused and confusing. We keep expecting a much more thoroughgoing continuity in the Cupid imagery; while this for Propertius is only another metaphor, looked at in more detail but no nearer to the real nature of love than the other metaphors of the poem.

Our appreciation of the final section of the poem depends even more on our grasping the—to us—curiously tentative and imprecise position Propertius adopts throughout. The mood changes as it did in passing from the first section of the poem to the second, and the poet's involvement in his theme deepens:

> quid tibi iucundum est siccis habitare medullis?
> si pudor est, alio traice tela tua!
> intactos isto satius temptare ueneno:
> non ego, sed tenuis uapulat umbra mea.   20

> *Why dwell in dried-out bones? What pleasure there?*
> *Have you no shame? Aim your shafts another place—*
> *against the unafflicted the poison better turned;*
> *not me but my wasted shadow they assail.*

Propertius and the Poetry of the Intellect

The love Propertius addresses in this passionate outburst is his Roman mixture of Senses 1 and 2, something he feels exists; not the Hellenistic Cupid of Sense 3 who, he knows, does not. The deep-rooted Roman belief in the existence and power of what we find it hard to regard as more than abstractions is abundantly vouched for. We may compare Propertius' impassioned address of Good Sense—*Mens Bona*—in iii, 24. There is no attempt to preserve imaginative continuity between the love Sense 2 now addressed and the fiction of love Sense 3 earlier entertained, because the reality of that fiction was never part of the poem's hypothesis. The metaphors chosen are simply those that seem most able to bring out the reality of love Sense 2.

We find a comparably vague personification of *amor* Sense 2 in ii, 30a. In that short piece (it is twelve lines long) a certain consistency is achieved by leaning on the *seruitium amoris* cliché (see the discussion of i, 1 in the previous chapter). Love is the harsh, watchful master; the lover the would-be runaway slave who finds escape impossible, however hard he tries. Love the power (*deus*, line 11) is a reality; the rest merely an attempt to state the impossibility of resisting this power in figurative language.

To describe love Sense 2 as a power that lives deep inside us and consumes us is by comparison genuine and natural. So, too, is the feeling that love Sense 1 is a physical wound inflicted by love Sense 2. We might say in modern scientific language that the relation between the two is that between symptoms and disease. Latin poetry found metaphors more effective, even if the images conflicted. Virgil uses the same technique as Propertius to describe Dido in love in the opening lines of *Aeneid* iv:

> At regina graui iamdudum saucia cura
> uulnus alit uenis et caeco carpitur igni.

*But the queen, stricken long since by a grievous passion,
nurses the wound with her blood, consumed by a deep-seated fire.*[1]

---

[1] For a discussion of these lines and the pattern of ambiguities built up in them, see Kenneth Quinn, 'Syntactical ambiguity in Horace and Virgil', *Aumla*, No. 14 (1960), pp. 43-4.

The Power of Love (ii, 12)

But since the power that has assailed us is not precisely visualized, the metaphor of a poison in our blood (*ueneno*) is as eloquent as that of armed assault (*tela*). And just as good again is the metaphor of the lover thrashed by love Sense 2 until he is more dead than alive (*tenuis uapulat umbra mea*). The images conflict too much for our taste; I think they must diminish the poem's stature in the eyes of a modern reader, however much their Roman looseness guarantees the integrity of Propertius' thinking.

The object of the final stanza is to bring the poem back into a more maturely ironic context as a corrective to the almost stridently unrestrained note in lines 17–20. Like the preceding stanza, Stanza 6 is of course addressed to the power of love (*amor* Sense 2):

> quam si perdideris, quis erit qui talia cantet,   21
>   (haec mea Musa leuis gloria magna tua est),
> qui caput et digitos et lumina nigra puellae
>   et canat ut soleant molliter ire pedes?

> *That destroyed, who will be your singer then?*
> *(My frivolous Muse has brought you much renown.)*
> *And who'll my black-eyed mistress sing, head and toe,*
> *when she walks, how her steps do melting go?*

The concluding lines bring the tone of the complete poem back under control admirably. It has much to offer: honest thinking; complex, ingenious argument about things not easy to discuss, handled with the concentrated techniques of poetry; a hint of morbid oversensitivity to show the poet is not trifling; finally, to correct any impression that the poet's thinking is too much centred on himself, a graceful acknowledgment of how much his mistress, too, figures in his thoughts, and inspires them.

The elegy is an example of a new and worth-while poetry of the intellect. We may see in it yet another development of Hellenistic epigram, the source of more than one kind of Roman new writing—the neat, succinct statement of hard ideas in Catullan elegiacs, or the elliptical presentation of dramatic context in Horace's odes, to name only two. The link here is with the conceit, the dextrous verbal point that is so often a feature of epigram. But where epigram plays with ideas instead of trying to tie them down, Propertius takes up a conceit to explore it at a truly poetic level, deploying a poetic fullness of responsive imagery, and a seriousness of tone that transcend epigram in a new direction.

Death of the Lover (ii, 27)

The link with epigram is closer in the second elegy of our trio, particularly in the final stanza, which bears the main emphasis. A slighter piece, it stands almost too close to epigram to count as poetry.[1] But it may serve as an instructive intermezzo between two fully developed poems.

The elegy falls into three sections. The connection is not explicit, a point that has aroused some criticism. For example, Butler and Barber (p. 237) call the elegy 'a jerky and ill-constructed poem, but not demonstrably a patchwork of fragments'. The text of the second section is variously printed by editors, some of whom suppose a lacuna. However, the uneasy feelings the elegy prompts are due less, I think, to the state of the text than to a failure to perceive that the poet is manipulating a series of epigrammatic clichés—and has not perhaps sufficiently assimilated them to make out of them a coherent poem.

The basic cliché is that human life is uncertain. We might expect Propertius to begin by saying so. Poetically, however, it is less effective to begin with an abstract statement than with a statement of something we can all see. So Propertius makes his starting point the effect on human beings of their uncertainty. They do all they can to circumvent it, probing the future, consulting the stars. The uselessness of astrology (another cliché—compare Horace *Odes* i, 11) is the theme of Propertius' opening stanza:

At uos incertam, mortales, funeris horam
    quaeritis, et qua sit mors aditura uia;
quaeritis et caelo Phoenicum inuenta sereno,
    quae sit stella homini commoda quaeque mala!

[1] Erich Reitzenstein, *Wirklichkeitsbild und Gefühlsentwicklung bei Properz*, Ph. Supplementband, xxix, 2 (1936), goes pretty fully into the relationship between epigram and elegy. He is mainly concerned, however, with differences in structure and content of epigram and elegy, stressing therefore such features of elegy as the narrative and emotional elements and the greater subjectivity of factual layout. One might add imagery as another important structural element of elegy that distinguishes it from epigram. I am concerned with what one might call the style or tone of a small group of Propertian elegies; the overall 'intellectual' impression they give, which seems to me a development of one feature of epigram.

Death of the Lover (ii, 27)

Yet, mortals, the hour you'll die (a thing past knowing)
is ever your enquiry, and the way that death shall come.
Enquiry, too, with Punic science, of untroubled sky,
which planet aids a man and which him harms.

Propertius makes it plain he believes even less in astrology than, in the opening elegy of the collection, he believed in the power of witchcraft to release the lover from his torture. The reticent *Phoenicum inuenta* is a sufficient expression of the poet's incredulity. And the second *quaeritis* at the beginning of line 3, catching up the first *quaeritis* at the beginning of the previous line, effectively underlines the folly of frantic efforts to know the unknowable. But as a result the second couplet swings on from the first with an emphasis that becomes disconcerting when the development of the initial idea is abruptly dropped.

The fear of death is one of the great Lucretian commonplaces. It is a fear from which, Propertius will argue in his third stanza, only the lover is exempt. But first he provides a series of illustrations of the dangers to which ordinary mortals, in their fear of death, feel themselves exposed. The illustrations add up to the basic proposition with which Propertius, if logical presentation of an argument had been his object, could have been expected to begin. Life is uncertain (except, remember, for the lover):

> seu pedibus Parthos sequimur seu classe Britannos,   5
>   et maris et terrae caeca pericla uiae;
> rursus et obiectum flemus caput esse tumultu,
>   cum Mauors dubias miscet utrimque manus,
> praeterea domibus flammam domibusque ruinas;
>   neu subeant labris pocula nigra tuis.   10

> *Marching into Parthia, taking ship to Britain,*   5
> *by land or sea perils lurk upon our way.*
> *Likewise to civil rising we bemoan a life exposed:*
> *unsure of the issue is each side Mars embroils.*
> *Then, too, houses burn, houses topple down,*
> *sinister-coloured potions see your lips reject!*   10

Propertius and the Poetry of the Intellect

However, for the moment Propertius, with ironical solicitude, identifies himself with the rest of mortals, switching from the second person plural of the opening stanza to first person plural—'you and I'. Getting little guidance from astrology—or mistrusting the guidance we receive—we try to forestall death, and see death lurking in every human enterprise.

The Roman citizen soldier is exposed to the risk of death at every moment of a foreign campaign: from the enemy on land, from the perils of the sea (always prone to arouse morbid apprehensions in a Roman) while journeying to the theatre of war (lines 5–6); the point is taken up again in inverse order in line 12, *Boreae flabra . . . arma*).

Even if we do not venture out of Italy, there is always the risk of getting caught up in revolution (*tumultus* is an armed rising within Italy). For a Roman this had been a real risk at any time for the last thirty years during which Italy had been devastated by civil war. The pentameter

cum Mauors dubias miscet utrimque manus,

unsure of the issue is each side Mars embroils,

a good example of Propertius' evocative imprecision of language, deserves more attention than it has received. The words *dubias* and *miscet* suggest a complex pattern of ambiguities. The primary meaning of *dubias* is not, I think, 'uncertain who will win'[1] (something that is true of all fighting, not peculiar to civil strife), though doubt on this score is intended, too; but 'hesitant', 'holding back'—partly through unsureness of the rights and wrongs of the struggle, partly because they are afraid of dying. And *miscet* is nearly always a stronger word in Latin than its seeming English equivalent. Here the surface meaning is 'pour together' (as if mixing fluids), a meaning supported by the common phrase *miscere proelia* which means little more than 'join battle'. But outside this phrase the meaning 'throw into confusion' is the commoner in poetry; and, with

---

[1] As Rothstein, p. 385: 'weil ihre Aussichten auf den Sieg unsicher sind'. Postgate, op. cit., p. 141, has 'hostility of uncertain issue'. If one has to tie Propertius down to one meaning, Butler's 'wavering ranks' (Loeb translation [1912], p. 143) seems preferable.

Death of the Lover (ii, 27)

a variation in the common phrase (*miscere manus* for *miscere proelia*), that meaning asserts itself here.[1]

But that is not the end of it. To the perils of war and revolution must be added the perils of everyday life in Rome: the house you live in may burn down or collapse (both appear to have been frequent occurrences). The repetition of *domibus*, which editors tend to find otiose (and some would meddle with), is in fact effective: one's own home at least one thinks of as safe, but even in one's own home death threatens. And even if your house remains intact, you can never tell when somebody is going to poison you—for your money, for your wife or for political reasons: poisoning was the favourite form of premeditated murder. Observe we now switch to the second person singular.

The second section, then, has an argument that hangs together and undergoes an effective development, passing from the most obvious and easiest avoided forms of violent death to those liable to strike down the most timorous stay-at-home. The manner, however, is that of satire rather than that of epigram, whose tool is irony; not the hammer-blows of rhetoric which satire may indulge in. Having more space to play with than epigram's tight confines permit, Propertius has perhaps let himself go a shade uncritically. The writing moreover is somewhat disjointed by comparison with the opening section, especially in the initial couplet (lines 5–6). The change from second person plural to first person plural and then to second person singular, on the other hand, does not, I think, deserve the interference it has received.[2] There is evident irony in the progressive narrowing of the focus: 'you—mankind in general'; 'we' (i.e., you and I—the poet identifies himself for a moment with his reader); 'you' (singular—he

---

[1] Propertius uses *miscere proelia* in iv, 1, 28. For the meaning 'throw into confusion' in a battle scene, see Virgil, *Aeneid* x, 721:
    hunc ubi miscentem longe media agmina uidit,
where *miscentem . . . agmina* is rendered by Mackail, p. 408, 'throwing the ranks into confusion'.

[2] I take lines 5–6 as an independent statement (*sunt* understood). Some link it to the preceding lines, but this spoils the development of thought: outside Italy, Italy, Rome. Editors indulge in a good deal of interference with the text in line 7, though no important change of meaning is involved. The first person plural *flemus*, for example, may be removed by Housman's rather too *ben trovato fles tu*, made up out of *fletis* and *fletus* (which occur along with *flemus* in the mss.).

suddenly deserts his reader, in preparation for the assertion in the next stanza of his immunity from the common anxiety). Moreover, Propertius is aiming, I think, at producing a hasty, confused tempo that will contrast sharply with the smooth, serene assurance (of syntax and idea) of the final stanza:

> solus amans nouit, quando periturus et a qua
>   morte, neque hic Boreae flabra neque arma timet.
> iam licet et Stygia sedeat sub harundine remex,
>   cernat et infernae tristia uela ratis:
> si modo clamantis reuocauerit aura puellae,   15
>   concessum nulla lege redibit iter.

> *Only the lover knows when he'll die and how meet*
> *death, fearing neither war nor stormy northerly.*
> *Even on reedy Styx, seated at the rower's bench,*
> *gazing at the gloomy canvas of the bark of Hell,*
> *let him catch a breath of summons from his mistress,*   15
> *and he will make the journey back no law allows.*

The final conceit depends in part on another cliché, asserting that the lover is protected from the dangers to which ordinary men are exposed; being under the protection of Venus, he bears a charmed life. We find this cliché worked out at length in iii, 16, 11–18 (*nec tamen est quisquam, sacros qui laedat amantis* . . .), and, more fully still, in Tibullus (i, 2, 16–32).[1] It is one of the most well-worn conceits of love poetry. But if the lover is protected from death, how is it he comes to die at all? Obviously of love, or when he is deserted by his cruel mistress. Yet another cliché lurks here, built upon the constant use of *pereo* ('I die') by the Roman poets to mean 'I am suffering the anguish of unrequited love'. When Propertius tells us only the lover knows when he'll meet death (*quando periturus*, line 11), this is how he expects us to take his words.

If we are innocent enough to suppose Propertius means what he says, a final piece of hyperbole will dispel our illusions. Even when he's dead and on his way to Hell, all that's needed to call the lover back among the living is for the breeze to waft along

---

[1] And, of course, the cliché stands behind Horace's miraculous escape in *Odes* i, 22 (*Integer uitae scelerisque purus* . . .).

The Lover's Dream (ii, 26a)

the voice of his mistress calling out for him (or for his mistress to concentrate her allure upon him once again—*aura* is used ambiguously, as in line 8 of the previous poem).[1] The climactic point is a good one, despite the strong flavour of epigram. It is treated, however, with a richness of imagery epigram cannot permit itself: lines 13–14 are good, especially the pentameter, and genuinely poetic.

Boiled down to essentials, stripped of extravagances, all the poem states is that the passionate lover's all-absorbing infatuation with his mistress makes him oblivious of all else. For her sake he sacrifices everything—and is, therefore, pretty immune from the dangers to which an active life, politics, ambition and the rest expose ordinary men. But a prose summary does little justice to this compact, ingenious, tellingly ironical meditation woven on to a coarse homespun of clichés.

Our final impression is surely mixed. The poem's most serious defect is that it leans so heavily upon its clichés. There is no harm in picking up a cliché, provided one can transform it and make oneself independent of it. But take away the scaffolding of clichés here, and the poem collapses into unintelligibility. Furthermore, the writing stands too close to origins outside the limits of serious poetry: both the ideas and the manner are too suggestive of epigram, or of satire. Above all, the intellectual element is inadequate. The elegy serves in fact as a useful test of the quality of the other two in the trio. We detect here and there the distinctive note that in them predominates. It is a transitional poem, making clear how much more the others have achieved. For, ultimately, we are left with the feeling that, despite the sustained ingenuity with which it is presented, this is a pattern of thinking that did not seriously involve the poet—as he was involved in thinking about the nature of love in ii, 12; or as we shall see him involved in a pattern of complex feeling towards his mistress in our third elegy.

The Lover's Dream (ii, 26a)

A poem may seriously involve its maker and yet not bear a solemn aspect. Gravity is not the only mood of the intellect. Words spoken lightly can hit true, if there is feeling behind

[1] On this use of *aura*, see my note on ii, 12, 8, above.

Propertius and the Poetry of the Intellect

them—and a craftsman's skill; this our third elegy will show. In it Propertius tells his mistress he dreamed he saw her drowning. He relates with elegant urbanity the thoughts that passed through his head and the emotions that accompanied them. Again we are asked to take it for granted that the poet is passionately in love. But again this is only an initial hypothesis (though one Propertius seriously intends us to make). What he offers us is an exercise in ingenious irony, mainly at his mistress's expense, but an irony we can feel deserved, and one that reveals sensitivity not coarseness in the poet. There is more than a touch of Ovid in this poem; but its intellectual strength and a note of genuine personal involvement make the elegy unmistakably Propertian and give the poetry a distinction that Ovid, the amorous entertainer, cannot equal.

An opening six-line stanza states the poem's subject, crisply fixing scene and moment with the tonal complexity which is one of the poem's features:

> Vidi te in somnis fracta, mea uita, carina
>   Ionio lassas ducere rore manus,
> et quaecumque in me fueras mentita fateri,
>   nec iam umore grauis tollere posse comas,
> qualem purpureis agitatam fluctibus Hellen,   5
>   aurea quam molli tergore uexit ouis.

> *I dreamed I saw you, darling, vessel wrecked,*
> *through Ionian spray stretching failing stroke;*
> *all the lies you'd told me now confessing,*
> *head bowed, as water loaded down your hair*
> *—and thought of Helle, on iridescent billows tossed,*   5
> *whom on golden fleecy back a sheep conveyed.*

Cynthia (let's assume it is Cynthia) is drowning in the Ionian. She is presumably on her way to or from Greece. At the moment when the dream and poem begin, the wrecked ship is in the background, and in the foreground Cynthia, struggling to keep afloat, the whole of her past life (as in popular belief) flashing before her. There is no suggestion for the moment that Propertius figures in the dream himself; though he knows that it is taking place in the Ionian sea, not somewhere else, with that

The Lover's Dream (ii, 26a)

immediate certainty we have in dreams. The tone is direct, but that of poetry. The phrase *uidere in somnis*, 'to dream', though it occurs, too, in serious prose, has a verse pedigree extending back to Ennius.[1] Of the four common words for 'ship' in Latin poetry (*nauis, puppis, ratis, carina*) *carina* is the most characteristic of high style;[2] *lassus* is also high style compared with *fessus* or *defessus*; and so is *ros* for 'sea'—a little precious even.[3]

Why does Propertius choose these words? Partly because his poem will contain more than a trace of flippancy and he is anxious to avoid an overall impression of mere persiflage. His immediate object, however, is contrast—the grand manner of the opening couplet is abruptly undercut by the next line:

et quaecumque in me fueras mentita fateri.

all the lies you'd told me now confessing.

Several times in the poem Propertius indicates that (at any rate in restrospect) he does not feel so very sorry for Cynthia in her danger. The danger was an imaginary one, of course, and a certain amount of light-hearted callousness is permissible afterwards. But Propertius wishes, I think, to go further. He wants us to feel how Cynthia's treatment of him rankles, eliciting a touch of malice in his recollection of her discomfiture. But we must no more than sense it. It is not the moment to air grievances. He will forfeit our sympathy if he attempts it. This one restrained outburst of bitterness in line 3 must sustain and justify the tone of malicious irony that permeates the remainder of the poem, ensuring the reader catches and interprets rightly each hint that is to come.

The first follows close on the savage *mentita fateri*. If Cynthia were making her confession under normal circumstances, we should expect her to hang her head in shame as she admits the

[1] The phrase *in somnis* has been studied by Einar Löfstedt, *Syntactica*, Vol. i, (2nd edn. 1942), pp. 55–9.

[2] Propertius uses the neutral word *nauis* 8 times; of the two conventional verse words, he prefers *ratis* (23 times) to *puppis* (5 times). He used *carina* 11 times, favouring it in more 'poetic' contexts, e.g. in introducing the theme of the battle of Actium, iv, 6, 17.

[3] Virgil does not use *ros* for 'sea', though he uses it once to mean 'water'. Propertius does not use *ros* elsewhere, but in iii, 2, 8 has *rorantis equos*, 'horses dripping with sea-water'.

Propertius and the Poetry of the Intellect

lies she had told Propertius. And hang her head she does now. Of course it is the weight of the water in her long, soaked hair that drags her head down, but we are meant all the same to feel the posture is appropriate. A series of verbal tricks ensures we do. First, *fateri* is held over to the end of the hexameter, so that it is easily associated with the pentameter following. Then echoes in the line of common phrases such as *attollere caput* ('to lift one's head'), a gesture of pride or defiance, and its opposite *demittere caput* ('to lower one's head'), a gesture of shame.[1] Finally the syntactical ambiguity involving *umore*: either true ablative with *tollere* ('raise out of the water'), or instrumental with *grauis* (hair 'heavy with water'). It would be pushing the line too far, of course, to extract these overtones of irony from it if our reactions were not sharpened by the previous line and underpinned by similar reactions to other lines in the poem. The cumulative effect fixes one aspect of the poem's tonal structure.

Propertius, on seeing Cynthia's danger, feels, to begin with, no impulse to do anything. Instead the scene stimulates his fancy, recalling a scene from legend: the beautiful Helle (legendary heroines are always beautiful), who, forced to run away from home, tried to cross the sea with her brother upon the back of the ram which produced the famous golden fleece. It could also fly; but Helle fell off midway, plunging into that part of the Mediterranean which was called after her the Hellespont. Propertius is going to make something of this last detail of the story in a moment.

For the present what he wants from the heroic parallel is a resumption of the formally poetic tone, which he proceeds once more to undercut delicately in the next line. Greek myth made it a ram that carried Helle and her brother, and Roman poets from Ennius onwards had spoken, too, of a ram (*aries*). There is something unheroic about a sheep, particularly if it is a ewe (*ouis* is feminine gender). The bantering note lies partly in the word used, partly in the way Propertius throws *ouis* into prominence by delaying it until the opposite end of the line from its adjective *aurea*, which the clichés of the legend are likely to cause the reader to take as neuter plural, anticipating some

---

[1] For *demittere caput*, see, e.g., Cicero, *Cluent.* 58, or *Dom.* 83; for the opposite, Livy, vi, 18, 14: *ut caput attollere Romana plebes possit*.

The Lover's Dream (ii, 26a)

such word as *uellera* ('fleece'). Any reference to the animal he would expect to involve *aries* (masculine gender). So that *uexit ouis* comes as an unexpected anticlimax.

But the heroic parallel serves as well a more poetic purpose. Propertius is after the colour contrast between golden sheep and the dark-blue waves, flecked with light, of a choppy sea (*purpureis . . . fluctibus*—a calm, sunny sea is *caeruleum*).[1] And the emotional contrast between the luxurious softness—and warmth perhaps—of the sheep's fleece and the unpleasantness—and cold perhaps—of the water into which Helle fell. The poetry is working fast in this short simile. To the responsive reader a great deal is suggested with impressive economy.

In the next four lines we come to Propertius' emotional response to Cynthia's danger:

quam timui, ne forte tuum mare nomen haberet,
    atque tua labens nauita fleret aqua!
quae tum ego Neptuno, quae tum cum Castore fratri,
    quaeque tibi excepi, iam dea, Leucothoe!   10

Was I afraid in case you, too, named a sea,
and sailors wept, across your waters sweeping!
How I prayed to Neptune then, to Castor and his brother,
beseeched you, too, goddess nowadays, Leucothoe!   10

There are two stages to his response, each alloted a couplet. First he was afraid. But once again the line does not turn out in accordance with the expectation aroused by its opening words. The words (*quam timui*) are urgent and direct, but the fear turns out to be neither. Instead it is indirect, prompted not by the scene of the opening line, but by a pattern of poetic reflection: 'She looks like Helle . . . Helle was drowned . . . they called the place Hellespont . . . if Cynthia got drowned they could call this place after her.' And, instead of an urgent fear, it is one attenuated by ingenuity and slightly ridiculous hypothesis. 'Was I afraid in case you, too, named a sea' of course

---

[1] The *locus classicus* for the use of colour words to describe different aspects of the sea is Cicero, *Acad.* ii, 33, 105. The best modern study is J. André, *Etude sur les termes de couleur dans la langue latine* (1949)—see especially pp. 100–2. In windy weather the sea is *purpureum* (glistening, streaky blue as the light catches the waves); in calm, sunny weather *caeruleum* (intense dark blue); in overcast weather *rauum* (grey); in stormy weather *nigrum* (black).

boils down to 'Was I afraid you might die!' But, robbed of its immediacy, the statement acquires a note of elaborately bantering irony, one the poet can sustain without undue heartlessness because the echo continues of that other line,

all the lies you'd told me now confessing,

which has fallen like a barrier between Propertius and Cynthia, enabling him to withhold any real depth of sympathy for her.

A couple of details before we leave this couplet. Observe first how tightly the words *tuum mare nomen haberet* cling to one another: we are not sure whether to take *tuum* with *nomen* or with *mare*. After all, if it had your name it would be your sea. The combination *tuum nomen* is slightly more probable, but *tua aqua* in the pentameter re-establishes the ambiguity. It is characteristic of a good line that the words seem so tightly interwoven analysis cannot prise them asunder. Then, what about the sailor in tears? Of course he could be in tears simply because he is afraid of the water. Roman sailors were prone to timorousness.[1] The assumption, however, is hardly flattering to Cynthia. But if we assume he is grieving for Cynthia, the hyperbole, inherent anyway in the conceit, becomes even more plainly ironical.

The second stage to Propertius' emotional response is to beseech the gods to spare his mistress. At first sight the couplet looks like straightforward high style writing aimed at regaining a suitable level of poetic dignity. The paraphrasis *cum Castore fratri* is conventionally poetic: Roman poets seem unable to restrain the impulse to play tricks with the Dioscuri.[2] Leucothoe, however, is not as innocent as she sounds. To begin with, the name starts off an unusual and striking sound pattern that will be picked up again in line 16. (She is more often called

---

[1] Remember, e.g., Horace *Odes* i, 3, 9-20:
illi robur et aes triplex
circa pectus erat, qui fragilem truci
commisit pelago ratem . . .
qui *siccis oculis* monstra natantia,
qui uidit mare turbidum et
infamis scopulos Acroceraunia?

The participle *labens* does not suggest a storm, but is consistent with a ship running fast before a strong wind in a swell.

[2] E.g., Catullus 4, 27: *gemelle Castor et gemelle Castoris*; Horace *Epodes* 17, 42-3: *Castor . . . fraterque magni Castoris*; etc.

The Lover's Dream (ii, 27a)

Ino: in a fit of madness she leapt into the sea and was transformed into a goddess.) Then she plays in the poem a kind of double role: first, as a divinity appealed to to save Cynthia from drowning; second, as a beautiful mortal girl who was herself drowned (*iam dea* reminds us she was not always an immortal). We are left with the feeling that no more can be expected of her, perhaps, than the posthumous salvation (plus deification) granted to herself.

Propertius will approach this idea from another angle in a moment. But by now he has got us adjusted obliquely to the idea that his mistress is beyond rescue. He sums this up in a neat, crisp couplet with no tricks:

>   at tu uix primas extollens gurgite palmas   11
>   saepe meum nomen iam peritura uocas.

While you, stretched-out hands only just protruding,
kept in the hour of death calling on my name.

Cynthia is going down for the last time with Propertius' name upon her lips. A pretty thought, undisturbed by any impulse to action. Instead, with Leucothoe in mind—and thoughts, therefore, of survival as a divinity of the sea (instead of the hollow, eponymous glory granted Helle)—the poet in Propertius turns back to legend and to the beautiful young sea-nymphs, the Nereids.

We reach the Nereids, however, by an oddly circuitous route. The four lines have woven into them more than one thread of irony, while Propertius lets his fancy play with thoughts of how nice it could have been for Cynthia, had she really drowned:

>   quod si forte tuos uidisset Glaucus ocellos,
>   esses Ionii facta puella maris,
>   et tibi ob inuidiam Nereides increpitarent,   15
>   candida Nesaee, caerula Cymothoe.

If only Glaucus now had seen those eyes of yours!
He'd have made you mistress in the Ionian sea,
touching off ocean-nymphs' envious chatter,
glistening white Nisaee's, gleaming blue Cymothoe's.

Propertius and the Poetry of the Intellect

Glaucus was a Boeotian fisherman. Something he ate gave him a mad desire to jump in the sea. There he became a god. We have by now quite a collection of spectacular drownings. All, too, involve people who took to the sea in peculiar circumstances. Just how much and what Propertius expects us to read into this is hard to say. But we may be sure his list of mythological characters is not assembled at random.

Glaucus' role in the poem at any rate is plain enough, and it is adumbrated with a nice irony. If Glaucus had seen you, says Propertius, *esses Ionii facta puella maris*. Now, to judge from Virgil's *senior Glauci chorus* and other hints, Glaucus acquired, with the passage of the years, a reputation for being something of a ladykiller.[1] The word *puella* (like our English 'girl') may be either free from overtones or saturated with them. The neutral sense is sustained by the reference to the Nereids in the following line: *Ionii puella maris* sounds almost like a title. But within its own line the word is wrapped up in a context which brings out all the echoes of Roman love poetry and the use of *puella* there as an equivalent of 'mistress'.[2] These echoes are then made to react upon *Nereides*. A realistic, everyday note is introduced into a legendary context by the double-edged *puella*, and that realism then heightened by *increpitarent*. The normal idyllic picture that the Nereids conjure up (beautiful serene goddesses) fades, its place taken by that of a bunch of chattering demi-mondaines, jealous of the beautiful newcomer. But—it is almost a virtuoso touch—the pentameter swings away from this realistic note. It is a formal Hellenistic line, balanced at the caesura round four words: two exotic proper

---

[1] Virgil *Aeneid* v, 823. Rothstein's dry comment, Vol. i, pp. 376–7, provides the sort of background we need to get Propertius' point:
  Besonders gefährlich ist der Fischergott Glaucus, dem ausser seiner unerwiderten Liebe zu Scylla, von der die Dichterin Hedyle von Samos erzählt hatte (auch Ov. met. 13, 904), auch andere Liebesabenteuer zugeschrieben wurden (Ath. VII, 296a), die vielleicht Callimachus in seinem Glaucus behandelt hatte.
Propertius' ingenious flippancy in the treatment of legend owes a lot, probably, to Callimachus. On this element in Callimachus, see K. J. McKay, *The Poet at Play* (1962).

[2] One is tempted, in so complexly ironical a context, to suspect a pun as well: 'mistress of an Ionian *male*' (taking *maris* as genitive of *mas*). And in Horace *Odes* i, 5, 15–16 *potenti maris deo could* mean 'the divinity with power over a male', as well as 'the powerful divinity of the sea'—Aphrodite in both cases. But puns of this kind are usually rejected by the native speaker's *Sprachgefühl*, except in contexts that stimulate his receptivity. It is wiser probably to reject both these.

The Lover's Dream (ii, 26a)

names (in Greek they mean 'island-dweller' and 'wave-swift'), two contrasting colour epithets,[1] each a dactyl and each beginning with the same letter. A serenely mellifluous line, contrasting with the clattering consonants of the second half of the preceding hexameter and their suggestion of female chatter.

This elegy illustrates well two different ways of using mythology exploited by Propertius. The simpler and commoner use is the mythological simile (here the Helle simile); it serves as ornament, adds stature to everyday reality, provides opportunities for verbal poetry (as in line 16). A less common and more poetically effective use results from the integration of legend and reality. Propertius' mistress and the Nereids are not merely compared or contrasted as in a simile. The real and the unreal are intimately interwoven as though both were equally real.

The last four lines of the poem bring action at last, introducing Propertius as an actor in his dream instead of some kind of spectator of it. (Dreams *are* of both kinds and often start one way and end the other, without warning.) Dream and poem conclude:

> sed tibi subsidio delphinum currere uidi,
>   qui, puto, Arioniam uexerat ante lyram.
> iamque ego conabar summo me mittere saxo,
>   cum mihi discussit talia uisa metus.   20

> *But racing to your rescue a dolphin I observed—*
> *the one, I expect, once carried Arion and his lyre:*
> *I was on top a rock, preparing for the plunge,*
> *when fear filled me so the vision fell apart.*

In a way that is characteristic of dreams, a dolphin appears from nowhere. It must, of course, in a poet's dream be a poetic dolphin. But in Latin the qualification *puto* ('I expect') introduces an ironical assumption more often than something one really does suppose (for which the formula is *ut puto*). Anyway, we are left to suppose that, although the dream now evaporates, Cynthia had a good chance of being rescued at the last moment.

---

[1] The first, *candida*, 'radiant, fair-skinned', is often used of women; with the second, *caerula*, Propertius ironically attributes to Cymothoe the colour of the sea on a sunny day.

Propertius and the Poetry of the Intellect

Propertius, too, now a participant in the dream, is on the point of rushing to the rescue. He stays on the point: discovering himself on top of a rock, he is 'starting to think of ways of getting down' (the imperfect *conabar* gives his efforts about that degree of urgency)

> *when fear filled me so the vision fell apart.*

The last word in the poem is *metus*, and fear was the last of the poet's responses to what he saw in his dream. One is left, however, less than sure of the reason for his fear. Was it fear for his mistress in her peril? Or was he afraid because plunging from the rock looked like proving a tricky business, to say nothing of the danger once he was down? The final ironical ambiguity rounds off the poem the more nicely because this time one edge of it is turned against Propertius himself.

The analysis of an intellectual poem tends always to stress the intellectual element at the expense of the poetry; and at the same time, by turning irony, innuendo and malicious hint into plain statement, the intellectual element is made to sound rather silly. Propertius gives to these just the degree of emphasis they can stand. Explain them and the edifice begins to totter: it is like trying to explain a funny story. But this elegy contains a great deal more than sophisticated leg-pull. It is more than a matter of words or style. It is a quality that resides ultimately, I think, in the poet's attitude to his mistress as expressed by the poem. She is not just any girl. We can sense between poet and mistress a complex emotional bond. The sort of bond that can produce, along with the many other responses love elicits, a train like this of malicious whimsy. There are always reasons for resentment, memories that nettle, in a protracted liaison, things that lie deep beneath the surface passion, intermingled with affection.

The poet's thinking, we feel, is rightly subtle, sensitive, double-edged in such a situation. There is produced in us a conviction, ensuring our collaboration in the experience the poem offers, that the poet is not just playing with ideas, carried away by the exhilaration that game produces. One keeps thinking of Ovid, and how brittle his bravura seems because we never sense feeling behind the cleverness—though this is unfair to

The Lover's Dream (ii, 26a)

Ovid, because he has other merits which cannot be considered now. But in these poems of the intellect of Propertius it is this element of personal involvement that gives his lines their satisfying, rewarding toughness. What might otherwise have remained ingenious verse fuses into poetry.

8

The Tempo of Virgilian Epic

We expect of epic a loose-knit style and a leisurely tempo. In Homer we find them. The dimensions of the form, the poet's emotional attachment to a departed gentlemanly age that subordinated efficiency to good manners, the genesis itself very likely of Homeric epic (to venture on conjectural ground)[1]— all made for a mellifluous fullness.

Virgil is different. The tempo of the *Aeneid* seems by comparison curt, swift-moving, matter-of-fact. The difference lies in the narrator's manner rather than in his story. His plot can hardly be said to be crowded with action. The *Aeneid* is shorter, admittedly, than the *Iliad* or the *Odyssey*; all the same, 10,000 lines—almost—are ample for the story told.[2] Virgil tells it, however, with an urgent economy that makes us feel every word counts. Naturally the pressure varies. Virgil's own narrative is terser and tighter than the speeches he assigns his characters. Within the narrative the sustained similes are fuller and richer in style; but in them a cohering density, likewise alien to old Greek epic, is substituted for brevity. In the narrative proper the tempo changes constantly. But take a couple of hundred lines of narrative at random and compare them with a similar sample from Homer: your impression will be that, however much Virgil appears to vary the speed of his narrative, his close-packed lines maintain a tempo consistently faster than Homer's.

Some of the pruning has a structural purpose: to reduce the

[1] See C. M. Bowra, *From Virgil to Milton* (1945), pp. 3–5.
[2] On the length of various epic poems, see Mackail, pp. xxxviii–xxxix.

The Tempo of Virgilian Epic

poem to proportions compatible with real artistic form and give it clear lines. But Virgil has another, more important object: to create a new style, one whose distinctive quality shall be terse excitement rather than the charm of leisurely fullness. What he is attempting is not pastiche, but a style founded on the resources of expression of his own day, refined by the craftsman in verse and raised to a new level by the poet's genius. We sense the influence of contemporary prose as often as that of contemporary verse. In prose the orator and the historian had each since Homer's day contributed much to the art of telling a story efficiently. As for verse influences, Virgil owes a lot to the Roman tradition since Catullus and the emphasis that tradition placed on a manner that was closely woven and allusive and yet light, and so shorn of unproductive adornment as to make it deceptively plain.

The drive for conciseness is easiest seen in Virgil's manipulation of the mechanics of syntax. The devices he employs form part of the repertoire of poetic syntax and are familiar enough to the student of Latin. But, though they are regularly pointed out and labelled in annotated editions, their purpose is seldom clearly stated or appreciated. Among them are the extensive use of an infinitive after a finite verb instead of a subordinate clause; the frequent excision of *est, sunt,* etc., in the perfect passive—leaving the past participle to act unsupported as a finite verb; a preference for simple verbs where compound forms of the same verbs are usual in contemporary prose; a considerable reduction in the incidence of prepositions—using the dative case instead of *ad* and the accusative, or leaving out the preposition that normally accompanies certain ablative forms.

Many of the devices are commonly written off as archaisms, as though it were enough for poetry, or enough for poetry of the quality that Virgil wished to write, to be old-fashioned. Virgil takes from older Latin poetry those features which help him to achieve simplicity and directness and a purity of diction that can predispose us to being moved in the ways in which it is poetry's function to move us, without recourse to the ostentatious sublimity of the grand manner. But above all Virgil concentrates on cutting down the incidence of the small, fussy, unproductive word, often reducing his hexameter to five or six

The Tempo of Virgilian Epic

solid, massy words, all pulling their weight.[1] The words, moreover, especially when the narrative is unusually elaborate or allusive, often cohere, linked together by patterns of syntactical ambiguity (the units mutually interlocking) to a degree that almost defies analysis.[2] For he wishes, as well as moving us by an austere simplicity of diction, to excite us (when excitement is appropriate) and to sustain our interest (when things less exciting must be dealt with expeditiously) by a style that will suggest a tight, urgent complexity of thought.

We shall see better how economy makes for speed by considering passages of some extent than by detailing the minutiae of poetic syntax. Take, for example, these lines from Book IV; it is the moment near the end when Anna reaches the pyre and takes her dying sister in her arms:

>   sic fata gradus euaserat altos   685
> semianimemque sinu germanam amplexa fouebat
> cum gemitu atque atros siccabat ueste cruores.
> illa grauis oculos conata attollere rursus
> deficit; infixum stridit sub pectore uulnus.
> ter sese attollens cubitoque adnixa leuauit,   690
> ter reuoluta toro est oculisque errantibus alto
> quaesiuit caelo lucem ingemuitque reperta.

A prose translation that preserves the grammatical structure of the Latin is necessary to bring out the point I wish to make:

Speaking thus, she had emerged from the high stairway, and, having taken in her arms her sister now near death, she was

---

[1] Though he does not strain after this effect as hard as Catullus does in Poem 64. Occasionally there are only four words in a Virgilian hexameter. The most striking of these is *Aeneid* ii, 549, a line that conveys the spendid bravura with which the arrogant young Neoptolemus taunts old Priam (who has reproached him for letting down his father):

'degeneremque Neoptolemum narrare memento!'

[2] See Kenneth Quinn, 'Syntactical ambiguity in Horace and Virgil', *Aumla*, No. 14 (1960), pp. 36–46. Since writing this article I find my arguments are lent considerable detailed support by R. S. Conway's commentary on *Aeneid* i (1935), *passim*. E.g., his comment on i, 75:

> to ask which of two possible constructions must be chosen for any one word is often like enquiring whether a particular figure in a picture is to be regarded as belonging to the left- or the right-hand side.

The Tempo of Virgilian Epic

caressing her in the midst of her grief and was stanching the dark blood with her dress. Dido, attempting to raise again her eyes, lacked the strength. There was a sharp sound from the wound inflicted deep in her chest. Three times, straining and leaning on an elbow for support, she raised herself; three times she rolled back onto the couch, and with her wandering eyes looked to high heaven for the light of day, and groaned on discovering it.

There is not one subordinate clause in these eight lines—something much more unusual in Latin than it would be in English. Confronted with so much action to describe, the Latin writer's problem is this: if he subordinates, the sense of urgency is lost; a series of simple sentences on the other hand is liable (in Latin) to result in a jerkiness that will break up the flow of the writing and destroy its dignity; a succession of *and*'s may prove equally disastrous. Virgil has attained the effect he desires by a construction normal enough in prose, but in prose much less common than a subordinate clause: the deponent past participle. There are four here (*reperta* is passive): *fata* ('speaking'), *amplexa* ('having taken in her arms'), *conata* ('attempting'), *adnixa* ('leaning'). Only one sentence is left as a single statement, the terrible *infixum stridit sub pectore uulnus,* and it stands out starkly in this smoothly articulated context.[1]

So concentrated an employment of the deponent past participle must naturally be reserved for special occasions if it is not to degenerate into mannerism. More frequent is the well-known Virgilian use of an accusative noun after a past participle,

---

[1] Even here the past participle *infixum* introduces a second verbal idea, binding the words tightly together and introducing a daring and effective ambiguity. Taking the words at their surface meaning *infixum uulnus* is the wound 'inflicted' by the sword Dido has just plunged into her breast. But behind the surface meaning lies the suggestion of a different kind of wound: the wound of passion, described in the opening lines of the book, and brought back to the reader's memory now by the echo here of Virgil's words in line 67: *tacitum uiuit sub pectore uulnus.* To this new meaning of *uulnus* a new meaning of *infixum* ('deep-seated') is appropriate. (Nor should we overlook the symbolism of the sword. The psychical wound was inflicted by Aeneas, the physical wound by his sword.) For *stridit*, see Mackail, p. 162 (approved by Austin, p. 198):

> *stridit* (a word over which commentators have bungled strangely) accurately expresses the whistling sound with which breath escapes from a pierced lung.

But with the breath escapes, of course, life itself, and with life the metaphorical wound that had 'been living deep-seated' within her.

201

The Tempo of Virgilian Epic

a simple, distinctive construction that usually obviates a subordinate clause.[1] Virgil naturally by no means denies himself the subordinate clause in setting out the steps in a complicated piece of narrative. It is striking, however, that nowhere in the poem does he use *cum* with the pluperfect subjunctive—perhaps the most characteristic subordinate clause of contemporary prose narrative. Clearly the construction seemed to him, somehow, irredeemably prosy—or insufficiently supported by tradition (it is not used in early Latin).[2] His favourite temporal conjunction is *ut*. But instead of using it to state a simple temporal relationship ('When X happened, A did so-and-so'), he is fond of using it as a kind of comment on motive, combining *ut* with a verb of perceiving (i.e., *ut uidit* . . ., 'When A *saw* that X had happened . . .')—looking at the action from inside his character, as it were, instead of as an impersonal, remote observer.[3]

Elliptical Narrative

But the drive for conciseness is seen also in the way the story is shaped for telling. The method of selecting events dictates the tempo of the narrative, no less than the techniques Virgil exploits for presenting these events once selected and fitted into the pattern of his story. All skilful writers do this to some extent. But not all take the trouble Virgil takes to sustain an impression of urgency and variety.

The procedure has an interesting and important consequence. The illusion is created of a story with an existence of its own, independent of Virgil's telling of it. This is something different

---

[1] E.g., iv, 589–91:

> terque quaterque manu pectus percussa decorum
> flauentisque abscissa comas 'pro Iuppiter! ibit   590
> hic,' ait . . .

> *Three times, four times she struck her fair breast with her hand,*
> *and tore at her golden hair. 'In Jove's name! shall*
> *he go,' she said . . .*

Three statements in one sentence, but no subordinate clause. On this construction see Quinn, pp. 66–7.

[2] He uses *cum* freely enough with the imperfect subjunctive. In more dramatic contexts he has a fondness (beyond prose usage) for the inverted-*cum* construction with the indicative.

[3] Of 53 examples of temporal *ut* in the *Aeneid*, 18 are of the type *ut uidet*, and 14 more involve equivalents of *uidet*. The usage seems peculiar to Virgil.

Elliptical Narrative

from the knowledge the reader may or may not possess of earlier differing versions, say, of the Aeneas or Dido legends. Quite apart from the aid it receives from any resources of allusion, Virgil's narrative itself makes us feel continually that his story neither begins nor ends with what he tells us. We seem all the time to catch hints of things left out. We sense explanations the poet might have given if he had had time.

At first sight Virgil's technique seems the opposite of that of the realist writer and his wealth of detail painstakingly recorded. The difference is more, however, that in Virgil the details are *suggested*, often, as much as they are recorded. The true opposite of realism is the story so clear-cut that the writer is able to present in his narrative everything the reader needs for the story to proceed. A story so simple that it elicits no curiosity for fuller information, no puzzlement about the causal relationships between events.

But Virgil expects of his readers this curiosity and this puzzlement, the realization that steps have been omitted, explanations not given. He relies on them to conjecture half-consciously about what is missing, but needed if they are to grasp the story properly.[1] Virgil in fact transfers to epic the evocative economy of Hellenistic epigram and Horatian ode. It is another instance of his reliance upon the reader's active collaboration. We saw, for example (in Chapter 2), how in *Aeneid* iv Virgil tells us practically nothing about the events at Dido's palace between the day of the hunt and the day of Aeneas' decision to depart. At the same time he makes us feel that time has gone by, that much has passed between Aeneas and Dido to complicate their relationship. Yet we haven't any feeling that something is missing. On the contrary, Virgil's story somehow acquires the solidity and depth of real life, where there is no limit to the data relevant to an episode, but only limits to our knowledge. A story that does not elicit the curiosity and puzzlement that real life elicits cannot ring true.

Let us look at some simpler examples with more care. In the story of the boxing-match in *Aeneid* v Virgil passes on from the braggart display of Dares (who looks like taking the prize

---

[1] We should remember, of course, we are reading an unfinished poem. What we are discussing, however, is something different from unintentional slips or oversights.

The Tempo of Virgilian Epic

without having to fight because no opponent comes forward) with the words (v, 387-8):

> hic grauis Entellum dictis castigat Acestes,
> proximus ut uiridante toro consederat herbae.

Here, Acestes, speaking sternly to Entellus, upbraided him, after he had sat down close beside him on the grass.

Two words—*grauis, consederat*—draw the reader out and set him putting together the details of the story the way Virgil intends. Why should Acestes speak 'sternly'? Why are we told so precisely that Entellus 'had sat down'—not merely that he 'was sitting'? The reader, sensitive to the precision of Virgil's narrative text, hardly needs to ask these questions consciously. The form of the verb *consederat* (the pluperfect tense, the preverb *con-*) bring action into what *sedebat* would have left as description of scene. Entellus, the recognized local champion (our filling-out begins) had come along expecting to compete. That is why he has his great gloves with him. But he is an old man; seeing the visiting champion brings second thoughts and he sits down. This action explains *grauis*: Acestes is not merely urging Entellus to fight, but upbraiding him for his decision not to fight (revealed by the action of sitting down).

Expansion like this of Virgil's text may seem high-handed until we realize how constantly his technique of elliptical narrative requires it. It illuminates, too, the conclusion of the boxing match, where obscurity has been felt:

> 'nate dea, uosque haec' inquit 'cognoscite, Teucri,
> et mihi quae fuerint iuuenali in corpore uires   475
> et qua seruetis reuocatum a morte Dareta.'
> dixit, et aduersi contra stetit ora iuuenci
> qui donum astabat pugnae, durosque reducta
> librauit dextra media inter cornua caestus
> arduus, effractoque inlisit in ossa cerebro: 480
> sternitur exanimisque tremens procumbit humi bos.
> ille super talis effundit pectore uoces:
> 'hanc tibi, Eryx, meliorem animam pro morte Daretis
> persoluo; hic uictor caestus artemque repono.'

Elliptical Narrative

'Just you look, goddess' son,' he said, 'you Trojans, too:
you'll see what strength my body had when I was young—
and the death your intervention saved your Dares from.'
With that he planted himself right before the bull—
there it stood, the winning fighter's prize—drew right hand
back, balanced the cruel gloves evenly between the horns, and
from his full height drove them through the splintering skull.
The bull fell to the ground to sprawl a twitching lifeless mass.
Standing over it, his voice lifting from his chest, he said:
'Here, instead of Dares' death, a better life I offer
to you, Eryx: my gloves, my craft, I the winner now renounce.'

What actually does Entellus do? The picture is far from clear on a first reading. A double hint is given by *duros . . . caestus* in lines 478–9. First the plural: how more than one glove on one hand (*dextra*)?[1] Then why *duros*? Is the epithet distinguishing or ornamental? An eye cast back over the preceding lines shows us how Virigil expects us to fill out his narrative. Clearly they are the gloves of Eryx, not the ordinary gloves Entellus wore in the fight. There is a distinct interval after the fight stops—the time needed for Dares' friends to carry him back to the ships and then return to recover the loser's prize. More than enough time for Entellus to remove his gloves and take up the gloves of Eryx which he had brought with him in the first place.

Virgil makes more than one use of these gloves of Eryx. If he had used them only for Entellus' gesture in accepting the challenge, it would have been a little flat to have them thrown aside when the fight began—though we could admire Virgil's taste in avoiding undue brutality. They are needed as well, however, in the last line of the episode: it is the gloves he has used throughout his career that Entellus dedicates to Eryx in his declaration of retirement, not the substitute gloves. A less compact writer might have included some specific statement of Entellus' resumption of the gloves of Eryx for the ceremony of dedication. Virgil, however, prefers to work by suggestion.

---

[1] Williams's suggestion, p. 134, that *caestus* is a poetic plural is implausible: (1) It falls too far outside the normal range of poetic plurals (see the discussion in E. Löfstedt, *Syntactica*, Vol. i (2nd edn. 1942), pp. 35–8); (2) it throws away the hint provided by *duros*. Mackail's explanation, p. 188, of the passage undoubtedly builds up the picture Virgil intended.

The Tempo of Virgilian Epic

The reader who wants to visualize the scene, instead of reading the passage quickly for its superficial excitement, is expected to look for the clues the poet has taken care to leave him. It is not Virgil's aim to provide a clear-cut image. He leaves it to the reader, aroused to responsiveness by his puzzlement, to assemble his own.

Next to be decided is the meaning to attach to *librauit* (line 479). If Entellus is carrying both gloves in one hand, they must be brought down on the bullock's skull with a swing, not a punch; *librauit* then is the preliminary calculation of the swing, not the poising of the clenched fist for a punch. A detail in Entellus' words before he struck the blow that ought to have puzzled us is now explained. How can Entellus show the strength of body he had as a *young* man now he is *old*? By some superhuman effort? No, really by a sort of trick. A theatrical gesture (a calculated swing with two gloves) demonstrates what he could have done once, he claims, with a normal punch. Today he has to resort to a trick to crack open the tough skull of a bullock. But Dares' skull he could still manage, he asserts, even with an ordinary glove and an ordinary punch.

Commentators on Virgil tend to be resentful at the lack of clarity which results from his technique of elliptical narrative. The fifth book, because of the wealth of complicated incident related, provides many examples of the sort of thing that annoys them. Details that seem important are left obscure. What use, if any, for instance is made of sail in the boat-race?[1] Details not mentioned at what one would take to be the proper time crop up afterwards. Mnestheus presents himself for the archery contest wearing an olive garland awarded in the boat-race, though we were not told in the narrative of the prize ceremony after the boat-race that he had won one.[2] Ascanius, before speaking to the women who had set the fleet on fire, throws down his helmet; but in the parade he was not wearing a helmet.[3] Even in an unfinished poem, the commentators feel, Virgil should not nod as often as this.

The questions they ask can hardly be dismissed as irrelevant or wrong-headed, like Professor Knights's model of the

---
[1] See the commentators on v, 211–12.
[2] See the commentators on v, 494.
[3] See the commentators on v, 673.

Elliptical Narrative

sort of question not to put to the text of Shakespeare: 'How many children had Lady Macbeth?'[1] At the same time it is obvious that, if Virgil had attempted to forestall all possible relevant questions, his narrative would have become intolerably crowded and slow-moving. Most of the apparent slips complained of are the results of omissions, not inconsistencies, and most details the sensible reader can supply for himself.

Sometimes, however, Virgil's method imposes omissions beyond the needs of economy. It is then as though he wished to observe on our behalf only what the actual spectators might have observed. For often *they* would be left unsure what exactly has happened even though they had been watching; often they would only realize afterwards that things they missed at the time must have occurred. Why shouldn't then the reader, too, be left to worry details out of the text on a second, a third and a fourth reading and still, here and there, be left unsure what happened?

But Virgil's narrative has more to it than the story. He wants us to understand the sort of people his characters are, how they are affected by the decisions they take, the rightness or wrongness of those decisions. None of this can be made clear-cut and remain convincing. Even the evidence for our judgments—what actually happened—must not be too neatly presented. Often, too, he wishes us to sense the symbolic significance of an episode. But we must no more than sense it. If the symbolism is too expressly implanted, it will lose its power to move us.

In *Aeneid* ii, while the Greeks are pouring out of the wooden horse into the streets of the sleeping city, Hector appears to Aeneas in a dream, to warn him of Troy's impending destruction and to tell him what he must do:

> 'heu fuge, nate dea, teque his' ait 'eripe flammis.
> hostis habet muros; ruit alto a culmine Troia.   290
> sat patriae Priamoque datum: si Pergama dextra
> defendi possent, etiam hac defensa fuissent.
> sacra suosque tibi commendat Troia penatis;
> hos cape fatorum comites, his moenia quaere
> magna, pererrato statues quae denique ponto.'   295

[1] L. C. Knights, 'How many children had Lady Macbeth?', *Explorations* (1946), pp. 1-39.

The Tempo of Virgilian Epic

*'Ah! flee, goddess' son,' he said, 'snatch yourself from these flames.
The enemy has the walls; Troy is crashing headlong down.
There's no more to do for country or for Priam. If Troy's defence
had lain in strength of hand, mine had so defended it.
To you Troy entrusts her holy things, her city's gods.
Take them to share your destiny, seek for them the fabric of
a mighty city you shall found, your ocean journeys ended.'*

The symbolism is as plain as Virgil dare make it. Aeneas is to replace Hector as the protector of the Trojans. But he is to be their protector in exile, and their religious as much as their military champion. Aeneas rushes to a vantage point and Hector's opening words are confirmed by the scene before his eyes: Troy is in flames. His natural instinct is to spring to the defence of the doomed city:

>arma amens capio; nec sat rationis in armis,
>sed glomerare manum bello et concurrere in arcem   315
>cum sociis ardent animi; furor iraque mentem
>praecipitat, pulchrumque mori succurrit in armis.

*Distraught I snatch up arms, though there's little sense in arms;
but to build a band for battle, to rush with comrades to the
citadel—thus the hot impulse; a mad anger tumbles over
reason, and the quick thought comes: how fine a fighting death!*

The stress Virgil lays on the folly of Aeneas' reaction should warn the sensitive reader he has in mind something other than the nobility of hopeless resistance. A moment later appears

>Panthus Othryades, arcis Phoebique sacerdos,
>sacra manu uictosque deos paruumque nepotem   320
>ipse trahit cursuque amens ad limina tendit.

*Panthus, son of Othrys, Apollo's citadel-priest;
the holy things, the vanquished gods, his little grandson,
these he clasps as he runs distraught toward my house.*

It is as though Hector's words were once again confirmed, as though the same power that sent Hector to Aeneas in vision is now sending Panthus to him in reality.

Elliptical Narrative

It is clear Virgil wishes us to understand that Panthus is bringing to Aeneas the gods that Aeneas must take with him into exile—the gods he eventually does take with him when he sets out at the beginning of Book III:

> feror exsul in altum 11
> cum sociis natoque penatibus et magnis dis.
>
> *An exile I put to sea;*
> *with me comrades, son, ancestral gods, mighty powers.*

It is equally clear Virgil cannot say so in as many words: the hand of fate must not appear too mechanical. And any identification of the images of the gods with the gods themselves must be no more than discreetly implied.[1]

But, though the reader senses the hand of fate when Panthus appears with the city's gods, Aeneas does not.[2] He assumes Panthus' appearance carrying the gods means that the citadel where they were kept (Panthus is carefully described as *arcis Phoebique sacerdos*) is being evacuated and another established:

> 'quo res summa loco, Panthu? quam prendimus arcem?' 322
>
> *'Where's the last stand, Panthus, what take we for our citadel?'*

---

[1] While he naturally avoids making things too specific, Virgil does imply a distinction between (1) the physical images of the gods which can be carried from place to place; (2) the divinities themselves with whom contact is made and whose protection is secured by the worship of the physical images. E.g., in iii, 148–55 the Penates appear to Aeneas in a dream in Crete. What he sees are the physical objects,

> effigies sacrae diuum Phrygiique penates,
> quos mecum ab Troia mediisque ex ignibus urbis
> extuleram. 150

But when the Penates address him, their words make it clear the actual divinities are speaking, sent to Aeneas by Apollo: *tua nos en ultro ad limina mittit*. Often there is initial ambiguity and we should not press for its resolution, e.g., iii, 11–12, and viii, 679.

[2] The hand of fate has been missed, too, by more than one modern editor without Aeneas' justification that his mind was distraught by the turmoil of disaster. They assume Panthus' own domestic Penates must be meant. Yet Richard Heinze put the matter beyond inadvertence by his admirably clear analysis of Virgil's elliptical narrative, *V.E.T.*, p. 35:

> Panthus rettet diese *sacra* von der Burg herab zu Aeneas . . .: so bestätigt sich unverzüglich der Traum. . . . dass [Panthus] die Heiligtümer . . . nicht mit sich genommen, sondern bei Aeneas zurückgelassen hat, brauchte wohl nicht besonders gesagt zu werden. Somit geht dann auf Aeneas die priesterliche Pflicht über . . . .

The Tempo of Virgilian Epic

It is clear from Panthus' despondent reply that there is no question of an organized stand. But Aeneas does not seem to grasp the hopelessness of resistance. Panthus, for his part, either does not know he is to commit the gods to Aeneas' care, or forgets. Both he and Aeneas are described as *amens*—'distraught', 'not thinking'. The impulse to fight is so strong that, despite Hector's charge, Aeneas joins the battle. So does Panthus, but, with characteristic economy of detail, Virgil does not say so. Only when Panthus is killed (lines 429–30) are we told he had fought till then by Aeneas' side. For the moment the tempo of events is too fast for them, or us, to grasp clearly all that happens.

The battle scenes follow (lines 336–587), lit up by the flames that join with the Greeks in destroying Troy. Before the end of this central and longest section of the three which comprise the book, we see Priam brutally murdered and Aeneas on the point of murdering Helen. The writing is magnificently vivid and moving; yet all the time, though we, like Aeneas, have forgotten it, Aeneas is out of step with destiny. He is neglecting what Hector told him he must do. Virgil has the courage to imply in his epic of Rome's greatness that death in battle is the easy way out. The implication underlies all the time the glamour of the battle scenes. It pervades the first words Aeneas speaks in the poem (i, 94–6):

> 'o terque quaterque beati,
> quis ante ora patrum Troiae sub moenibus altis
> contigit oppetere!'

> '*O three times blessed and more they
> that before their fathers' eyes, by Troy's towering walls,
> were granted death!*'

But the easy way out is denied Aeneas. His mission, as Hector told him, was to save his people and their gods, not to fight for the doomed city. At the very moment when his hand is raised to murder Helen, his divine mother Venus intervenes, makes him realize at last that Troy is doomed, and restores him to his destined mission:[1]

---

[1] Needless doubts about the authenticity of the Helen episode have been finally dispelled by R. G. Austin, *C.Q.*, xi (1961), pp. 185–98.

Elliptical Narrative

> 'eripe, nate, fugam finemque impone labori' 619

> *'Clutch your chance of escape, my son, end your struggle.'*

Throughout the epic heroics of the night of fighting, Virgil intends us to preserve this sense, not merely of the futility of fighting, but of its misguidedness. He has gone as far as he dares. A lesser poet might have imperilled our acceptance of his message by reintroducing the images of the gods at this point. That would make it all just too contrived. Virgil instead sets Aeneas about preparations for exile and keeps the gods back until the moment of departure. Aeneas' words then to his father

> 'tu, genitor, cape sacra manu patriosque penatis' 717

> *'You, father, clasp the holy things, our ancestral gods!'*

echo Hector's words[1]

> 'sacra suosque tibi commendat Troia penatis;
> hos cape fatorum comites, his moenia quaere
> magna'. 295

> *'To you Troy entrusts her holy things, her city's gods.
> Take them to share your destiny, seek for them the fabric of
> a mighty city'.*

And in the next book we have the final reminder (iii, 11-12):

> feror exsul in altum
> cum sociis natoque penatibus et magnis dis.

> *An exile I put to sea;*
> *with me comrades, son, ancestral gods, mighty powers.*

---

[1] The verbal echoes make it clear it is Troy's Penates and not Aeneas' domestic Penates (or even Priam's domestic Penates, as some have oddly supposed from ii, 514) that are meant. For Roman domestic Penates in historical times, see C. Bailey, *Religion in Virgil* (1935), p. 31ff.; for the city's Penates, ibid., p. 91ff.

The Tempo of Virgilian Epic

Interweaving

Another device for suggesting ramifications of the story beyond the framework of the actual narrative is a technique we shall call *interweaving*. Its function is to prepare for the main appearance of an important secondary character by an anticipatory glimpse of him in action—sometimes a whole series of glimpses. When his main scene comes, we feel that, though the tempo of the action has not given the opportunity for more than an occasional glance, he has been there all the time.

Virgil makes use of this technique in building up the character of Mezentius. Mezentius does not come into the foreground until Book X, but the pattern of reference to him and glimpses of him taking part in the fighting begins as far back as Book VII. His name occurs first in the list of princes opposing Aeneas (vii, 647–8):

> primus init bellum Tyrrhenis asper ab oris
> contemptor diuum Mezentius . . .
>
> *First into battle goes a formidable Etruscan,*
> *god-despising Mezentius. . . .*

Nothing is said of him here beyond the arresting comment *contemptor diuum*. Instead Virgil tells us about his son Lausus, who gets six lines to his father's two: a short panegyric ending with the remark that he deserved a better father. The reader's interest in this striking and vaguely sinister character is economically aroused—and then no more is said of him until the beginning of the next book.

This time we have a brief glimpse of him in action, marshalling his forces with other princes (viii, 6–8),

> ductores primi Messapus et Vfens
> contemptorque deum Mezentius undique cogunt
> auxilia et latos uastant cultoribus agros.
>
> *First the leaders Messapus, Ufens, and*
> *god-despising Mezentius comb the countryside for*
> *troops, stripping fields far and wide of husbandmen.*

Interweaving

—the reference again vague but menacing and an echo of the same intriguing phrase. Then no more about him for nearly five hundred lines. His name now crops up while Evander is talking to Aeneas (viii, 481ff.), and at last we learn something about this cruel, bizarre prince living in exile from his own people. Evander, in bidding farewell to his son Pallas, who is going to fight with Aeneas, mentions Mezentius again (viii, 569–71) and again it is his cruelty and barbarity that are stressed.

The name Mezentius is becoming familiar. We start to feel we know something about the man. In Book IX Virgil is content to remind us that Mezentius is present, taking part in the fighting. We catch sight of him a couple of times, both action shots (ix, 521–2 and 586–9). In the first he stands out among a group attempting to set fire to the ramparts. In the second we see him kill a man with a spectacular sling shot. Book X brings in his name again by yet another device. A glimpse of Aeneas journeying through the night to rejoin his men is followed by a recapitulatory passage telling us of his negotiations with the present Etruscan prince. Once more the name of Mezentius crops up. We are made to feel, not only that he is there all the time fighting, but also that he is present in the thoughts of the other characters—a man to be reckoned with.

We glimpse him again for a moment at x, 204. Then, at x, 689, he comes at last into the foreground to take a major part in the fighting during the absence from the battle of Turnus. He is mentioned again at x, 714. Then for the first time he is allotted a scene of some importance at x, 729–46: the dying Orodes predicts to his assailant standing over him that death will seek him out, too, before long. Mezentius despatches him with a smile—though irritated by Orodes' words, he is still sufficiently master of himself to treat the Jupiter he despises with heavy irony, addressing the god by his full traditional title:

> ad quae subridens mixta Mezentius ira: 742
> 'nunc morere. ast de me diuum pater atque hominum rex
> uiderit.'

> *Smiling and angry, too, Mezentius replied,*
> *'Now die: as for me, the king of gods and men will give*
> *the matter his attention.'*

The Tempo of Virgilian Epic

Virgil's touch is subtle. We begin to understand why Mezentius is known as *contemptor diuum*. And when god-despising Mezentius, with a gesture of uneasy bravado, invites the wrath of Jupiter upon his own head, the thrill of presentiment we feel is accompanied by a fresh insight into the much talked of cruelty of Mezentius. This is no unfeeling brute, we sense, but a man made ruthless by embitterment.

Virgil has now prepared us for Mezentius' main scene, his first fight with Aeneas, in which he is wounded and saved from death by the intervention of his son Lausus—the son who deserved a better father. Aeneas kills the boy and his body is brought to where his father is resting by a stream, urgently asking for news of the duel. Shamed beyond endurance, Mezentius calls for his horse (for whom he feels an affection shown no human companion), determined to face Aeneas in a fight he does not hope to win.[1] After a fierce encounter, he meets death with the hard, realistic courage we expect of him, no more willing to beg quarter from Aeneas than he was willing to extend it to Orodes.

Our concern, however, is not with the main episode, which is magnificent and moving, but with the way Virgil has woven it into his story. Nor is Mezentius forgotten about as soon as his big scene is over. We hear of him again during the burial of the dead at the beginning of Book XI in a final pathetic echo: Mezentius, who had boasted he would array his son as a living trophy with the arms of Aeneas (x, 775), is now himself offered as a trophy to the god of war (xi, 7). The whole pattern of interweaving repays the closest study, not only as an example of economical presentation of a fully rounded and highly individual secondary character, but also as a sustained illustration of an important narrative device.

The same device on a more limited scale is used many times. Nisus and Euryalus, for example, are first presented to us in a minor episode during the games in Sicily as contestants in the sprint (v, 294ff.), so that, when their major scene comes four books later (ix, 230ff.), two things will have been achieved. First, we shall see them come forward, not as characters

---

[1] Mezentius' affection for his horse (858–66) stresses his isolation. Toward his son he recognizes obligation and is humiliated by his failure to discharge it; but his words (846–56) show no affection for Lausus.

Interweaving

suddenly created, but as people we have seen before, whose presence all along among Aeneas' men we can believe in, and into whose characters we feel we already possess some insight. Second, the two episodes four books apart provide one of the bonds that hold together the main structure of the narrative.

The two Palinurus episodes are closer together, standing at either end of Book V. Their main function is to underline, by a clear piece of symbolism, the progress of the rehabilitation of Aeneas in the eyes of his men. The opening lines of Book V show clearly how their misgivings about the rights and wrongs of their commander's quarrel with Dido have imperilled Aeneas' moral ascendancy (see Chapter 2). In the crisis of the storm immediately following, Palinurus assumes the initiative and Aeneas merely acquiesces. At the end of the book the Trojans are at sea once more. But it is a calm night, not a night of storm (a further piece of symbolism). The eventual happy outcome of events in Book V has restored Aeneas' confidence in himself. When the crisis comes now, he springs to assume control of the situation (lines 867–8).

But symbolism apart, the second Palinurus episode relies for its vividness on the reader's memory of the first. It becomes unnecessary to burden the second with a delineation of Palinurus' character: we feel we know the man already. And, knowing him as a seaman of resource and authority, we can appreciate the importance of his loss to Aeneas. These are facts the reader needs, to grasp the magnitude of the crisis when Palinurus is lost. But they are facts he feels he can supply from his own knowledge, not facts suddenly created and asserted by the poet.

This is not the end of Palinurus. We meet him again in Book VI. Nor is this by any means a full account of the patterns of interweaving in the poem. The more one comes to know the poem, the clearer the more subtle patterns stand out. The patterns do not always work forward to a main scene. For example, the description of the *Lusus Troiae* in Book V breaks off a description of the leaders with a short apostrophe to the father of one of them, Polites (v, 563–5):

> una acies iuuenum, ducit quam paruus ouantem
> nomen aui referens Priamus, tua clara, Polite,
> progenies, auctura Italos!

The Tempo of Virgilian Epic

*One column of exulting youngsters is led by a little
Priam (named after his grandfather)—your stock, Polites,
famous now, to have Italian descendants soon!*

The touch is characteristic enough of Virgil's manner. But it helps as well to draw out on this happy occasion our recollection of the brutal murder, described so vividly in Book II, of the boy's father, followed by the murder of his grandfather, King Priam.[1] The grandfather's name comes in almost casually because it is also the boy's name. But in a sense the whole story of the poem (murder and destruction in Troy, a new bright future in Italy) echoes through these two and a half lines.

Allusion

Another of Priam's sons who died the night Troy fell is Deiphobus. His role in the story illustrates. not so much interweaving, as a narrative technique which we may call *allusion*. In Virgil's own story Deiphobus occurs only twice. Indeed the first time hardly ranks as an occurrence. His name is mentioned to localize one detail in the panorama of destruction that Aeneas surveys from his roof-top before his meeting with Panthus. While he watches, the house of Deiphobus crashes to the ground, engulfed in the fire destined that night to consume Troy (ii, 310–11):

　　　　　　iam Deiphobi dedit ampla ruinam
　Volcano superante domus.

But the reader who knows his Homer catches an echo here that others miss. In *Odyssey* viii Odysseus, at the banquet given by King Alcinous, asks the Phaeacian minstrel Demodocus to relate to him the destruction of Troy. Demodocus provides in fact no more than an excerpt from the story. As reported by Homer, his lay occupies a mere twenty lines (*Odyssey* viii, 499–520). A paraphrase of the episode of the wooden horse occupies nearly the whole. One detail only of the ensuing destruction is high-

[1] The murderer Pyrrhus, we learn, met a like fate at the hands of Orestes (iii, 332), who
　　　　excipit incautum patriasque obtruncat ad aras
—another example of interweaving. Later in the same book (iii, 469) his name occurs once more when, as a final act of retribution, his armour is given to Aeneas by Helenus.

Allusion

lighted: how Odysseus himself, Menelaus with him, made for the house of Deiphobus and there fought courageously a particularly bloody battle.

Virgil says nothing of this, relying on his readers to catch the echo of Homer and feel they know what has happened to Deiphobus. In Book VI, however (lines 494–534) Aeneas meets Deiphobus among the shades of the dead, his body cruelly mutilated, and is told the story of how the brutal Ulysses and Menelaus burst in that night upon Deiphobus and Helen.[1] The second reference picks up the first, by the normal process of interweaving—except that the first really only exists as the result of the process we have called allusion. Moreover, the information Virgil expected his readers to draw from Homer is now corrected: what Homer had presented as a heroic deed is now shown to have another, less attractive side. The correction is the more effective for being delayed: instead of retelling the story his way at the time (which might have tempted us to dismiss his version as partial, or an attempt to rewrite Homer), Virgil allows allusion to implant the Homeric version, and the truer version, we feel, of what happened to come out later.

Basically it is one more device for making Virgil's story sound real by implying the endless ramifications of reality. Set against an implied pattern of endless, conflicting detail, Virgil's own narrative sounds urgently selective. Allusion is, of course, an aspect of Virgil's constant imitation of Homer; but it represents a considerable refinement on the more normal techniques. Episodes, similes, tricks of language and style borrowed from Homer may pass undetected without much harm to our enjoyment. Something usually is lost if we miss Homer's words behind Virgil's; but success does not depend on recognition of the borrowing. Allusion, however, deliberately challenges our memory of Homer. Details are incorporated often that are dependent on our knowledge of Homer's story. When, for example, in recounting his vision of Hector the exclamation is wrung from Aeneas (ii, 274–5),

> ei mihi, qualis erat, quantum mutatus ab illo
> Hectore qui redit exuuias indutus Achilli!

[1] Deiphobus' marriage to Helen after the death of Paris is un-Homeric, but justified by Homer's reference to the two in *Odyssey* iv, 276ff.

The Tempo of Virgilian Epic

*Alas! how he looked! He was not the Hector now
that returned wearing the captured armour of Achilles!*

a detail is built in to arouse our active collaboration with the poet. We are challenged to remember it was not Achilles whom Hector killed, but Patroclus, who was wearing the armour of Achilles. Stimulated by our perception of this detail, we feel the whole story of Hector's own death flooding back with a fullness and a pressure that Virgil could not achieve by any explicit statement without destroying the narrative tempo.

Or take Priam's words to Neoptolemus, who has just killed Priam's son before his eyes (ii, 540-3);

> 'at non ille, satum quo te mentiris, Achilles
> talis in hoste fuit Priamo. sed iura fidemque
> supplicis erubuit corpusque exsangue sepulcro
> reddidit Hectoreum meque in mea regna remisit.'

> *'You lie when you claim Achilles was your father: he did
> not treat his enemy Priam so. Shamed, he acknowledged
> my suppliant's right to claim for burial Hector's body;
> restored it, life poured from it, sent the royal father home.'*

Our recollection is summoned of the compassion with which Achilles at the end of the *Iliad* received the grief-stricken Priam when he came to beg for the body of his son. Neoptolemus has shown, by his brutal disregard for Priam's feelings, that he is no son of such a father. Virgil's second sentence does not so much retell the story (retold so briefly it has little emotional impact on us) as guide us back to the reminiscence, so that allusion can do its work.

The most interesting type is that in which the new context implies a reversal of attitude, a correction of Homer. In the *Odyssey* the killing of Deiphobus is recounted with brief gusto as one of the manly exploits of Odysseus. In *Aeneid* vi, it is set against the initial picture of Deiphobus' mangled body as yet another instance of the barbarous brutality of the Greeks, and the role of Odysseus reduced to that of the contemptible accomplice (*comes additus una hortator scelerum*, vi, 528-9) of Menelaus. Naturally the story is seen from the Trojan side, but there is

Allusion

more to it than that: we feel in these passages the contrast between Virgil's melancholy revulsion at violence in an age that was sick of violence and Homer's neutral acceptance of it.

Another type uses allusion to create a fresh emotional context. When Dares comes forward as challenger in the boxing-match in *Aeneid* v, his name elicits two allusive touches (v, 370–4):

> solus qui Paridem solitus contendere contra,
> idemque ad tumulum quo maximus occubat Hector
> uictorem Buten immani corpore, qui se
> Bebrycia ueniens Amyci de gente ferebat,
> perculit et fulua moribundum extendit harena.

> *He was the only man who would take on Paris in a fight, and it was he, by the grave where mighty Hector sleeps, knocked out giant champion Butes (who had come, passing himself off as descended from Amycus of Bebrycia), and sent him sprawling on the yellow sand, as good as dead.*

After the quick implicit correction of Homer in the first line (we see a more manly Paris), the allusion to the grave of Hector at this point in Virgil's story is aimed less at stirring our memories of Homer than at making us understand how the Trojan exiles who are watching Dares must feel. On this festive day in Sicily they have temporarily forgotten their past. The sight of Dares with gloves again on his fists bring it all back. And then comes the thought that mighty Hector sleeps now outside a city that does not exist, linked only by memories with Aeneas' men and their present fate.

Finally, allusion may aim (apart from its central purpose of adding solidity to the story) at conciliating the reader by the fullness of his response. The real winner of the archery contest in *Aeneid* v, for example, Eurytion, is introduced as the brother of Pandarus (v, 495–7):

> . . . tuus, o clarissime, frater,
> Pandare, qui quondam iussus confundere foedus
> in medios telum torsisti primus Achiuos.

The Tempo of Virgilian Epic

> . . . *your brother, famous Pandarus*
> (*you they told that time to wreck the truce, when
> you fired first shot slap into the Achaeans*).

The reader who catches none of the allusions simply feels that Eurytion's prestige is somehow enhanced. The reader who remembers the role of Pandarus in breaking the truce in the *Iliad* (iv, 85ff.) is likely to appreciate, too, the rather Alexandrian way in which the build-up is underplayed. The words *telum torsisti* do not even make it clear that Pandarus was an archer, but in Homer there is an elaborate description of Pandarus' bow and the shot he fired to break the truce. And *iussus*, too, underplays the allusion—'ordered' is mysteriously vague: it was the goddess Athene, disguised as a comrade, who persuaded Pandarus to take a sniping shot at Menelaus. This is the sort of pleasure recognizing an Homeric simile behind one of Virgil's offers. At the same time Virgil's story acquires depth, without sacrifice of the narrative tempo.

The Narrative Sentence: Tenses

Despite his reliance upon the techniques of allusion, suggestion and implication, Virgil's story is still very long. In the actual telling of it devices are needed to maintain and vary the tempo, so that it neither flags nor becomes monotonous. Virgil's narrative sentence ranges constantly from staccato statement of essentials, notes for a sentence, almost, rather than a rounded sentence, to sustained, flowing narrative period. The middle and commonest course is a series of simple narrative statements linked by co-ordinating *and*'s. In the longer sentence he favours certain distinctive patterns in the arrangement of the steps in a narrative.

One of the major problems of the longer narrative sentence is to secure freshness in the temporal clause. Virgil, as we have seen, avoids the *cum* and pluperfect subjunctive of contemporary prose. He prefers *ut* for the lightly sketched-in recapitulation of preliminaries to the main action of his sentence. The rather grander *postquam* is used for the more significant step forward, or the more complete break with what went before. The opening lines of Book III are an example:

The Narrative Sentence: Tenses

Postquam res Asiae Priamique euertere gentem
immeritam uisum superis, ceciditque superbum
Ilium et omnis humo fumat Neptunia Troia,
diuersa exsilia et desertas quaerere terras
auguriis agimur diuum.   5

After the overthrow of Asia and Priam's undeserving house
by decision of the gods above, after proud Ilium's
fall when Neptune's Troy was all a smoking ruin,
a life of exile in all manner of distant, empty lands
the gods to us in prophecy commended.

He is fond of 'inverted' *cum* and an emphatic *donec* 'until' clause (usually with the perfect indicative) to round off a longish narrative sentence.[1]

Virgil's use of the narrative tenses to vary and enliven the tempo of his story is an aspect of his technique that has not received the attention it deserves.[2] He has four tenses at his disposal: the perfect indicative, the historic present indicative, the imperfect indicative, and the historic infinitive—leaving out of account the pluperfect indicative. Two of the four call for little comment. The historic infinitive serves as no more than an occasional variation by comparison with the other tenses—three or four examples (perhaps all together) per book.[3] In force it resembles the imperfect, denoting a process or state of affairs consequent upon action rather than action. The imperfect indicative represents a rather more frequent departure from the basic narrative tempo, which is built upon variation and

---

[1] We saw in Chapter 5 that Tacitus imitates this.

[2] The variation between historic present and perfect is seldom noticed by commentators, most often neglected in reference grammars, or at best made the subject of inaccurate generalization. The only systematic attempt to deal with the historic present known to me is that in Kühner-Stegmann, *Ausführliche Grammatik der lateinischen Sprache, Satzlehre*, Vol. i (3rd edn. 1955), pp. 111–17: they remark that in verse the historic present is the normal narrative tense and the perfect used mainly for convenience, but add the perceptive observation:

> aber es lässt sich auch nicht verkennen, dass die Dichter (besonders Vergil) das Perfekt als ungewöhnliches tempus gern zur Hervorhebung bedeutsamer Momente eintreten lassen.

The examples given, however, do not probe the question at all deeply. Cf. the brief remarks of E. Norden, *Vergilius, Aeneis VI* (2nd edn. 1915), p. 113 on 3ff.

[3] See Williams, p. 166.

The Tempo of Virgilian Epic

contrast between the two main narrative tenses, the perfect and the historic present.

The commonest narrative tense is the historic present, though it does not preponderate in Virgil's narrative to the extent implied by some reference grammars. The overall proportion of historic present to perfect in the actual narrative fabric of the poem (excluding dialogue, similes, flash-backs and other interpolations, but including description strictly within the narrative) is about three to one. The incidence of perfects rises markedly, however, with an increase in the excitement or the complexity of the narrative.[1]

We see this clearly if we take as an example the three sections of *Aeneid* ii. In the first section, the story of the wooden horse and the preliminaries to disaster, the narrative moves quickest and quietest, mainly in the present tense. In the central section, the story of the night of fighting, where the variation in tempo is much more marked, the proportion of perfects rises to the normal level for sustained narrative, about three to one. In the final section the proportion of perfects is even higher, in keeping with the greater structural complexity of this section. There are more imperfects, too.

Virgil's use of the two main narrative tenses shows a marked and individual refinement on the practice of his predecessors. The historic present is not used at all by Homer (as a literary device it appears to have been invented by Herodotus) and it remained unexploited in Greek epic.[2] On the other hand, Homer makes freer use of the aspectual contrast between aorist and imperfect than the nature of the Latin tenses permitted. Variation is also possible in Homer between augmented and un-

---

[1] A count of the narrative tenses in Book V gives 308 presents to 108 perfects; in Book II there are 243 presents to 82 perfects. The figures are necessarily rather arbitrary. Forms which, out of context, could be either present or perfect (*soluit*, etc.) can usually be assigned the tense of other verbs in the immediate context. A breakdown of the three past tenses in the narrative section of Book II, arranged according to the three sections of the book, looks like this:

	Present:	Perfect:	Imperfect:
Section I (to 267)	76	11	5
Section II (to 633)	122	44	13
Section III (to 804)	45	27	19
	243	82	37

[2] See J. Humbert, *Syntaxe grecque* (2nd edn. 1954), pp. 137-8.

The Narrative Sentence: Tenses

augmented past tenses. Latin epic, however, uses the historic present from the beginning, though it is hard to tell from the fragments that survive what principles guided the practice of the first epic poets. Catullus in his hexameter epyllion, Poem 64, is clearly conscious of the stylistic possibilities of a variation in the narrative tenses, but his practice differs completely from Virgil's.[1] The main structure of the narrative has perfect verbs.[2] Only in one short passage do we find anything approaching Virgil's alternation of tenses within a single piece of narrative.[3]

The effect of the historic present is to represent past action as actually taking place before the narrator's eyes—a description of action rather than action reported. It represents, of course, the literary use of a very common device of conversational narrative. The perfect has more than one use—at least three in Virgil. The relationship between the different uses is elusive, to be accounted for in part perhaps by the double origin of the form, which morphologically, is both a true perfect and an aorist.

In a narrative otherwise uniformly conducted in the historic present we find, not uncommonly, an isolated verb in the perfect, apparently with the force of a genuine perfect—for example (ii, 252–3):

> fusi per moenia Teucri
> conticuere; sopor fessos complectitur artus.

> *Sprawled in their fortress the Trojans*
> *have fallen silent; sleep clasps their tired limbs.*[4]

Much more frequent is the *instantaneous* use of the perfect: a perfect breaking into a series of presents (occasionally imperfects)

---

[1] Catullus makes much freer use of imperfects and of reported action: e.g., the section preceding Ariadne's speech, 124–31, is all infinitives and participles.

[2] Except for one section, the bridge passage between the first wedding-day scene and a description of the picture of Ariadne on the beach (31–67). These 37 lines contains 29 historic presents, 2 perfects and a concluding imperfect.

[3] The infinitives of 124–31: perfect, present, present, perfect.

[4] Another example probably is to be found in v, 680–2:

> sed non idcirco flammae atque incendia uiris
> indomitas *posuere*; udo sub robore *uiuit*
> stuppa uomens tardum fumum, etc.

to denote sudden, abrupt action.[1] The present being a descriptive tense, expressing, as we have said, what is going on before the narrator's eyes, and the imperfect the past equivalent of this, neither is suited to the expression of an action begun and completed in an instant. Such instantaneous perfects in Virgil are common, but usually occur in isolation, or in groups of two or three perfects at most. The effect may be very vivid. For example, the battle scene in *Aeneid* xii, 289–310, is conducted throughout in historic presents (eighteen of them) —except for a sentence in the middle, describing how Corynaeus dashed a smouldering brand from the altar in Ebysus' face:

> olli ingens barba reluxit   300
> nidoremque ambusta dedit.

> *His great beard burst into*
> *flame with a sudden stench of burning.*

The inherent aptness of the perfect *reluxit* for expressing a sudden flash of flame is increased by the unexpected change of tense; the perfect *nidorem . . . dedit* expresses the sudden odour of singeing.[2]

Most examples of the instantaneous perfect are of this kind. It is the tense used, for example, of Laocoon abruptly hurling a spear at the wooden horse and the sinister noises produced when it struck (ii, 50–3). Or the tense used when the wooden horse stuck in the gateway as the happy Trojans were drawing it into the doomed city (ii, 243). More interesting is the

---

[1] In ii, 1–2,
> Conticuere omnes intentique ora tenebant.
> inde toro pater Aeneas sic orsus ab alto,

conticuere, followed by *tenebant* (imperfect) and *orsus* (= perfect), is *instantaneous*: 'all fell silent', i.e. there was a sudden hush as Aeneas began to speak. Both here and in ii, 252 (just quoted) the preverb *con-* denotes the *action* of falling silent (as opposed to the *state* of silence, denoted by the simple verb *tacere*); in ii, 252 the force of the perfect is what grammarians sometimes call *resultative* (silence reached), here *ingressive* (silence beginning).

[2] Some see in these instantaneous perfects the influence of the Greek instantaneous aorist. They can equally well be regarded as true perfects—just as in English, in an animated commentary on a race, say, ('they're coming fast up the straight', etc.) the commentator may lapse into a perfect tense to describe something sudden or unexpected ('X has fallen').

The Narrative Sentence: Tenses

description of the beginning of the boat-race in *Aeneid* v, and the simile of a chariot-race that supports it:

> inde ubi clara dedit sonitum tuba, finibus omnes,
> haud mora, prosiluere suis; ferit aethera clamor   140
> nauticus, adductis spumant freta uersa lacertis.
> infindunt pariter sulcos, totumque dehiscit
> conuulsum remis rostrisque tridentibus aequor.
> non tam praecipites biiugo certamine campum
> corripuere ruuntque effusi carcere currus,   145
> nec sic immissis aurigae undantia lora
> concussere iugis pronique in uerbera pendent.

*Then when the clear trumpet sounded, from their starting-point
all bounded straightway forward. An uproar of sailors strikes
the air, arms strain in a stroke that turns water to foam.
In line they plough forward, the whole stretch of water
yawns, churned by oars and three-pronged prows.
Not like this the sudden bound onto the track of the racing
chariots that stream along once poured out of the starting pen.
Not like this the charioteers' sudden jerk of the snaking reins
over teams that then, stretched forward, they belabour with whip.*

Virgil's purpose is to stress in both scene and simile the contrast between the abrupt springing into action of the contestants and the continuity of the action that follows. There is the sudden trumpet-peal (*dedit sonitum*), the sudden surge forward from the starting-line (*prosiluere*); then the protracted uproar (*ferit clamor*), the continuous disturbance in the water (*spumant, infindunt, dehiscit*). Likewise the charioteers hurl themselves on the track from the starting pens (*corripuere*), then race on along the track (*ruunt*); there is the sudden slap of the reins on the horses' backs to get them under way (*concussere*), and then the continuous urging on (*in uerbera pendent*).[1]

The instantaneous perfect produces a momentary marked change in the narrative tempo. It seems probable it was the

---

[1] The use of the perfect tense in the simile seems strange to us in English, because the chariot-race is not, like the boat-race, a past event. It depends, perhaps, on the *gnomic* use of the perfect in such cases, though its force here is clearly instantaneous.

The Tempo of Virgilian Epic

effectiveness of this device that led Virgil to experiment with the use of the perfect on a more sustained scale—not for the single isolated action, but for a whole section of the narrative where he wished to vary the tempo. The section in perfects no longer necessarily relates actions more abrupt than those surrounding them. The narrative simply acquires a greater rapidity of movement, the object of which may be to increase excitement or to produce the opposite effect: a break in the excitement while details of minor importance are run through quickly.

For example, in the narrative of the first encounter between Aeneas and Mezentius (*Aeneid* x, 762–802) the main line of narrative runs again in historic presents. But at 783–6 we have three perfects, relating how Aeneas' spear pierced Mezentius' shield and inflicted a minor wound. The three perfects do not describe things that happen with especial speed. Indeed the action in both the preceding sentence and that following is more quick-moving. The effect of the perfects is rather to create a parenthesis on a different emotional level. The narrator's voice drops, as it were, for a moment from a level of excited description to tell us quickly and tersely the effects of the blow, and then the tone of excited description is resumed.

The device enables Virgil to break up a long narrative section into blocks. The change of tense represents the kind of change in tempo and emotional level that an experienced reader makes in reading sustained narrative, in order to avoid monotony. We have a good simple example in the description of the Troy game in Sicily (v, 553–602). After twenty-four lines of precise description in the historic present of the opening march-past, ending with the round of applause with which the riders are greeted, comes a short block of six lines containing six perfects. This section, at a quicker tempo and a more restrained emotional level, briefly recounts the complicated manoeuvres with which the performance begins—a respite in the excitement before the description of the actual battle-game, for which the historic present is resumed.

The imperfect indicative may also be used to vary the tempo of the narrative. It can, for example, mark the change from detailed narrative, where much is related as happening within a short space of time, to more slow-moving narrative. A good

The Narrative Sentence: Tenses

example is the story of the settlement Aeneas and his men established in Crete and the pestilence which eventually forced them to leave (iii, 132–46). The opening lines are full of action, the *preparations* for construction. The tenses are historic presents. A change comes at line 137. The *process* of construction is about to get under way. This is marked by a single imperfect. Then abruptly the work is suspended by the sudden outbreak of a mysterious disease (instantaneous perfect):

> subito cum tabida membris   137
> corrupto caeli tractu miserandaque uenit
> arboribusque satisque lues et letifer annus.

> *Suddenly to waste our limbs*
> *from a corrupt quarter of the sky there came to trees*
> *and crops a hideous disease and a year of death.*

Then come three lines describing the months of pestilence (*letifer annus*): the narrative occupies only three lines, but the tempo is retarded by four imperfects and an historic infinitive. After that the tempo quickens again: the decision is taken that something must be done. A single historic present (*hortatur pater*) cuts this section off from what precedes. The change of tense makes it clear, without further comment, that what Virgil means is not that Anchises 'kept on urging' Aeneas to act, but that he 'finally urged' him to act. With it thus established that a single occasion is meant, the imperfect *nox erat*, 'it was night', which begins the next sentence (line 147) is also defined without need of further explanation: it is the night after Anchises advised Aeneas to do something to stop the pestilence that the Penates appeared to Aeneas in his sleep. Often, as here, the change in tempo produced by the change in tense fixes the meaning as much as any inherent force of the tense itself.

The other main use of the imperfect is to set the background to action. The contrast here may be between imperfect and perfect, or between imperfect and historic present. Virgil often uses these narrative resources with great delicacy within the space of a few lines, sometimes within a single sentence. Here are the opening lines of *Aeneid* v:

The Tempo of Virgilian Epic

Interea medium Aeneas iam classe tenebat
certus iter fluctusque atros Aquilone secabat
moenia respiciens, quae iam infelicis Elissae
conlucent flammis. quae tantum accenderit ignem
causa latet; duri magno sed amore dolores 5
polluto, notumque furens quid femina possit,
triste per augurium Teucrorum pectora ducunt.
ut pelagus tenuere rates nec iam amplius ulla
occurrit tellus, maria undique et undique caelum,
olli caeruleus supra caput astitit imber 10
noctem hiememque ferens et inhorruit unda tenebris.

*Meanwhile Aeneas was holding his fleet, now well under way,
upon its course, resolutely biting into waves blackened by the
northerly,
gazing back at walls on which the fire unhappy Dido lit
sheds flickering flames. What caused so great a conflagration
remains obscure; but, aware how harsh the grief when great
love is poisoned, and what a frenzied woman may essay,
the Trojans feel foreboding of disaster pervade their hearts.
When the ships reached the open sea and land no more coursed up
at their approach—everywhere the ocean, everywhere the sky—
a sombre blue squall took up position just above his head,
bringing night and storm, and the water shuddered at the dark.*

The book begins quietly: an evening scene viewed from a distance. A fleet in movement (imperfects *tenebat, secabat*). In line 3 the present participle *respiciens* picks out the figure of Aeneas whose presence as commander we no more than sensed in the first two lines (*tenebat* and *secabat* imply no particular action on his part). The historic present *conlucent* in line 4 almost startles us. We have that feeling which we get in a film when the camera, after steadily tracking closer to a scene, suddenly is close enough for us to feel we are not viewing the scene from a distance, but are present in it. The second sentence of the book (two historic presents) studies Aeneas and his men and their feelings as though from close up. Then the third sentence switches to perfects and fast-moving narrative:[1] they reach

---

[1] Reckoning *occurrit* as perfect.

The Death of Priam (ii, 506–58)

the open sea, the remainder of the day passes, and with evening comes storm.

The Death of Priam (ii, 506–58)

It is difficult to discuss the structure of Virgilian narrative if we confine ourselves to short examples. We need to consider a complete episode to appreciate the interplay of the narrative tenses. At the same time we can point to some of the structural devices Virgil makes use of to reduce his story to manageable shape—and yet create the illusion of unending ramifications.

The account of the death of King Priam (ii, 506–58) stands outside the basic, fast-moving narrative structure of Book II. Within that structure Priam is already dead before our episode begins, his death related with the terse rapidity appropriate to the main structure:

> uidi ipse furentem
> caede Neoptolemum geminosque in limine Atridas,   500
> uidi Hecubam centumque nurus Priamumque per aras
> sanguine foedantem quos ipse sacrauerat ignis.

> *I saw Neoptolemus myself*
> *murder-mad in the doorway, the Atrid brothers with him.*
> *I saw Hecuba, the hundred princesses, Priam by the altar,*
> *defiling with his blood the fire he himself had consecrated.*

Aeneas now comes back on what he has already told, at a slower tempo, with the words

> forsitan et Priami fuerint quae fata requiras.   506

> *You ask perhaps how Priam met his destined end.*

Before we examine the account Aeneas proceeds to give, let us consider what the reader has so far been told of Priam. It does not in fact amount to a great deal. All the same, when the old king at last comes to the foreground, a pattern of interweaving makes him seem a familiar figure. His name has cropped up a dozen times in the poem. Most often it has been no more than a glancing reference. An exception was the Sinon episode. There we saw the refugee appeal directly to Priam

The Tempo of Virgilian Epic

(ii, 141) and the old king assume command of the situation.[1] Since then the night's fighting has brought Aeneas inevitably to the royal palace and progressively closer to Priam.

This is the sort of picture we have when Aeneas' detailed narrative of Priam's death begins. It starts on a quiet but rising note, as we look back over the last 250 lines of the main narrative through Priam's eyes:

> urbis uti captae casum conuulsaque uidit   507
> limina tectorum et medium in penetralibus hostem . . .

> *When he saw the captured city's fall, the palace-gate*
> *hacked down, the enemy within the central shrine . . .*

The three predicates of the *ut uidit* clause are arranged in an increasing triad, each longer than its predecessor and each more precise and emotionally stronger: first the city taken, then Priam's palace overrun, then the enemy within the inner sanctuary itself—one can feel Priam's despairing anger mount.[2] Note incidentally how the delayed *uidit* binds the first and second members of the triad together. They are arranged in a chiasmus: dependent genitive followed by object (*urbis captae casum*), then object followed by dependent genitive (*conuulsa limina tectorum*). The tense is perfect, as often in temporal clauses when their function is to set the stage for the main action.

The narrative now slides into graphic description and historic presents. Priam determines to die fighting—no more able than Aeneas to resist the useless heroic gesture:

> arma diu senior desueta trementibus aeuo
> circumdat nequiquam umeris et inutile ferrum   510
> cingitur, ac densos fertur moriturus in hostis.

> *the old man upon shoulders age-enfeebled sets*
> *unavailing armour long unused, straps on futile*
> *steel, makes for the invading horde, there to die.*

---

[1] Priam figures, too, fairly prominently in the scenes from the Trojan war that Aeneas saw depicted on the temple at Carthage (i, 455 ff.).

[2] See the introductory section of this chapter for a discussion of Virgil's use of *ut uidit* clauses.

The Death of Priam (ii, 506-58)

Each of the two really descriptive words, *circumdat* and *cingitur*, is emphasized by its position at the beginning of the line, the sense flowing over from the previous line. The picture of determined activity these verbs conjure up forms an ironic contrast with the dominant note of futility. The first of these three lines is loaded with words suggesting age and feebleness: *senior* (he is an old man), *diu desueta* (his armour feels strange— it is so long since he last fought in battle), *trementibus aeuo* (his limbs shake with age). In the next line we pass from implication to plain statement: *nequiquam, inutile* (an old man's attempt at heroics is bound to fail).

His narrative already in motion, Virgil now suspends it while he fills in the details of the scene:[1]

> aedibus in mediis nudoque sub aetheris axe
> ingens ara fuit iuxtaque ueterrima laurus
> incumbens arae atque umbra complexa penatis.
> hic Hecuba et natae nequiquam altaria circum   515
> praecipites atra ceu tempestate columbae
> condensae et diuum amplexae simulacra sedebant.

> *At the palace centre, bare to the pole of heaven,*
> *a great altar stood, beside a most ancient laurel*
> *leant upon the altar and clasped the Penates in its shade.*
> *Here Hecuba and her daughters round the unavailing shrine*
> *like doves clustered in refuge from black storm*
> *huddled together sat, clutching the images of their gods.*

Three lightly end-stopped lines, each of the first two with a clearly marked caesura, move in more closely upon the scene as they proceed, the third line flowing on to fill out this crisp statement of detail. The perfect verb (*fuit*) emphasizes more clearly than an imperfect could that this is something over and done with. Then, after these slow-moving lines, three that flow on with hardly a pause, held together by the simile which is woven in by a double ambiguity of construction: *praecipites* ('clustered in refuge') refers to Hecuba and her daughters as

---

[1] For another example of the same device, see v, 124–31: the contestants in the boat-race are already rowing up to the starting-line, then the narrative is suspended while the turning-point is described.

The Tempo of Virgilian Epic

much as to the doves; *condensae* ('huddled together') refers to the doves as much as to Hecuba and her daughters. The tone is one of quiet description (imperfect *sedebant*), but with an overtone of disaster introduced by the menacing echo, *nequiquam*, repeated from five lines above.

Our attention now reverts to Priam, whom we left about to join the fighting (*fertur in hostis*). He is restrained from making a useless gesture by his wife Hecuba. Omitting the dialogue and concerning ourselves only with the narrative, we have:

> ipsum autem sumptis Priamum iuuenalibus armis 518
> ut uidit, . . .
> . . . sic ore effata recepit
> ad sese et sacra longaeuum in sede locauit. 525

When she saw her Priam take up the armour his youth had known, . . .
. . . With these words she brought the old man back to her and seated him at the holy place.

The perfect tenses *uidit, recepit, locauit* indicate how Virgil wishes us to take the passage.[1] Quietly, gently Hecuba holds the old man back. It seems for a moment the crisis has passed.

The fighting, however, comes to Priam:

> ecce autem elapsus Pyrrhi de caede Polites, 526
> unus natorum Priami, per tela, per hostis
> porticibus longis fugit et uacua atria lustrat
> saucius.

Imagine then Polites just escaped from the murderous Pyrrhus, alone of Priam's sons. In a hail of enemy spears he comes down the long colonnade running, crosses the great empty hall, wounded.

We are back in the tempo of dramatic narrative, the scene related as though it were still present before the narrator's

[1] Leaving the present *inquit* in 520 out of consideration—Virgil regularly makes verbs introducing direct speech present—perhaps because direct speech always increases the excitement and slows up the action. The perfect or pluperfect (*dixit, dixerat*) is used to indicate the end of direct speech ('he had spoken'), not to introduce it.

The Death of Priam (ii, 506–58)

eyes (historic presents *fugit, lustrat*). Observe how the rattle of short syllables and sharp consonants in *porticibus longis fugit* suggests the clatter of Polites' feet along the paved colonnade; and how the single word *saucius* carried over to the following line suggests the breathless effort of the wounded man.

Virgil introduces Pyrrhus (also called Neoptolemus) without explanation, relying on a pattern of interweaving. We caught our first glimpse of him in line 263, climbing down from the wooden horse. We saw him next leading the assault on the palace (line 469)—a detail of the fighting fixed in our minds by the ensuing simile, in which he was likened to a venomous snake. A few lines later (line 500), we saw him burst into the palace with Agamemnon and Menelaus.[1] Polites, however, is named for the first time and allotted, therefore, a brief descriptive phrase. He is *unus natorum Priami*: *unus* (the word is always emphatic in Latin) reminds us that, of all the more famous sons of Priam and Hecuba, not one is there on this night of crisis to help his father. Except for Polites, old Priam has only his wife and daughters around him.[2] The detail is important. It explains a vital point in Virgil's story that would have seemed implausible if left unexplained: why Aeneas (a secondary member of the royal household and a minor character in Homer) was singled out by Hector to succeed him as protector of the Trojans.

Virgil has now two actors in the foreground of his narrative, Priam being reduced for the moment to the role of helpless onlooker. But as this is a poem, not a drama, and Virgil's medium words, not spectacle, it is impossible to present both contestants simultaneously. All Virgil can do is make the narrative alternate between them. He began with Polites, devoting three lines, in which Pyrrhus is no more than named, to a description of his headlong flight. Now he turns from pursued to pursuer, utilizing a device that we might perhaps call *parallel narrative*:[3]

---

[1] Virgil never mentions Agamemnon by name and Menelaus rarely, preferring to lump the two together in what one feels to be the slightly contemptuous collective *Atridae*. In *Aeneid* xi, 266–8, Agamemnon is alluded to in a grandiloquent periphrasis that lapses into something like a sneer.

[2] For subsequent interweaving involving Polites, see earlier in this chapter.

[3] Virgil's technique at this point is analysed with clarity and vigour by James Henry, *Aeneidea*, Vol. ii (1878), in his note on lines 526–32:

. . . there is another actor on the stage, whose action—although synchronous

The Tempo of Virgilian Epic

>illum ardens infesto uulnere Pyrrhus
>insequitur, iam iamque manu tenet et premit hasta.   530

>*Hot in pursuit, poised for a cruel blow Pyrrhus
>comes, at each stride his hand outstretched, his spear raised.*

As Polites runs along the portico out into the courtyard, Pyrrhus is just behind him.[1] The picture complete, our attention returns to Polites:

>ut tandem ante oculos euasit et ora parentum,   531
>concidit ac multo uitam cum sanguine fudit.

>*When at last he emerged, facing his parents, before their eyes
>he fell and poured his life out in a bloody stream.*

The transition from pursuit to death scene is marked by a change of tense (perfects *euasit, concidit, fudit*).[2] The change of tense marks, too, a change in tempo. The effect of the perfects is

---

[1] The phrase *infesto uulnere* is inclined to suffer from the habit of attaching stock English equivalents to Latin words: 'with hostile wound' sounds vaguely ridiculous. But *uulnus* is often used of what we should call 'a crippling blow' rather than the wound produced. In *infestus* the basic idea is that you mean business (perhaps 'menacing'). Cf. Caesar *B.C.* iii, 93, 1 (*infestis pilis*) and 5 (*infestis signis*), where 'hostile' is clearly not enough—any army is hostile to the enemy.

[2] Regarding the ambiguous form of *concidit* as perfect since it is preceded and followed by a perfect.

---

with that of Polites, yet being a distinct and different action—cannot be described synchronously, but must in description either precede, or follow, or be introduced in the middle. Being that of Polites' pursuer, it can neither precede nor follow; preceding, it would be unintelligible, impossible; following, it would be too late, the interest would be over. It is therefore placed in the middle, and the narrator suddenly leaves the one actor in the midst of his action, takes up and follows to the end the action of the second, and then returning to the action of the first proceeds . . . also to the end, to that point where the two actions which had all along been synchronous terminate together. . . . readers, misled by the rapidity of transition, have fallen into the mistake of connecting together as parts or consequences of one action things which were parts or consequences of another. It is by such mistake arising from such cause that in our text UT TANDEM . . . CONCIDIT has been taken with PREMIT HASTA, and Polites supposed to die not in consequence of his original wound, the wound of which when he first came into view he was already SAUCIUS, but in consequence of a new wound inflicted on him at the end of the chase, and imagined to be found described in PREMIT HASTA. . . .

As Henry points out, the narrative of the attack on Priam's palace has alternated between description of besiegers and description of besieged.

For the use of parallel narrative by Tacitus, see Chapter 5.

The Death of Priam (ii, 506–58)

complex. They suggest partly how quickly the end comes. No further blow is needed, Polites simply collapses and dies. At the same time it is as if we heard the narrator's voice drop, as though it were indecent to describe death with the same animation as the pursuit.

The perfect remains the basic tense for the rest of the episode, sustaining this note of restrained, tight-lipped statement of horror. There is in fact little action before the final narrative sentence (lines 550–3). Till then the drama lies in the dialogue between Pyrrhus and Priam, upon which the perfects serve as a terse, quietly-spoken commentary.

Our attention switches from the dead Polites to his father:

> hic Priamus, quamquam in media iam morte tenetur, 533
> non tamen abstinuit nec uoci iraeque pepercit.

Then Priam (though death is now closing its grip upon him) made no effort to check his voice or restrain his indignation.

In the explanatory *quamquam* clause, where a continuous tense is necessary, Virgil chooses the more dramatic historic present instead of the imperfect. Somehow the narrator's tone rises in this parenthesis. It contains a comment on the situation rather than a report on a step in the action. The effect is of an outburst of feeling accompanying the realization, 'Priam is going to be killed'.

Priam's angry outburst (introduced by a present *exclamat*)[1] seals his fate. Here occur the lines studied earlier in this chapter as an example of allusion (lines 540–3), in which Priam contrasts Pyrrhus' brutality with the civilized compassion shown him by Pyrrhus' father Achilles. The emotions aroused by his own words provoke Priam to a gesture of defiance:

> sic fatus senior telumque imbelle sine ictu
> coniecit, rauco quod protinus aere repulsum,   545
> et summo clipei nequiquam umbone pependit.

With these words the old man cast his harmless spear, no force behind it. Checked quickly with a brassy clang it hung unavailing, lodged in the shield's centre.

[1] For the present tense introducing direct speech, see above.

The Tempo of Virgilian Epic

When at the beginning of the episode Priam gathered up his weapons in order to die fighting, though warned of the futility of his gesture, we could hardly have foreseen how utterly futile it would prove. The third *nequiquam* drives the point home. These lines contain the first real action since line 532—a single action studied in three aspects: the faltering throw of the spear, the harsh clang on the shield, the spear hanging useless.

Pyrrhus' brief reply, full of panache and heartless self-confidence, flashes out, rising to a climax in the contemptuous rhetoric of the four-word hexameter:

>   cui Pyrrhus: 'referes ergo haec et nuntius ibis
>   Pelidae genitori. illi mea tristia facta
>   degeneremque Neoptolemum narrare memento.
>   nunc morere!'   550

To him Pyrrhus, 'Here's an errand you can run: repeat your story
to my father Achilles. Give him the whole sorry tale
of me, Neoptolᵒmus, the degenerate. Don't forget to tell.
Now die!'

For the administration of the death-blow and the steps leading up to it we might expect the staccato phrases and the vivid historic presents Virgil more usually employs in dramatic narrative. That was his technique in describing how Pyrrhus burst into the palace earlier:

>   instat ui patria Pyrrhus; nec claustra nec ipsi
>   custodes sufferre ualent; labat ariete crebro
>   ianua, et emoti procumbunt cardine postes.
>   fit uia ui; rumpunt aditus primosque trucidant
>   immissi Danai et late loca milite complent.   495

Pyrrhus fights forward like his father of old: bars, guards
even, are powerless to check him; ceaselessly battered,
the door totters and the uprights give, torn from their sockets.
Nothing resists brute force; bursting inside, the Greeks
butcher the first rank of defenders, pack the palace with soldiers.

But there the note of urgent excitement came from the situation as a whole. The individual acts were not more dreadful

The Death of Priam (ii, 506-58)

than war necessitates. It was legitimate, therefore, for the narrator, watching the scene of horror to which the individual actions contributed, to heighten our excitement by revealing his own. Here the actions can be left to speak for themselves. Each individual act is horrible. Virgil therefore continues to use the restrained perfects which he began using at line 531. And, instead of a staccato, disjointed narrative, he gives us a long, tightly-woven sentence that binds the successive actions together in a complex picture.

Three brusque, ruthless actions precede the death-blow:

> hoc dicens altaria ad ipsa trementem   550
> traxit et in multo lapsantem sanguine nati,
> implicuitque comam laeua, dextraque coruscum
> extulit ac lateri capulo tenus abdidit ensem.

So speaking he dragged the shaking Priam,
slithering in his own son's blood, right to the altar;
twined left hand in Priam's hair; with right, in a flash of steel
drew and hilt-deep in Priam's ribs plunged his sword.

The first verb *traxit* is preceded and followed by participles (*trementem, lapsantem*), telling us what we need to know of the old man's appearance and movements while keeping Pyrrhus the subject of all four finite verbs. His second action, *implicuit*, is carried on into the third by the chiasmatic arrangement of *laeua* and *dextra*, implying the simultaneous action of left and right hand. But the final action, the blow, follows hard upon the drawing of the sword. Both actions, therefore, are bound together by the epithet *coruscum*, which precedes its noun by more than a line, epithet and noun forming a further chiasmus— epithet-verb : verb-noun (*coruscum extulit : abdidit ensem*).[1]

Priam's brief epitaph follows:

> haec finis Priami fatorum, hic exitus illum
> sorte tulit Troiam incensam et prolapsa uidentem   555
> Pergama, tot quondam populis terrisque superbum
> regnatorem Asiae.

---

[1] Similarly Tacitus uses the perfect tense in the concluding steps of the murder of Agrippina (see Chapter 5).

The Tempo of Virgilian Epic

*Such was Priam's fated end, destined in death's hour
to see Troy blazing, to see Pergamum fall destroyed—
he who once over many peoples, many lands, had proudly
ruled in Asia.*

Then a final sentence:

> iacet ingens litore truncus,   557
> auulsumque umeris caput et sine nomine corpus.

*A great trunk lies on the beach,
a head torn from its shoulders, a body without a name.*

The present tense comes as a surprise after the long run of perfects until we realize how much Virgil succeeds in conveying. First of all, the present tense brings us back to the point (line 506) where Aeneas broke off, with Priam already dead, to give us this detailed recapitulatory narrative of his death. The return to the main narrative is smoothed by the intervening epitaph sentence. By now, it is implied, Pyrrhus and the invaders have swept on. Priam's corpse has been trampled over and its identity forgotten. But the present tense also stands outside time, as though, when Aeneas tells his story to Dido years later, the corpse lay there still upon the devastated beach where once Troy stood—the *campos ubi Troia fuit* of iii, 11, from which all the living, Greeks and Trojans, have long ago withdrawn. It is one of those sentences that illustrate the difference between poetry and prose. Restated with the calm logic of prose, what Virgil has tried to convey sounds at best fanciful, at worst simply untrue. But poetry can sometimes disregard logic: time ceases to have anything to do with the picture impressed on Aeneas' mind, and on ours, of Priam's mighty, headless corpse.[1]

---

[1] It has been suggested that Virgil wishes to imply as well an allusion to the corpse of Pompey murdered in Egypt after Pharsalus.

9

Persistence of a Theme: The Propempticon

THE propempticon, or *bon voyage* poem, marks the forthcoming departure of a friend, expressing the poet's mixed feelings—he wants to rejoice for his friend's sake, but is sad, too, at losing him.[1] It seems an obvious enough form, but we have to remember how late a development this sort of easy, intimate personal poem is in ancient literature. The use of a Greek name is apt to mislead.[2] For, though in Greek we find the theme adumbrated from the earliest period (Calypso's parting words to Odysseus, for example),[3] we get nothing

---

[1] Though the term is often used, the propempticon does not appear to have been made the object of any detailed study since Felix Jäger's *Das antike Propemptikon und das 17. Gedicht des Paulinus von Nola* (Diss. München, 1913). The first two chapters (pp. 4–36) contain an excellent brief summary of the history of the classical Greek and Latin propempticon. More information may be found in studies of particular poems, especially G. L. Hendrickson, 'Horace's Propempticon to Virgil', *C.J.*, iii (1908), pp. 100–4, and other discussions of this ode (i, 3), e.g., Pasquali, pp. 260–78, and Heinze, pp. 19–20. Among numerous brief discussions may be mentioned L. R. Palmer's article in the *Oxford Classical Dictionary*, and Luigi Alfonsi's note, 'Sui propemptici' in *Poetae novi* (1945), pp. 193–5.

[2] The label 'propempticon' has more ancient authority than some other names used by critics as labels for ancient poetic genres (e.g., epyllion), but is current only among late Greek writers whose recognition of the genre is based on their familiarity with its development at Rome: the scholiast on Aristophanes, *Knights*, 498, Stephanus of Byzantium, *s.v.* Κώροκος, and Menander Rhet., Spengel, *Rhet. Graeci*, iii, p. 397.

[3] *Odyssey* v, 203ff.; cf. *Od.* xv, 125–9 (Menelaus' farewell to Telemachus).

Persistence of a Theme: the Propempticon

like a real propempticon till we come to Hellenistic times—and then only a couple of very unpretentious pieces.[1]

All the half dozen Roman poems from Propertius to Statius to which the label is customarily applied are on a more ambitious scale.[2] Horace's farewell to Virgil, *Odes* i, 3 (*Sic te diua potens Cypri* . . .) seems typical of what became at Rome the basic pattern. Like the other Roman poems, it represents the exploration at a sophisticated and consciously literary level of a theme which possessed humbler origins. The term propempticon serves as no more than a preliminary classification: though we shall see, once the lay-out was settled, the form and some of the clichés appropriate to it displayed a remarkable tendency to persist.

The Roman propemptica and their Hellenistic antecedents provide one more illustration of the difference between occasional verse and poetry. Catullus in Latin might have given us an example of an occasional propempticon. His *bon voyage* poem would have possessed, we may suppose, the warmth, simplicity and directness we find in Poem 9—not a propempticon, but the counterpart to one: a welcome-home poem. Partings, of course, arouse more complex emotions than home-comings. No doubt

---

[1] Jäger, op. cit., Chapter 1, cites a fragment of Sappho (frag. 94 L.-P.), one couplet of which (7–8) contains a suggestion of the propempticon theme, and a few lines from Aristophanes (*Knights*, 498–502) which (as the scholiast saw) contain the theme in embryo. A short lyric in an Idyll of Theocritus (vii, 52–62) and an epigram of Meleager (*A.P.* xii, 52) may be regarded as complete miniature propemptica. Fragments cited are Erinna (in Athen. vii, 283 d) and Callimachos (frag. 114 and 126)—each a couplet. Parthenius (a Greek contemporary of Catullus) seems to have written a more ambitious propempticon, but nothing survives.

[2] Surviving Latin propemptica include: Propertius i, 8 and perhaps ii, 26 (some echoes of the theme in i, 17); Horace, *Epodes* 1 and 10; *Odes* i, 3; iii, 27 (and perhaps i, 14—see R. C. Kukula, 'Quintilians Interpretation von Horaz' Carm. I 14', *Wiener Studien*, xxxiv [1912], pp. 237–45); Ovid *A.* ii, 11; Statius iii, 2; Tibullus i, 3, while not a propempticon, contains a number of echoes of the theme.

An early Latin development seems to have been the expansion of the propempticon into a kind of guide-book, telling the departing friend what he will see while abroad. Jäger suggests a connection with the Greek hymn to a departing divinity, where a list of places about to be visited was customary. He maintains that fragments of a satire of Lucilius (the one used by Horace for his 'Journey to Brundisium') belong to such a propempticon. At any rate a propempticon written by Catullus' friend, Cinna, to mark a journey to Greece and the East made in 56 B.C. by Asinius Pollio seems, to judge from the meagre fragments surviving, to have taken this form. See H. Bardon, *La littérature latine inconnue*, Vol. i (1952), p. 346. So, too, apparently did Parthenius' poem (see previous Note)—the poem is cited by Stephanus of Byzantium in his gazetteer. We shall see a trace of this theme in Ovid's propempticon.

Persistence of a Theme: the Propempticon

it is the greater opportunities for emotional conflict that led to the development of the *bon voyage* poem as a literary form far beyond the comparatively limited success of the welcome-home poem in Latin.[1]

The fact remains that no surviving Latin propempticon is a *bon voyage* poem pure and simple.[2] Of what value then is the label to the critic? Does it merely authorize an initial gesture of classification? A gesture moreover of which he should perhaps beware. For while classification by origin legitimately concerns the literary historian in his investigation of the genesis of forms, the literary critic should remember that the poet—if he is worth his salt—will contribute something of his own to the stock material. Unless we take into account his reshaping of tradition as well as his acceptance of what tradition offered him, we shall misjudge, and perhaps misprize, his poem.

We saw in Chapter 3 how an adherence to stock forms was natural during the infancy of the short personal poem in Latin. Some awareness of formal factors accepted and struggled against is clearly required in considering such transitional poems. The comparative study, however, of a number of poems by different writers, linked by traces of a common origin and by echoes, conscious or unconscious, of a traditional thematic development, suggests a method likely to stimulate ingenuity more than appreciation.

Its justification lies in the willing and unusually detailed acceptance of the formative force of a literary tradition displayed by the Roman propempticon, or at any rate by the three examples of the genre we shall consider in this chapter. We may compare the readiness with which Horace and all three elegists accepted what must seem to us a much more wooden and restricting form, the *paraclausithyron*: the serenade of complaint before the locked street-door of the poet's mistress.[3] Our three pieces are, of course, independent poems, not mere literary exercises. They are different in important, characteristic

---

[1] As examples of the literary exploration of the welcome-home theme, one may mention several odes of Horace: i, 36; ii, 7; iii, 14; and perhaps the political ode iv, 5.

[2] Statius comes nearest to this: his poem is a protracted exercise on the conventional clichés with little personal involvement or thematic originality.

[3] This history of the *paraclausithyron* as a poetic form has been studied in detail by F. O. Copley, *Exclusus amator* (1956).

Persistence of a Theme: the Propempticon

ways, despite the acceptance of a common basic pattern—and the oddly precise reproduction of some details of that pattern.

Propertius, the Passionate Lover (i, 8)

The three we shall discuss are all love poems—which introduces, of course, an additional formal limitation. Of the three, Propertius' Propempticon for Cynthia is probably the earliest in date. Another reason for taking it first is that of the three it follows closest what came to be regarded as the proper pattern for a propempticon. Who created the formula is a bit of a mystery. The best guess we can make (supported, we shall see, by an observation Servius made on Virgil's tenth Eclogue) is that Propertius followed the lay-out worked out by Cornelius Gallus in a propempticon he wrote for his mistress Lycoris about 40 B.C.—ten years or so before Propertius' poem. Horace's Propempticon for Virgil adopted a similar lay-out. So did others—and the genre was created.

At any rate the existence of rules remarkably like those we might deduce from these two poems (Gallus' poem is conjecture) is pointed to by an odd piece of evidence. Menander, a writer on rhetoric of the third century A.D. (a period when the rigid imitation of classical models was becoming fashionable), lays down these rules for a propempticon on the departure of a friend. First you announce your theme. Then you wax indignant (σχετλιάσεις) with the departing friend for his heartlessness in deserting you. Then you attempt to talk him out of going. Then you give in gracefully, and wish him well.[1]

To this formula Propertius adheres pretty strictly. The individual twist is provided by giving the poem an unforeseeable contrasting second half. In the first half, if one element in the formula is stressed at the expense of the others it is the poet's indignation. It is on that note that he begins:

> Tune igitur demens, nec te mea cura moratur?
> an tibi sum gelida uilior Illyria?
> et tibi iam tanti, quicumque est, iste uidetur,
> ut sine me uento quolibet ire uelis?

---

[1] Menander, Spengel, *Rhet. Graeci* iii, pp. 396–7. See Hendrickson, art. cit. He shows how Horace conforms to this pattern in *Odes* i, 3. The Menander passage is also quoted and discussed by Jäger, op. cit., pp. 11–15, and by Enk, p. 75.

Propertius, the Passionate Lover (i, 8)

This is madness then? Does affection not hold you back?
Do I mean less to you than Illyria's icy cold?
And he, whoever he is, so much apparently that you
would leave me, whatever winds prevail eager to depart?

Indignation is, however, held in check with a fine show of smouldering resignation. Propertius is playing the lover's role that we discussed in Chapter 6: aware intellectually of the lopsidedness of the affair, but passionately attached to the woman just the same, wanting only to be with her.

But first let us get the situation clear—a precaution commentators on the poem seldom take. The dramatic moment is fixed by the concluding words of the stanza:

> ut sine me uento quolibet *ire uelis?*

Cynthia is so infatuated with her new lover[1] that she is *eager to depart* (with him or to join him on the other side of the Adriatic —the detail is unimportant and left unstated). But the sailors on the ship on which she has taken passage (line 14 implies it is one of a convoy of ships) are not, like her, bereft of their senses: and they will not put to sea in winter, a season of storms when all regular navigation was suspended.

It is taken for granted that Cynthia's affection is not adequately returned by the man for whom she is throwing over whatever Propertius and Cynthia had come to mean to one another. For, though Propertius' love was the fiercer, we should not suppose he means us to think of Cynthia as utterly indifferent to him—until the other man came along. There is, I think, a nice double edge to *mea cura* in line 1 which I have tried to bring out by omitting the pronominal adjective. Primarily it is Propertius' affection for Cynthia; it might, he feels, have held her back. But we are meant to sense at the same time a little residual disillusionment in Propertius on realizing that she is not held back either by any affection for him.

We have in fact a nice reversal of the situation Propertius described in the introductory elegy to Book I (discussed in Chapter 6). This time it is Cynthia who is throwing over a *tutus amor* (i, 1, 32) for one that can bring her only misery. It

---
[1] He may be the praetor of Illyria who crops up in ii, 16.

Persistence of a Theme: the Propempticon

is her turn to fall victim to love's folly (*demens*, line 1). Propertius foresees what will happen, but cannot hope she will listen to him. He feels the helplessness the *amici* feel in i, 1, 25 when they try too late to rescue their friend. Except that the insight Propertius had won into his own infatuation enables him to sense more acutely than they what it feels like to be infatuated. His verse crisply conveys this attitude of sensitive, affectionate concern.[1]

The opening stanza, then, captures our attention by the neatness and precision with which the theme is introduced—and by the freshness of the theme itself. For too often the Roman elegist is inclined simply to complain his mistress is unfaithful to him, not sensing (or at any rate not troubling to make us sense) that the emotions which draw her away from him may be as worth while as those who draw him to her. The quality of the writing now deteriorates however:

> tune audire potes uesani murmura ponti 5
> fortis, et in dura naue iacere potes?
> tu pedibus teneris positas fulcire pruinas,
> tu potes insolitas, Cynthia, ferre niues?

Have you heart to face the maddened ocean's
growl, while on hard deck you lie?
What when your poor foot treads the frozen lying snow?
What, Cynthia, when it snows as you've never seen it snow?

After the display of indignation comes the section of the propempticon devoted to talking the traveller out of his journey. As in Horace's Propempticon for Virgil, the dangers that lie ahead are stressed.

The writing in this stanza is adequate, but not convincing— perhaps because Propertius is following a detail of the formula that did not appeal to him. We feel, too, his intellectual impatience with scene. His interest is in argument and in emotion, not in description. The repeated questions, each beginning with *tu*, are correctly laid out. The striking *uesani* in line 5 and the

---

[1] Propertius, Cynthia and the other man are, of course, involved in just the sort of *ronde de l'amour* that Horace in *Odes* i, 33 describes as the normal state of affairs. The difference is that Propertius takes it seriously.

Propertius, the Passionate Lover (i, 8)

personification it implies (the adjective is normally used only of persons) make for a good, but conventional line. But in the next line the promising *dura* (with its suggestion of the discomforts awaiting Cynthia whatever the weather) is thrown away on the vague *naue* ('ship')—unless the whole phrase *in dura naue iacere* is intended to imply that Cynthia would be better off lying *in molli lecto* (compare line 33).

The next couplet runs better, but, while it is well enough to remind Cynthia of the barbarous winter climate of Illyria, our attention is distracted from the sea-voyage to the destination—a distinct blemish in a poem in which elsewhere all centres around Cynthia's ship in port waiting to depart. It looks at first glance like one more instance of Propertius' slackness about detail. As it happens we possess the real explanation. It is presented to us by Servius, the ancient commentator on Virgil. In Eclogue 10 Virgil restates, according to the conventions of pastoral allegory, an unhappy episode in the liaison of his friend Gallus with the actress Lycoris. Lycoris has run off with another man to foreign parts (line 23), and Gallus pictures her struggling through the snows of Gaul or Germany (the Rhine is mentioned)—and feels pity well up for her at the thought of her tender feet cut about by the jagged ice (lines 46-9).[1] Servius, in a note on lines 46-9, says the lines are taken from a poem written by Gallus himself. They come perhaps from a Propempticon for Lycoris.[2] At any rate the details closely resemble those in Propertius' Propempticon for Cynthia. Substituting Cynthia for Lycoris, Propertius conjures up the same picture of the unaccustomed discomforts the mistress who deserted him will have to face amid the snow and ice of a provincial winter.

This sort of compliment to a fellow-craftsman is common in

---

[1] Eclogue 10, 46-9:

>tu procul a patria (nec sit mihi credere tantum)
>Alpinas a, dura, niues et frigora Rheni
>me sine sola uides. a, te ne frigora laedant!
>a, tibi ne teneras glacies secet aspera plantas!

[2] A famous controversy has long raged about what Eclogue 10 can be made to tell us about the poetry of Gallus. See H. J. Rose, *The Eclogues of Vergil* (1942). It may be taken as certain that Propertius' couplet contains an echo of Gallus; but that the lay-out of Propertius' poem is based on that of a poem of Gallus cannot be regarded as more than a sensible guess.

Persistence of a Theme: the Propempticon

Latin poetry and perhaps almost *de rigueur* in a strictly conventional form like the propempticon. Ideally you recast the borrowed lines slightly, giving them a fresh slant while preserving a distinct verbal echo. Thus Propertius' *pedibus teneris* echoes without reproducing the *teneras plantas* of Virgil's version of Gallus' lines. But the upsurge of compassion (Virgil's *a, te ne frigora laedant*) is checked—or rather transferred to a later section of Propertius' poem. We are entitled to complain, however, that Propertius has allowed his respect for the rules to blur his argument. One may in general attempt to talk a friend out of a proposed voyage by representing its dangers and discomforts to him, because one's friends are assumed to be reasonable. Cynthia, however, is *demens* and cannot be expected in her infatuation to listen to reasonable argument.

The next section is both more coherent and more relevant to the poem's development:

> o utinam hibernae duplicentur tempora brumae,
>   et sit iners tardis nauita Vergiliis,   10
> nec tibi Tyrrhena soluatur funis harena,
>   neue inimica meas eleuet aura preces!
>
> atque ego non uideam talis sibsidere uentos,
>   cum tibi prouectas auferet unda ratis,
> et me defixum uacua patietur in ora   15
>   crudelem infesta saepe uocare manu!

If only winter time could be to winter added,
the Pleiads slow to rise, sailors unemployed,   10
no painter cut on beach in Tuscany,
no enemy breeze to undo all that I entreat!

I'd not then see these present winds subside—
When your craft will put to sea, over ocean disappear,
leaving me rooted to an empty shore,   15
upraised fist reproaching you repeatedly.

The lines are troubled by a loose, involved structure that is characteristic of Propertius' impatience with perfection of phrasing when a good idea draws him on. It has caused some

Propertius, the Passionate Lover (i, 8)

manuscript confusion and encouraged editors to resort to more extensive repair than a study of the poem's development of thought shows to be justified.[1] The lines take us back to the situation sketched in at the end of the first stanza. There Cynthia was *eager to depart*, but the sailors would not put to sea till spring. 'If only it could always be winter,' says Propertius, and proceeds for the remainder of the stanza to elaborate the idea. The four lines are simply strung together, but the order is logical: no spring, no action by the sailors, no departure, no separation.

In the next stanza wishes merge into dreams of their realization:[2]

> atque ego non uideam talis subsidere uentos,   13
>
> *I'd not then see these present winds subside.*

The line brings us back to the actual dramatic moment of the poem, the storm before our eyes (*talis ... uentos*). But *subsidere*, despite the negative, reminds Propertius that in reality the present storm will subside. The day-dreaming cannot banish the nagging thought. And with its return comes the thought: 'and then ... '. The inverted *cum* clauses in lines 14-16 finally face up to the reality that the propempticon has to pretend it hopes to avert.

We are now ready to slide into the next section of the typical propempticon, in which the poet says, 'Well, if you must go, I hope no harm comes to you':

> sed quocumque modo de me, periura, mereris,
>   sit Galatea tuae non aliena uiae:
> ut te, felici praeuecta Ceraunia remo,
>   accipiat placidis Oricos aequoribus.   20

---

[1] Bailey, p. 23, fairly speaks of a *locus uexatissimus*. The latest editor, W. A. Camps, *Propertius Elegies Book I* (1961), offers a fresh version of the text. But E. A. Barber's Oxford text (1953) seems to me, though loose, comprehensible and translatable. The inverted-*cum* clause explaining what will take place in a future situation (implicit in *talis subsidere uentos*) is like that in i, 5, 14ff. Personally I prefer a second *cum* clause in line 15.

[2] The transition is easy in Latin from wish to realization. The present subjunctive is appropriate to both.

Persistence of a Theme: the Propempticon

Yet, faithless, whatever your deserts,
may Galatea not view your journey with disfavour.
May your oars round Ceraunia rock triumphantly,
and Oricos receive you with a placid sea.

The literary historian can point to echoes of these lines in the other versions that have come down to us of this oddly conventional form—echoes so numerous, and so easily avoided, they are unlikely to be inadvertent—the unwished-for betrayal of a blind adherence to stock material. The promontory of Acroceraunia crops up in Horace's Propempticon for Virgil (*Odes* i, 3, 20) and in Ovid's Propempticon for Corinna (*A*. ii, 11, 19). The nymph Galatea is found in the Ovidian poem (*A*. ii, 11, 34); and Galatea is actually the name of the girl to whom Horace addresses his Europa ode (iii, 27, 14). Propertius can hardly have been the first to introduce all these details; some at any rate are taken, pretty surely, from his predecessors in the genre—an acknowledgment to the lettered reader that the form *is* a stock one, that the poet has accepted the challenge to make a poem out of it that can display its acceptance of tradition and still succeed as a poem.

Tradition, moreover, is not only accepted, but intelligently exploited. The idea that the poet's affection for his faithless mistress remains, whatever her deserts,

> sed quocumque modo de me, periura, mereris,

has its origin in Cornelius Gallus (or in Virgil's recasting of Gallus' lines). But in Propertius the idea is more explicit (a welling-up of feeling is analysed into rational statement) and made to fit in well with the poet's *persona* established in the opening stanza. We are thus led on smoothly to the contrast between her faithlessness and his fidelity with which the first half of the poem concludes:

> nam me non ullae poterunt corrumpere, de te
>   quin ego, uita, tuo limine uerba querar;
> nec me deficiet nautas rogitare citatos
>   'Dicite, quo portu clausa puella mea est?'
> et dicam 'Licet Atraciis considat in oris,   25
>   et licet Hylleis, illa futura mea est.'

Propertius, the Passionate Lover (i, 8)

Me no wench shall so infatuate that I
will cease, love, from lamentation at your door,
or from plying sailors with my eager questions:
'Tell me, what harbour shelters my love now?'
And I'll add: 'Though she's in Atracia now,   25
or some Hyllean town, the day will come she's mine.'

So much for the first half of the elegy. We cannot escape the feeling, I think, that, after the conventional second stanza, the control over statement and idea established in the opening lines is not regained. The poem flounders through a sequence of contrasting emotions that we might have difficulty in retracing if we did not possess the formula. At this point it seems irresponsible to accept Ussani's often quoted appraisal—'one of the finest examples of passionate, emotional poetry handed down to us by antiquity'.[1] We are tempted to explain dissatisfaction by pointing to the signs that we have seen of tradition taking charge at the expense of the poet's own personality. Propertius wanted to do, I think, what we shall see Horace do: to embed the first part of his poem firmly in what was becoming a recognized form, and then give his propempticon a new and unexpected twist. I think we shall see that Horace succeeded where Propertius really did not.

The second half of the poem is usually printed as a separate elegy; the manuscripts make no division, and there are those who insist we should make none.[2] Clearly 8b (as the second half is usually designated) presupposes 8a: it cannot stand alone. It is equally clear we are expected to assume a dramatic break, a sufficient interval for Cynthia to give up her plans for running away with the other man and for Propertius to hear of this. Whether we regard the juxtaposition as two connected poems or a single poem in two parts hardly matters.

The break is there because the propempticon has come to an end. It has served its purpose. Cynthia has decided after all to abandon her trip abroad. Propertius is elated:

---

[1] 'Questa elegia è uno dei piu begli esempi di poesia concitata e appassionata che abbia lasciato l'antichità.' Quoted, e.g., by Enk, p. 74.
[2] The most recent advocate of unity is R. E. White, 'Dramatic unity in Propertius', *C.Ph.*, lvi (1961), pp. 217–29. It is generally agreed that the manuscripts of Propertius are liable to omit divisions between elegies.

Persistence of a Theme: the Propempticon

    hic erit! hic iurata manet! rumpantur iniqui!
        uicimus: assiduas non tulit illa preces.
    falsa licet cupidus deponat gaudia liuor:
        destitit ire nouas Cynthia nostra uias.   30

She's not going! She's sworn she'll stay! My enemies to hell!
I've won. I pleaded and I pleaded and she gave in at last.
The bawdy and the jealous can call their celebrations off;
my Cynthia has renounced her journey off the beaten track.[1]

The lines achieve at once an almost lyric emotional intensity for which we may suspect Propertius was holding himself in check, to the detriment of the first half of the poem.

The exclamation of joy is followed by a more reasoned section:

    illi carus ego et per me carissima Roma
        dicitur, et sine me dulcia regna negat.
    illa uel angusto mecum requiescere lecto
        et quocumque modo maluit esse mea,
    quam sibi dotatae regnum uetus Hippodamiae,   35
        et quas Elis opes ante pararat equis.

It's me she loves. Because of me she loves, she says,
Rome best, finds no pleasure reigns where I am not.
She'd rather pass the night on narrow bed with me,
rather feel she's mine on any terms at all,
than own a kingdom, Hippodamia's dowry once,   35
or the wealth horses brought to ancient Elis.

The moment of delight and triumph past, Propertius brings himself under control, in order to analyse the reasons Cynthia gives for not going (lines 31 and 32). The most important is that she has said she does not want to be without him (*sine me*). A couplet expands what is implied by that. Another draws on mythology to add stature and romance to the plain assertion (lines 33–4) that the liaison will be resumed.

---

[1] The *iniqui* of line 27 are jealous of Propertius. For the idea, cf. Catullus Poem 5; for this meaning of *iniquus*, cf. Cicero *Pro Balbo* 56 where *iniquus* is coupled with *maliualus* and *inuidus*.

250

Propertius, the Passionate Lover (1, 8)

The reference to Hippodamia's dowry is intended to set us thinking of the riches Cynthia has rejected in order to remain with her poet-lover:[1]

> quamuis magna daret, quamuis maiora daturus,
>   non tamen illa meos fugit auara sinus.
> hanc ego non auro, non Indis flectere conchis
>   sed potui blandi carminis obsequio.   40

Despite his many presents, despite the likelihood of more,
greed did not send her headlong from my arms.
It wasn't gold I changed her mind with, or Indian pearls:
I courted her with coaxing verses, and succeeded.

The figure of the *diues amator*, that stock villain of Roman love elegy, lurks behind these lines, making them less uncomplimentary to Cynthia than they are likely to seem to us. Once again tradition shows signs of taking charge, but Propertius brings the poem more or less back under control by pointing to a connection between first and second half: it was the *blandum carmen* of the first half that won his Cynthia back for him.

At the thought the lyrical note of lines 27–30 is resumed:

> sunt igitur Musae, neque amanti tardus Apollo,
>   quis ego fretus amo: Cynthia rara mea est!
> nunc mihi summa licet contingere sidera plantis:
>   siue dies seu nox uenerit, illa mea est!
> nec mihi riualis certos subducit amores: 45
>   ista meam norit gloria canitiem.

There are Muses then! When you love Apollo's never slow.
On them my passion can rely. Rare Cynthia is mine!
Now may I touch with toe the topmost stars.
By day, and equally by night, Cynthia is mine!
Our love's too certain for rivals to subvert.   45
There's a glory my grey hairs will be able to recall!

---

[1] The train of thought is confused, however: Hippodamia would have lived in luxury whomever she married, because her father provided a rich dowry. Cynthia could only live in luxury by giving up one lover for another (Propertius for her *diues amator*). What is offered as an illustrative parallel turns out, upon investigation, not to be one at all.

Persistence of a Theme: the Propempticon

The cry 'she's mine!' rings out twice. The words have echoed down the poem with increasing fervour, helping to bind the two parts together. They occurred first in line 24; in a question, not an exclamation:

> 'Dicite, quo portu clausa puella mea est?'
>
> *'Tell me, what harbour shelters my love now?'*

For she remained *his* love, even though at this stage he thought of her as already departed with another. In line 26 the words take on a more confident sound. Somehow she is going to be his despite everything: *illa futura mea est!* The first half of the poem ends with this prediction. In the second half prediction becomes fact (*maluit esse mea*, line 34), and the words that asserted the prediction are repeated in a cry of triumph (*Cynthia rara mea est!* line 42). And then repeated again in a fresh prediction:

> siue dies seu nox uenerit, illa mea est!   44

The present tense is used to preserve the echo of the four preceding occurrences of *mea est*, but the future perfect *uenerit* projects the whole statement indefinitely into the future:

> *By day, and equally by night, Cynthia is mine!*

Such, then, is Propertius' attempt to make the propempticon serve a turn in love poetry. The poem as a whole is exposed to the risk run by all divided poems. If the contrasting themes are not of equal weight, one will spoil the other. Horace's first Spring Ode (*Soluitur acris hiems . . .*, discussed in Chapter 1) is an excellent example of contrasting themes successfully juxtaposed. His poem continues to move us long after the abrupt transition from first half to second half has ceased to take us by surprise. The successive moods are equally intense and equally valid. In Propertius' poem the two halves are steps in a story, told as a study in emotion. But once we know the story has a happy ending, it becomes hard to take the emotional turmoil of the first half seriously. And if we cannot, the first half fails, because its only function is to provide a conventional lay-out

Horace's Cautionary Tale (Odes iii, 27)

for a sequence of conflicting emotions. Worse still, Propertius has made the mistake of writing for a climax. The propempticon is subordinated to the second half; the emotional level is held in check in order to make the lyrical exhilaration of the second half sound a convincing climax. In a single, coherent poem this could seem natural and effective. In a poem made out of two juxtaposed halves it is liable to prove fatal.

There is another solution to the problem of the poem in two halves. It involves establishing between them a true organic interrelationship, each half illuminating the other in a fresh light. Horace, it seems to me, has managed this in his adaptation of the propempticon.

Horace's Cautionary Tale (Odes iii, 27)

Horace's Propempticon for Galatea, more often referred to as the Europa ode, one of the longest of Horace's odes, is apt to be singled out for special condemnation by Horace's critics and damned with faint praise by his admirers. Wilamowitz's contemptuous dismissal ('utterly tasteless and absurd') is hardly offset by Dr. Fraenkel's lukewarm defence.[1] He finds it a heavy ode, lacking unity, a failure to be 'judged on its merits'.[2] Campbell (pp. 206-7) and Wilkinson (p. 134) express misgivings no less grave. Enthusiasm for the ode is conspicuously lacking.

The poem has suffered mainly because it has not been understood. The fault is a little Horace's. In the construction of a long and subtle poem, he has counted too much on his readers' ability to recognize themes and put two and two together. The first part of the ode is based on the propempticon theme.[3]

---

[1] Wilamowitz's words are quoted by Fraenkel, p. 196:
[Horace's ode] ist wirklich im ganzen und in jedem Zuge geschmacklos und absurd; er selber hätte sich's nicht verzeihen dürfen.

[2] Fraenkel, p. 196:
If he failed, his poem must be judged on its merits, but of the poet himself we still should like to say 'den lieb ich, der Unmögliches begehrt'.
Its main merit seems to him to lie in an attempt to reinvest the Europa legend with something like its original majesty.

[3] Even this much is not always realized. See, however, the first paragraph of Heinze's introduction, p. 363, which is sensible and adequate. Also Pasquali, pp. 278-86.

Persistence of a Theme: the Propempticon

The second relates a cautionary tale. So much is plain sailing. Two things now upset the critics. They do not realize that in the second part of his poem, as in the first, Horace is following a stock form with elaborate rules. And they do not perceive the complexity of the relationship between the two parts, taking it to be one of simple subordination. For the first reason they find the poem unbalanced and disjointed; for the second dull.[1]

The essential features of a good cautionary tale are that it should be long and that it should not make its point too bluntly. A favourite form seems to have been an elaborately retold legend, introduced with the hint that *de te fabula narratur*. The Europa ode and the Hypermestra ode (iii, 11) are often compared; but the closest parallel is actually Propertius' Hylas elegy (i, 20), in which the story of the kidnapping of Hylas is recounted at length with mannered gusto after a broad hint to the addressee, Gallus, that the theme touches him closely. Propertius tried the cautionary tale again in iii, 15, a delightfully urbane recasting of the story of Dirce and Antiope as a warning to his mistress of the dangers of misdirected jealousy. These two poems of Propertius stand closest among Roman elegies to Greek love elegy, if the modern assumption is correct that the Greek elegists did not write real love poems, but erotic συμφοραί, in some of which at any rate the mythological story was grafted on to a contemporary erotic situation which it pretended to illustrate.[2]

Horace, then, has combined the propempticon, for which no one metrical form was specially indicated, with the mythological cautionary tale, which seems to have had its origin in elegy. The link with elegy accounts perhaps for the greater length and complexity of the Europa ode, in comparison with the typical love ode. Within the mythological part there are affinities again

[1] An exception is W.-H. Friedrich's intelligent and sensitive reading of the poem, 'Europa und der Stier: angewandte Mythologie bei Horaz und Properz', *N.G.G.*, phil.-hist. Klasse, No. 5 (1959), pp. 81–100. He makes the parallel with Propertius i, 20, regarding both as comparable examples of the detailed exploration of legend.

[2] The nature of Greek elegy (now mainly lost) has long been hotly debated. The view expressed here is that of A. Rostagni, 'L'elegia erotica latina' in *L'influence grecque sur la poésie latine de Catulle à Ovide*, Fondation Hardt, *Entretiens sur l'antiquité classique*, Vol. ii (1956), pp. 59–90. This feature of elegy may be an expansion of what Fraenkel, pp. 185–6, calls 'paraenetic lyric'.

Horace's Cautionary Tale (*Odes* iii, 27)

with the epyllion and its mannered, ironical narrative.[1] At least one Hellenistic poet, Moschus, used the story of Europa for an epyllion, and it was used again by Ovid in the second book of the *Metamorphoses*. A poet is entitled, of course, to impress his individual stamp upon the legend he retells. The curiously ambiguous ending we find in Horace seems to have been devised by him for his own ironical purpose.[2]

But if Horace relies a little too much on the literary sophistication of his readers, the critics for their part might, by the exercise of some imaginative responsiveness, have avoided the pitfalls into which they have stumbled in approaching this subtle poem. They have been especially unsubtle in deciding what view to take of the poem as a whole. Is it a Propempticon for Galatea, they ask, and the Europa bit dragged in as a cautionary tale? Though how it can be a cautionary tale they cannot see because it appears to have a happy ending. Or alternatively is the Europa tale told for its own sake and the propempticon dragged in only as an excuse to get the poem going? The second is the more popular view.[3] The greater length of the Europa half appears to lend it support. But the view implies, too, a line of argument which we may reconstruct as follows:

> First proposition: It is to be taken for granted that Galatea, like the rest of Horace's girl friends, does not really exist.
> Second proposition: Horace's odes, being occasional verse, need an addressee.
> Conclusion: Galatea is that addressee and a mere peg.

The first proposition is very likely correct.[4] The second, as we saw in Chapter 4, is open to two objections. First, it makes

---

[1] The connection between the Propempticon for Galatea and the Ariadne episode in Catullus Poem 64 has been noticed, but it has not been remarked, I think, that one of their most important common features is the sympathetically ironical presentation of character. [2] See Heinze, p. 364.

[3] Wilkinson, p. 134, considers the first possibility, but on the whole favours the second. Fraenkel agrees, pp. 193-4:
> we should admit that Horace did not take much trouble when he invented a situation which might serve as a prelude to his fine story.

[4] Very different judgments may be based, however, on the acceptance of this proposition. For example, the fictitious character of Horace's girl friends was laid down by Lessing in the eighteenth century to preserve Horace's moral reputation —and then taken over by Romantic critics in the nineteenth century as a stick to beat Horace with—a poet whose love poetry was sham. See Chapter 6.

Persistence of a Theme: the Propempticon

a hard and fast rule out of what is no more than a general tendency. If Horace had really wanted only to write about Europa, he could have done so: *Odes* i, 15 (*Pastor cum traheret per freta nauibus* . . .) shows he can retell a legend without a peg to hang it on when he wants to.[1] If then he takes the trouble to invent Galatea and talk to her for several stanzas, it seems reasonable to assume he wants her to be something more than a peg. Second, Heinze confused form with purpose. A traditional form does not have to have a traditional purpose or a traditional content. The fact, therefore, that Galatea is the addressee of Horace's poem does not mean that the poem conveys a message intended primarily for her which Horace has made available for our inspection. It may be primarily intended for us.

A point these critics of the Europa ode overlook is that the first proposition destroys the validity of the second. If Galatea is only pretence, then the occasional form is only pretence, too. You can't have a real occasional poem to a non-existent girl. The poem you have *may* answer in all respects to the formula for a real occasional poem. But it is much more likely not to. And in dealing with a poem in which, as here, there is abundant evidence that a traditional shallow form has been invested with a new depth of content, we should be particularly chary about arguments that take its status as occasional verse for granted.

So long as we assume the first half of the poem is not merely addressed to its addressee but directed at her, the organic connection between the two halves that makes them a single poem can hardly be perceived. For it lies in the sensitive reader's ability to relate Galatea's situation to Europa's and thereby to savour Horace's ironical insight into both situations. This Galatea can hardly be expected to do; but the experience the poem offers is offered to us not to her. Horace, in other words, has written a poem, not a piece of occasional verse.

Galatea, like Europa at the outset of her adventure, is doubtless all excitement.[2] She feels she must be a very lucky girl,

---

[1] See Fraenkel's eminently sensible comments, pp. 188–9.

[2] While analysing the poem it is convenient to talk as though Galatea actually existed and as though the poem were actually addressed to her. Speaking more accurately we should perhaps say that Horace intends us to accept this hypothesis, in order that he may set us thinking about Galatea in the way in which it is the poem's object to make us think. In fact, of course, the poem is addressed to us, its readers.

Horace's Cautionary Tale (*Odes* iii, 27)

but she is apprehensive, too. A little imaginative collaboration on the part of the reader, some small acquaintance with stock themes, and her story quickly falls into shape. Like Cynthia in Propertius' propempticon, she is about to desert her poet-lover to bolt with a newly-found *diues amator*. He is, we may presume (for Europa's story is intended to fill out the details of Galatea's), a man of influence and rank as well as money. That won't stop her from feeling very sorry for herself when she ends up (this is the implicit prediction of the Europa legend) honoured but unloved. And being of course, Horace politely assumes, not only young and pretty but innocent as well, she is likely to be overwhelmed by the disgrace when the infatuation evaporates along with the cause of it—forgetting what an honour it was to be chosen by so important a man, even if it meant being left in the lurch the moment the voyage was over. Given Horace's attitude to love, it is not a cynical prediction, but simply one that accepts realistically the way the world works.

The second part of the poem has this backward-working organic connection with the first. But Galatea and her new lover (whose existence we assume from the second half of the poem) work forward, too, suggesting, without overtly asserting, that rational reassessment of mythology which Euripides and Alexandrian intellectualism had introduced into the presentation of the old stories.[1] With Galatea in mind, we can see the humour as well as the pathos in Europa's predicament. And with Galatea in mind and the realities of contemporary Roman life (viewed, at any rate, from Horace's standpoint of whimsical irony about love's tragedies), we can see that Europa's tragedy is not as tragic as she thinks. We can agree in short with Venus.

In constructing such a poem, one of the most important things is to get the tone just right. Horace aims at creating a mood in the first half that will cause us to approach the second half ready to accept its irreverent debunking without protest, but sensitive all the same to the poetry and the moral comment he wishes to imply. He begins with twelve lines of elaborate, earnest-sounding technical discussion of omens, inauspicious as well as

---

[1] So long as the stories were genuinely believed in, their relevance to the realities of human problems was not pressed too systematically. Systematic critical scrutiny of the implications of legend was introduced by Euripides. For the Alexandrians it became a game rather than a serious moral enquiry.

Persistence of a Theme: the Propempticon

auspicious. The mass of detail and the fearsome sound of the inauspicious omens (they include a screech owl, a pregnant bitch and a newly delivered vixen) should quickly warn us that our leg is being gently pulled—and therefore, probably, Galatea's too.[1] Particularly when we observe that Horace begins his poem by calling for unfavourable omens to dog those who behave badly; and reflect that Galatea, being on the point of deserting Horace for another man, may well consider herself included among the poet's enemies. He opens with the alarming word *impios*, followed by a horrific list of animals of ill omen. It is not until line 7 that he gives the game away and drops the first reassuring hint to Galatea:

        ego cui timebo
  prouidus auspex,
  antequam stantis repetat paludes
  imbrium diuina auis imminentum,   10
  oscinem coruum prece suscitabo
    solis ab ortu.

  When I've at heart a person's safety,
I'm a gifted omen-reader, and

before she seeks again the stagnant swamps,
that winged divine of rain to come, I'll   10
conjure a prophetic raven up from the
region of the rising sun.

The favourable omen, likewise described in detail, sounds only a little less repulsive. It is introduced with a promise that looks impressive, though not easy, one would suppose, to fulfil: for a person like Galatea, whose safety he has at heart, Horace undertakes, not merely to pray for a successful omen, but to *produce* it.

By the end of the third stanza, then, Galatea may begin to feel somewhat reassured. The reader is still in the dark, having

---
[1] Heinze gravely remarks, p. 366:
 Dass übrigens H. diesen ganzen mit ernster Miene vorgetragenen augurale Hokuspokus nicht selbst ernst nimmt, versteht sich.
His suggestion that Galatea was addicted to omens is ingenious, but hardly necessary.

Horace's Cautionary Tale (*Odes* iii, 27)

been vouchsafed no word of explanation. Horace can hardly tell Galatea what her relationship was and now is with him. The reader, however, needs this information, and Horace now contrives to supply it obliquely.

'You are entitled to happiness wherever you prefer to be,' the next stanza begins.[1] The words *ubicumque mauis* tell us enough. Galatea has changed her mind about *where* she wishes to spend her life—and therefore, we may take it, about *with whom*. The words carry just the right note of dignified acceptance of betrayal. The next line ('And I hope you'll remember me') sounds innocent enough. It was one of the traditional notes to strike in propemptica and other poems about friends separating.[2] But in the context of our present poem the irony is patent. If Galatea is going where she prefers to be, and if there is any sort of parallel at all between the propempticon half and the Europa half of the poem, then Galatea is leaving with her lover. When we realize this, we can detect the playful malice in Horace's innocent-sounding valediction.

Horace has now got his love propempticon going. He has taken over the basic data used by Propertius and doubtless other poets, and can therefore evoke a typical situation with the briefest of hints. The situation is invested, however, with a characteristically Horatian flavour, the philosophical basis of which we discussed in Chapter 6. Instead of the smouldering indignation of Propertius, we have that mixture of whimsy and irony, toughened by a thread of malice natural in one who knows that mistresses (and lovers) cannot be expected to be faithful. The sensible lover, Horace implies, has no illusions, but that need not make him spineless. Hence the sharp edge to his good wishes.

Propertius' Dream Elegy (ii, 26a, discussed in Chapter 8)

---

[1] The paratactic *licet* is emphatic, but to be taken only with the first jussive subjunctive *sis*.

[2] We find the 'remember me when you're gone' theme first in Sappho (frag. 94 L.-P., 7-8):

Χαίροισ' ἔρχεο κἀμέθεν
μέμναισ', οἶσθα γὰρ ὥς σε πεδήπομεν.

That there is perhaps an echo of Sappho's words here is suggested by what sounds an even clearer echo in Ovid's propempticon (*A.* ii, 11, 37):

uade memor nostri, uento reditura secundo.

Cf. Tib. i, 3, 1-2:

Ibitis Aegaeas sine me, Messalla, per undas,
  o utinam memores ipse cohorsque mei!

Persistence of a Theme: the Propempticon

comes much closer to the mood of Horace's poem. All the same we can sense a difference in the attitudes implied in the two. Propertius offers us the slightly morbid malice of the passionate lover who has had much to endure, Horace the tolerant, urbane malice of the realist: he is not going to pretend he isn't mildly annoyed, but his annoyance is tempered by an assessment of the outcome. Propertius expects our sympathy, our admiration at the sensitivity of feeling he displays. Horace expects us, on the whole, to agree with him.

He must be careful, however, not to overdo things. The leg-pull has the effect of putting Galatea's departure in what the lover-poet half regards, and half wants us to feel he pretends to regard, as the proper perspective. The ode must now move forward into a more subtle theme if it is going to be a worthwhile poem. Its development proves consistent with the attitude that has been built up. The poet-lover, though under no illusions, cares enough to make an effort to restrain Galatea. We slip naturally into the next section of the traditional propempticon, that devoted to an attempt to get the traveller to abandon his journey.

Horace is here faced with the problem that faced Propertius. His traveller is infatuated with another man, not therefore much disposed to listen to arguments, and the real arguments moreover are tricky to state. You are not going to get very far with a girl in Galatea's frame of mind by talking of the dangers of the journey or by telling her how much you love her. This is what Propertius does, and he leaves us, I think, at the end of i, 8a with an uneasy feeling that, though he has demonstrated he loves Cynthia passionately, he is not really behaving very sensibly.

Horace for a moment looks like heading in the same direction:

>   sed uides quanto trepidet tumultu
>   pronus Orion. ego quid sit ater
>   Hadriae noui sinus et quid albus
>   peccet Iapyx.   20

*You see of course how boisterous the storms
now Orion's setting. I know all about rough weather
in the narrow Adriatic—and in fair, what tricks
that Nor'-westerly can play!*

Horace's Cautionary Tale (Odes iii, 27)

The ingredients are Horace's; a characteristic mixture of Hellenistic tradition (we find setting Orion in the earliest surviving propempticon[1]) and the Italian scene (Iapyx is the wind that conveyed Italian travellers to Greece). The flavour ostentatiously matter-of-fact and self-centred. 'I wouldn't care to be at sea this time of year' is the drift of the second half of the stanza. 'It's not a time of the year in fact,' he goes on in the next stanza, 'when I'd like *any* friends of mine to have somebody they care for at sea.' The statement is made up with all Horace's studied obliqueness. He wants to build up the *persona* of himself as a reasonable, affectionate fellow, while implying the *persona* of a Galatea who is not responsive to reason or to Horace's affection for her.

This mood of lukewarm, almost avuncular reasonableness and affection enables Horace to slide without further ado into the Europa story, as though just reminded of it by his thoughts of an innocent young girl facing the perils of the sea in order to elope with her lover. *That* is the parallel to which the *sic* points:

>   sic et Europe niueum doloso   25
>   credidit tauro latus et scatentem
>   beluis pontum mediasque fraudes
>   palluit audax.
>
>   nuper in pratis studiosa florum et
>   debitae Nymphis opifex coronae,   30
>   nocte sublustri nihil astra praeter
>   uidit et undas.

Thus Europa entrusted snowy flank
to guileful bull; then at the teeming,
monstrous sea, the deception all about her, she,
though a girl of courage, paled.

In a field a while before, her thoughts all flowers
(she owed the nymphs a wreath), the garland-maker now   30
in night's dim light had nothing save the stars
to gaze at and the waves.[2]

---
[1] Theocritus vii, 54.
[2] Friedrich, art. cit., p. 85, points out that Propertius' Hylas is busy picking flowers when he falls victim to the amorous attentions of the water-nymphs (i, 20, 37–40). Flower-picking is, of course, pre-eminently an innocent occupation.

Persistence of a Theme: the Propempticon

We may read as much as we feel inclined into the ambiguously stylized language with which Horace launches into the Europa legend—and apply it all to Galatea. But the poetry is genuine. At the same time, behind the heroic, non-realistic picture of star-filled night and 'teeming, monstrous sea'[1] Galatea's unheroic story lurks all the while. The result is that kind of interlocking of legend and reality that Catullus exploits in his description of Ariadne on the beach in Poem 64.[2] Looked at this way, the picture loses some of its legendary sublimity, seems even a trifle ridiculous; but our sympathy for Europa is aroused to an extent that was hardly possible so long as she remained a mere figure of legend, tragically un-absurd.

The point of the Europa story (considering for the moment only the run of the argument and not that we are dealing with a poem possessing poetic qualities that are far from negligible) is left unstated, and Horace's failure to state it has frequently puzzled editors.[3] Yet it is an essential feature of a cautionary tale that it should not openly moralize. The discerning, sensitive reader is relied on to put two and two together. He usually then discovers the point is contained in that part of the story which is given prominence, but expressed with studious irrelevance. And here, of course, the point lies in relating to Galatea, not Europa's journey (which occupies only a couple of stanzas), but the story of what happened when she got to her destination (which occupies eleven stanzas).

For once in Crete, Europa is quickly deserted by her bull-

---

[1] Another traditional detail of the propempticon, we gather, for it occurs also in Horace's Propempticon for Virgil, *Odes* i, 3, 18.

[2] See my discussion of this in J. P. Sullivan, ed., *Critical Essays in Roman Literature*, Vol. 1, *Elegy and Lyric* (1962).

[3] E.g., Fraenkel, p. 193:
Horace's warning to Galatea could be boiled down to a simple 'beware of the coming storm'. But did Europa, after being tempted to cross the sea, experience any bad weather? . . . The difficulty has not escaped the commentators; their embarrassment is remarkable.

The difficulty only arises if we allow our attention to be distracted by the transitional passage, lines 16–24 (a bridge passage enabling Horace to move smoothly out of the first stock theme and into the second), and miss the force of the opening *sic*. What Galatea and Europa have in common are the circumstances that induced them to put to sea. Fraenkel, however, is not prompted to relate the two stories at all closely (ibid.):
My own experience at any rate is that when I have reached Aphrodite's serene speech at the conclusion of the poem I seem to have forgotten all about the girl Galatea.

Horace's Cautionary Tale (*Odes* iii, 27)

lover. She proceeds to lament her fate in the stylized language of high tragedy: 'Where am I? .. Dead or alive?. . . Where is the wretch?. . . What a shameless girl I am! . . Better death than shame. . . .' And so on. A recent critic remarks: 'I cannot take Europa as tragically as she takes herself'.[1] Like the majority of commentators he complains Europa succeeds only in sounding vaguely ridiculous. He is, of course, quite right. But that does not make her a mere figure of fun with no claim on our sympathy. Europa deserves our sympathy; if we have a heart, we feel it go out to her, even though an ironical smile accompanies it. The parallel with Ariadne's long speech in Catullus (Poem 64, 132–201) and its packed tragic rhetoric is close.

There is a distinction between burlesque and irony, though Horace's critics seldom draw it. Translations are perhaps to blame. They coarsen so much the fabric of poetry as delicate and as complex as Horace's. When not translated into what H. W. Fowler called Wardour-Street English (its usual fate), Horace's love poetry is made to sound like something out of *Punch*.[2] So much turns on *tone*. The complexity of attitudes, the humane stature of the observer degenerate so easily if the tone is degraded, or merely simplified.

The effect Horace aims at here is many-sided. To begin with, he wants us to read his retelling of Europa's story with a new critical awareness of the way the old legends neglected realism in their pursuit of the sublime and the pathetic—simplifications of reality that Horace never finds congenial. At the same time he wants us to feel sorry for Europa—without of course sharing her assessment of her misfortune. It is the way we feel often about real people when misfortune overwhelms their sense of proportion. At this point we remember Galatea. When her wonderful new lover throws her over, she is likely (if she is, as we politely assume, an honest, modest girl) to feel just as sorry for herself as Europa did—and look rather a bigger fool, lacking the stylized language of poetry to express her grief, and the goddess of love to console her.

---

[1] Collinge, p. 121.
[2] See, e.g., Edward Marsh's spirited translations. It is noticeable that an honest critic like Collinge finds himself tempted to abuse the term 'Gilbertian' (e.g., pp. 15 and 68).

Persistence of a Theme: the Propempticon

The moral now starts to suggest itself. The conclusion makes it plain. Europa has got to the point where she is working herself up to commit suicide by reminding herself that in poetry in the grand manner dishonour leaves no alternative. The verse is excellent—more than adequate to the occasion, supposing Horace were entirely serious, as of course he is not. But he does not intend the lines he gives Europa as burlesque either. For all the mockery, there is more than that to Europa. This is the way tragic heroines must behave if tragedy is to work. It just happens that Europa's is the sort of tragedy that can be looked at with the cool, sophisticated irony with which (as we saw in discussing his ode to Tibullus in Chapter 6) Horace greets all who make a tragedy out of love.

For, while Europa was lamenting, the goddess of love herself was there watching with an ambiguous smile, her son Cupid at her side, bow unstrung:

>   aderat querenti   66
>   perfidum ridens Venus et remisso
>   filius arcu.

Venus is there as the *dea ex machina* if you like, but her resolution of the tragedy is hardly intended to bring much consolation to Europa:

>   mox, ubi lusit satis: 'abstineto'
>   dixit 'irarum calidaeque rixae,   70
>   cum tibi inuisus laceranda reddet
>   cornua taurus.

>   uxor inuicti Iouis esse nescis:
>   mitte singultus, bene ferre magnam
>   disce fortunam; tua sectus orbis   75
>   nomina ducet.'

> *Then when she'd fun enough, 'You will remember*
> *to refrain,' she said, ' from hot and angry brawl*   *70*
> *when that bull you hate comes back to offer*
> *those horns of his to maul.*

Horace's Cautionary Tale (*Odes* iii, 27)

You're Jove Almighty's consort, don't forget!
Stop your tears and sobs—learn instead to bear
rightly your great fortune: half the world   75
will take its name from you.'

Observe first Venus is in no hurry to console. And when she speaks, she ignores the threats of suicide (not taking them very seriously, Horace perhaps implies); and from Europa's long speech (it occupied 33 lines) she singles out her threat (lines 45–8) to do all manner of murderous violence to her absconded lover—if she can only lay her hands on him. The future imperative *abstineto* suggests not only Venus' royal dignity, but also that the bull's return is hardly imminent. 'Lay murderous hands upon your lover?' she says, 'that would never do: you forget your position, my dear. You are now the consort' (*uxor*, remember, covers a very wide range of relationships) 'of an extremely important person.[1] Dry your eyes, you're going to be famous.' Venus' point of view is, of course, Horace's, and what she says is intended as much for Galatea's ears as Europa's. Galatea is not likely to see her lover again either once he deserts her, and all she will have to console herself with will be the notoriety her liaison has brought her.

Here we have poetry used for a genuinely poetic purpose. The stimulus provided by the quality of the verse and the complex, condensed pattern of innuendo the verse embodies commend to our serious consideration attitudes of mind in the poet to a relationship between reality and romance which, if stated as a series of propositions in prose, would appear flat and cynical. Moreover the argumentative character of prose would provoke us to agreement or disagreement. And we should probably disagree with Horace if, by reasoning with us, he

---

[1] I prefer to take line 73,
                uxor inuicti Iouis esse nescis,
to mean '*you do not know how to be* the consort of unconquered Jove', as originally argued, I think, by J. P. Postgate, *C.R.*, xxx (1916), pp. 190–1. Heinze continued to favour the traditional interpretation of the words as a nominative and infinitive construction: 'You do not know you are . . . '. His arguments are rather prosaic, but so is his discussion of the whole episode, p. 364:
    Ebenso singulär ist die Wendung, dass Jupiter, statt sich, wie bei Moschos, schon während der Fahrt oder wie bei anderen unmittelbar nach der Landung als Gott zu bekennen [a difficulty which Postgate's interpretation removes] sich zunächst den Blicken des Mädchens entzieht.

appeared to force his views upon us. Whereas poetry, by revealing his thoughts instead of stating his arguments, enables him to secure that sympathetic half-agreement which is all Horace wants.

Ovid, the Poseur (Amores ii, 11)

Coming to Ovid's Propempticon for Corinna, we are struck at once by the poet's failure to adopt a clear-cut, settled point of view. Horace has a point of view clearly formulated and earnestly, if gently, advanced. He would like us to feel, as he does, that the romantic attitude to love is unrealistic. Propertius' point of view is rather different. He is not concerned with making us feel as he does, but with expressing an exhilarated state of mind, intense and convincing enough to evoke our sympathy. We are prepared to believe while we read the poem that Propertius really feels the way he claims to feel. By comparison Ovid's poem seems oddly purposeless.

The love elegies of Ovid do reflect an attitude to love, but it is not one we believe in—or are expected to believe in. With occasional exceptions[1] the Ovidian pose is easy to define. Ovid puts on an act. In it he plays the role of the competent, blasé virtuoso, in both making love and writing verse. The verse is excellent entertainment, but it has almost no effect on our opinions, or on our understanding of human relationships.

In adapting the propempticon to this pose, Ovid has not resolved the difficulties that faced him in making the traditional theme his own. To begin with, the Don Juan *persona* imposes a flippant attitude that is difficult to reconcile with any of the states of mind appropriate to a propempticon addressed to a departing mistress. Propertian anguish is ruled out. It can have no place in love poetry where it is taken for granted that sensuality is the basis of love. Anger, too, is ruled out because it is incompatible with the Ovidian pose of male superiority. Indeed the pose hardly allows Ovid to admit the existence of a rival. Corinna's departure, therefore, is left unexplained—a serious weakness: the jealousy theme is sacrificed and nothing substituted. And with the jealousy theme gone, Horace's malicious irony is also excluded. In any case, the pose requires

[1] E.g., iii, 11—an elegy based on the Catullan *odi et amo* dilemma and accepting, therefore, the Catullan convention.

Ovid, the Poseur (*Amores* ii, 11)

superficial, clear-cut, slightly theatrical attitudes; neither Ovid's pose nor his flamboyant verse can cope with gentle complexity of tone.

In the last twenty lines of his poem we shall see Ovid finds a solution to his difficulties, but the central part of the poem totters. He begins not badly:

> Prima malas docuit mirantibus aequoris undis
> Peliaco pinus uertice caesa uias.

> *Evil were the ways (the ocean waves looked on amazed)*
> *which the first pine-tree taught, felled on Pelion's top.*

There are obvious echoes of the beginning of Catullus' Poem 64, but the mood of joyful confidence with which Catullus launched into the legend of the first ship that ever sailed is rejected by the emphatic *malas*, effectively placed after the opening *prima* and separated by almost the whole couplet from its noun *uias*. The Catullan wonder is there (*mirantibus undis*), but also a new contrasting note that travel by sea is wrong.

What Ovid has done is really rather clever. He has got his propempticon under way with an idea based on one of the tritest of propempticon themes ('If only ships hadn't been invented!')[1] disguising that well-worn exclamation for the moment as a piece of reflective didacticism[2]—and then stripping off the disguise at line 5, in order to start again, in the conventional way. In addition, he has evoked the optimism of epic poetry, its belief in progress and action, and simultaneously undercut it by evoking the distrust of progress and the pessimism of elegy. In elegy the wrongness of all forms of progress, because they lead to commerce and war and interfere with the lover's unambitious individualism, is a common theme.[3] He might have left it at that. Instead he sweeps on into four lines of virtuoso writing (3-6), filled with echoes of famous versions of the Medea theme.[4]

[1] Cf. Propertius i, 17, 13-14; Tibullus i, 3, 35-40.
[2] He got this idea from Horace *Odes* i, 3, 9ff.
[3] See A. Guillemin, 'Sur les origines de l'élégie latine', *R.E.L.*, xvii (1939), pp. 282-92.
[4] Echoes in the opening six lines of Catullus, Apollonius and Euripides are pointed out by L. P. Wilkinson, *Ovid Recalled* (1955), p. 22. The poem, as Wilkinson shows, is a veritable mosaic of literary reminiscences.

Persistence of a Theme: the Propempticon

At line 7 comes the formal statement of the propempticon theme:

> ecce fugit notumque torum sociosque Penates   7
> fallacisque uias ire Corinna parat.

> *See! familiar bed forsaken and the gods we'd pooled,*
> *on hazardous journey Corinna makes ready to embark.*

But the elegantly matter-of-fact couplet comes as a shock. The reader is troubled by the gulf between the six lines of legendary evocation and the abrupt announcement of the personal theme. If this had been Horace, we would have known that his object was to undercut the heroics of legend. Propertius would have tried to fuse the two worlds of heroic and personal romance. Ovid leaves us feeling a little embarrassed. The one grandiloquent touch (*sociosque Penates*) can hardly be taken seriously after the sham pathos of *notumque torum*. We begin to suspect mock heroics. The next couplet, with its flamboyantly pathetic hexameter,

> quid tibi, me miserum, Zephyros Eurosque timebo,   9

> *What! must I, poor wretch, fear for you winds west and east,*

and its diabolically ingenious pentameter,

> et gelidum Borean egelidumque Notum?   10

> *and northerly chill, and unchilled southerly?*[1]

in which Ovid completes his round of the cardinal points of the compass, rather confirms this. It is high time the poet made his attitude to his theme clear to the reader and fixed the tone of his poem. Ovid now attempts to do so, turning to address Corinna directly.

In obedience to the traditions of the propempticon he applies himself to dissuading Corinna. Precluded by his pose from

---

[1] It was one of Ovid's favourite lines, according to Seneca's well-known story: see H. Fränkel, *Ovid: A Poet between Two Worlds* (1945), p. 7.

Ovid, the Poseur (Amores ii, 11)

pleading with her, he represents to her the dangers of her sea journey—the stock approach—adopting the slightly supercilious, bantering tone appropriate to his pose. 'You'll find,' he says, 'a journey by sea is not the fun you think it is':

> non illic urbes, non tu mirabere siluas; 11
> una est iniusti caerula forma maris.
> nec medius tenuis conchas pictosque lapillos
>   pontus habet; bibuli litoris illa mora est.

No cities there, no woodlands will enrapture you:
the sea's uniformly, cruelly blue to look upon.
In mid-ocean you'll find no dainty shells, no little
coloured stones: that pastime's for the gurgling beach.

Corinna, it seems, is looking forward to some sight-seeing. 'Scenery and foreign places are all right,' Ovid warns, 'but the sea is dull and unpleasant even though it looks attractive enough when enclosed by a pretty stretch of beach.' Four excellent lines—taken out of context; *bibuli*, vivid and ironical, is particularly good. But the argument the lines purport to develop is unconvincing.[1]

The next six lines move forward with a swing, the Ovidian pose in control at last. Ovid is fond of the fast-moving parenthesis that develops a specious *ad hominem* argument, as it were on the spur of the moment, with a wink at the reader. He pretends the reference to 'beach' in line 14 suggests the argument, 'Yes, stick to the beach, girls, get your knowledge of the sea from others'. But it is an aside that continues, as the second person plurals indicate, at least until line 21. He is able to work in some good fun about sailors' tales, but Corinna and the development of the propempticon are rather lost sight of.

When we do get back to Corinna (probably at line 23), Ovid develops (for a further ten lines) the theme, 'It's safer to stay

---

[1] What seems to have happened is that Ovid has built into his love propempticon a reminiscence of the guide-book type of propempticon written, we gather, by Parthenius and Helvius Cinna. See Note on p. 240. Ovid's
   non illic urbes, non tu mirabere siluas
could be an echo of a line of Cinna's, the first of a four-line fragment describing the wonders of the east:
   nec tam donorum ingenteis mirabere aceruos . . .

Persistence of a Theme: the Propempticon

at home'. The writing is at times excellently imaginative and evocative, as in this fine hexameter:

> currit in inmensum panda carina salum,   24
>
> *out on to the boundless main runs the swelling hull.*

Other lines bear the clear stamp of Ovid's cool ingenuity, as in his picture of the sailor growing anxious in the rising storm:

> et prope tam letum quam prope cernit aquam,   26
>
> *and death as close he sees as the waves are close.*

In others we are offered mock grandiloquence:

> tum generosa uoces fecundae sidera Ledae   29
>
> *then you'd invoke fertile Leda's well-bred stars.*

He means Corinna will invoke Castor and Pollux, the twin gods, later twin stars, that protect those in peril at sea. Ostensibly this is the purport of a periphrasis in the grand manner. But the grandiloquence is tellingly undercut by the unexpected adjective *fecundae*. Leda produced a remarkable number of important children (Clytemnestra and Helen of Troy as well as Castor and Pollux); but somehow the moment to be reminded of the heavenly twins' family life is not when we are struggling to take seriously the dangers that will confront Corinna.

It is all great fun. Ovid possesses a facility of imagination and a precision of diction never matched by Propertius. But his poem is not really moving forward. The brilliance obscures the poet's attitude to his theme instead of clarifying it. Then in the last twenty-four lines Ovid suddenly strikes form. He brings in another commonplace of the propempticon (duly acknowledged by a reference to Galatea), the cliché, 'Well, if you must go, I wish you luck':

> aequa tamen puppi sit Galatea tuae!   34
>
> *May Galatea just the same give your ship a chance!*

Ovid, the Poseur (Amores ii, 11)

This is followed by another cliché:

> uade memor nostri, uento reditura secundo. 37

> *farewell, remember me, the winds speed your return.*[1]

Then comes, as though spontaneously, a neat evocation of Corinna on her return voyage, all eagerness to reach her lover's arms. The poem concludes with a superbly vivid picture of their passionate reunion, striking just the right note of Ovidian naughtiness:

> primus ego aspiciam notam de litore puppim
>   et dicam 'nostros aduehit illa deos!'
> excipiamque umeris et multa sine ordine carpam   45
>   oscula. pro reditu uictima uota cadet,
> inque tori formam molles sternentur harenae,
>   et tumulus mensae quilibet instar erit.
> illic adposito narrabis multa Lyaeo,
>   paene sit ut mediis obruta nauis aquis,   50
> dumque ad me properas, neque iniquae tempora noctis
>   nec te praecipites extimuisse Notos.

> *I'll know your ship, be first to spot it from the beach.*
> *'It's bringing all I worship home,' I'll say, and take*
> *you on my shoulders, and—uncircumspectly—cover you*   45
> *with kisses. In celebration of return will the desired*
> *victim fall—we can smooth the sand to form a bed.*
> *A dune somewhere will do duty for our table.*
> *The wine will flow while you relate your tale at length*
> *—how your ship almost foundered in the deep, how*   50
> *(eager to rejoin me) you faced undaunted those*
> *awful nights at sea, that roaring, southerly gale.*

The lines are successful on several levels. First, they express the emotion Ovid best enjoys expressing: eager sensuality, with no nonsense on either side. Second, they achieve a light-hearted grandiloquence that refines the sensuality by investing

---

[1] See Note on Horace, *Odes* iii, 72, 14, p. 259.

Persistence of a Theme: the Propempticon

it with a gay elegance. Third, they sparkle with parody, the grand manner deftly evoked in an unexpected context.

Ovid's sense of fun is sometimes irrepressible. We can see, I think, how a witty idea occurred to him—and forced its way into these lines. In line 44,

> et dicam 'nostros aduehit illa deos!'

we have the germ of the idea, a simple reversal of the normal. Instead of, 'The gods I worship are bringing her ship to me', we have that turned inside out: 'The ship is bringing back the gods I worship'—in other words Corinna (in Latin the plural can more easily refer to a single person). This sense is supported by a familiar cliché—that the lover's mistress is for him a divinity. So far so good, but at this point the grand manner, which Ovid is using to shape these lines, introduces a completely extraneous echo: Virgil's Aeneas and the ships that brought the Trojan gods to Italy. The echo is so faint we should hardly catch it if it were not supported by the *excipiamque umeris* immediately following—words that inevitably conjure up the centuries-old legend Virgil used of Aeneas carrying his father from burning Troy.[1] The process of free association is further reinforced if we remember that Aeneas gave old Anchises the images of the city's gods to hold in his arms before he lifted him onto his shoulders. The association of ideas is ludicrously inappropriate, but it is hard to doubt that these are the images Ovid wants to lurk in our thoughts while we picture him wading heroically ashore with his mistress perched on his shoulders.

The images, of course, do no more than lurk, but they underpin a fresh parody in the succeeding lines. With gay impropriety the details of Corinna's landing suggest scenes in the *Aeneid* where Aeneas and his men land and camp on the beach. First, the sacrifice that sounds so solemn—and is really so naughty: can we doubt that the 'desired victim' that 'will fall' is Corinna herself?[2] Then the improvised bed and table and the discussion of the storm while they drink. It all sounds just

---

[1] Terracottas, ascribed to the fifth century B.C., have been found representing Aeneas carrying Anchises on his shoulders. See A. Rostagni, *Storia della letteratura latina*, i (2nd edn. 1954), p. 18.

[2] Observe the ambiguity in *uota*: 'vowed' (i.e., 'offered by me to the gods') and 'desired' (i.e., 'by me').

Ovid, the Poseur (Amores ii, 11)

sufficiently like Virgil to thrust superbly extraneous half-images into the typically Ovidian central picture of Ovid reunited with his mistress on the sand.

He ends, however, a little disappointingly with an ironical withdrawal from both passion and parody in a couplet of coolly detached self-analysis. 'I shall of course believe every word she says,' he tells us, '(about the dangers she faced at sea to get back to me), though doubtless what she'll tell me will be a pack of lies':

> omnia pro ueris credam, sint ficta licebit.   53

A good example of Ovidian epigram: the line of statement limpid, the sense arrestingly unexpected. The epigram is then capped by the pentameter, 'Why shouldn't I believe you if you tell me things so flattering they seem an answer to my prayers.' One moment we have Ovid pretending to be as gullible as he would have the girls who listen to travellers' tales (lines 21–2); the next the cynic is back again, pointing out the need to practise calculated self-deception. Ovid had got us to the point where we were almost prepared to believe him really in love. With a dazzling pirouette the Don Juan pose is resumed and the propempticon rounded off with a casually formal concluding couplet in the high style:

> haec mihi quam primum caelo nitidissimus alto   55
> Lucifer admisso tempora portet equo.

This day the morning star will bring, I hope, and very soon, galloping through the sky—none brighter than he.

[1] As if to mark the final resumption of the pose, the final couplet is framed as a bare-faced imitation of a couplet with which Tibullus concluded his description of his reunion with Delia (i, 3, 93–4):
> hoc precor, hunc illum nobis Aurora nitentem
> Luciferum roseis candida portet equis.

List of Poems and Passages Discussed

Short passages briefly referred to are not included, but are listed in the Index.

Catullus
  Poem 14: 71–3
  — 43: 69
  — 86: 66–73
  — 101: 80–3

Horace
  Odes i, 4: 14–28
  — i, 8: 137–40
  — i, 27: 89–90
  — i, 33: 155–8
  — ii, 9: 158–62
  — ii, 14: 99–107
  — iii, 13: 75–8
  — iii, 27: 253–66
  — iv, 7: 14–28
  — iv, 9: 87–9
  — iv, 12: 7–14
  — iv, 13: 90–9

Ovid
  Amores ii, 11: 266–73

Pliny the Younger
  Epistles iv, 11: 117–8

Propertius
  i, 1: 131–2, 150–1
  i, 7, 1–8: 132–4
  i, 8: 242–53
  i, 9, 17–24: 151
  ii, 1: 163–4
  ii, 2, 5–10: 67
  ii, 3: 164–5
  ii, 3, 9–16: 70–1
  ii, 12: 168–82
  ii, 26a: 187–97
  ii, 27: 182–7

Tacitus
  Annals xiv, 8–10: 115–29

Tibullus
  ii, 4, 1–10: 153–4

Virgil
  Aeneid ii, 268–720: 207–11
  — ii, 506–58: 229–38
  — iii, 132–46: 227
  — iv: 29–58
  — iv, 685–92: 200–1
  — v, 1–11: 227–9
  — v, 139–47: 225
  — v, 387–484: 203–6

Index

Addressee of a poem, 79, 85, 87, 91
Aeneas, character of, 29
— lineage, 233
— stoicism of, 41
Agrippina, 114–28
Alcaeus, 65
Alfonsi, Luigi, 135, 239
Allen, A. W., 143, 144, 152, 163
Allusion, 216–20
Ambiguity, 21, 41, 50, 89, 94–5, 139–140, 175, 176, 178, 180, 184–5, 187, 190, 192, 196, 200, 201, 209, 231, 272; puns, 194
amor, 172–3
Anacreon, 65
André, J., 191
antiquus, 50
Antony, Mark, and Aeneas, 35
Apollonius, 8
Apuleius, 170, 173
Aristophanes, 240
Aristotle on tragic error, 34, 38–9
Augustine, St., 33
aura, 176, 187
Austin, R. G., 31, 41, 50, 201, 210
Axelson, B., 9

Bailey, Cyril, 147, 211
Bailey, D. R. S., 132, 134, 170, 175, 176, 247
Barber, E. A., 247
Bardon, H., 240
Barr, William, 20
Bateson, F. W., 6, 32, 63, 106
Bekenntnisdichtung, 64
bellus, 67
Benn, Gottfried, 59–60
Blaiklock, E. M., 143
Boetticher, W., 111
Bowra, C. M., 9, 198
Boyancé, Pierre, 135
Brouwers, A., 155
Burck, Erich, 173, 176

Buscaroli, C., 38
Butler, H. E., 37, 184
Butler, H. E., and Barber, E. A., 149; Chapter 7 passim

caeruleus, 191
Caesar, Julius, 128
Callimachus, 135, 194, 240
Campbell, A. Y., 77, 253
Camps, W. A., 247
candidus, 195
carina, 189
Catullus as craftsman, 64
— indecency of language avoided, 147
— influenced by Lucretius, 145
— preciseness of narrative technique, 122
— Romantic attitude to, 64
— Poem 3: 68, 80
— — 4: 9
— — 4, 27: 192
— — 5: 250
— — 8: 142
— — 9: 240
— — 11: 147
— — 11, 11–14: 176
— — 13: 14
— — 14: 71–3
— — 16: 147
— — 43: 69
— — 46: 8
— — 58: 147
— — 64: 9, 200, 223, 255, 262
— — 64, 19–21: 39
— — 76: 97, 142
— — 85 (*odi et amo*): 49–50, 266
— — 86: 66–73, 96, 98–9
— — 86, alluded to by Horace, 148
— — 96: 81
— — 101: 80–3
Cicero, 96, 110, 190, 191, 250
Cinna, Helvius, 269
Cleopatra and Dido, 35

Index

Cliché in poetry, 187
Coleridge, S. T., 63; on Lucretius, 30
Collinge, N. E., 11, 12, 27, 99–100, 263
Comedy, love in, 156
Conington, J., 30–1
Conway, R. S., 36, 200
Copley, F. O., 145, 241
Corbett, P. E., 38
Critics of modern literature, their attitude to classical poetry, 62
culpa, 38
cum, 202, 220, 221
Cupid, 170–1
cupido, 94–5

Deiphobus, 216–19
diues amator, 155–6, 160, 251, 257
docta puella, 70
Domitian, 117
donec, 126, 221
Donne, John, 74
Doyle, Conan, 166
Dramatic monologue, 78
—— in Horace, 84–109
Dudley, D. R., 29
durus, 133, 161

Elegy, Greek, 254
Eliot, T. S., 47
Elliptical narrative, 202–11
Enk, P. J., 143, 242, 249
Ennius, 189
Epic poetry, resemblance to tragedy, 35–6
Epicureanism, 108, 146
Epigram and Catullus, 181
—— elegy, 181–2, 187
—— Horace, 181
—— poem, 71
—— satire, 185
—— Virgil, 203
— hellenistic, 74
Epyllion, 255
Erinna, 240
Erlebnisdichtung, 64
Euripides, 257

felix, 97
Ferrero, L., 67
Fordyce, C. J., 72, 80
formosus, 67, 93
Fowler, H. W., 263
— Warde, 37

Fraenkel, Eduard, Chapters 1, 4 passim; 253, 254, 255, 256, 262
Fränkel, H., 268
Friedrich, G., 145
—— W.-H., 254, 261
Fronto, 111
fugax, 101

Galba, 112
Gallus, Cornelius, 149, 160, 242, 245–246, 248
Goethe and classical poetry, 63
— on Horace, 6–7, 30
Gow, James, 146
Graves, Robert, 74
Gray, Thomas, 'Elegy', 104, 106
Guillemin, A., 38, 133, 267

Harvey, Paul, 31
Heinze, Richard, 84, 135
—— on characteristics of Horace's *Odes*, 84–7
—— quoted, Chapters 1, 4 passim; 29, 35, 140, 157, 159, 209, 239, 253, 255, 256, 258, 265
Hellenistic poetry, 39
Hendrickson, G. L., 239, 242
Henry, James, 233–4
Herescu, N. I., 80
Highet, Gilbert, 135, 137
Historic infinitive in Tacitus, 125
—— Virgil, 221
— present, 126–7
Holmes, Sherlock, 166
Homer, narrative tempo in, 198
— *Iliad* iv, 85ff.: 220
—— xxiii: 8
—— xxiii, 147: 77
— *Odyssey* v, 203ff.: 239
—— viii, 499–520: 216–17
—— xv, 125–9: 239
Horace as craftsman, 64
— assault on love elegy, 154–62
— coarseness in early treatment of love, 146–8
— contrasted with Propertius, 259–60
— Epicureanism of, 7
— influenced by Philodemus, 147–8
— love poetry as social comment, 137–140
— Romantic attitude to, 64
— *Epistles* ii, 2, 99–101: 141
— *Epodes* 1: 240

278

Index

Horace, *Epodes* 7: 90, 108
—— 10: 240
—— 13: 108
—— 15: 155-6
—— 16: 90, 108
—— 16, 27: 9
—— 17, 42-3: 192
— *Odes* i, 3: 240, 248, 262, 267
—— i, 3, 9-20: 192
—— i, 4: 4-7, 14-28, 252
—— i, 5: 88
—— i, 5, 11: 176
—— i, 5, 15-16: 194
—— i, 6: 88
—— i, 8: 137-40
—— i, 9: 108
—— i, 11: 182
—— i, 14: 240
—— i, 14, 9: 9
—— i, 15: 256
—— i, 22: 186
—— i, 27: 89-90
—— i, 28: 82, 90, 108
—— i, 33: 155-8, 244, 264
—— i, 33, 8: 21
—— i, 36: 241
—— ii, 3: 108
—— ii, 7: 241
—— ii, 8, 24: 176
—— ii, 9: 158-62
—— ii, 14: 99-107
—— iii, 2: 137
—— iii, 9: 109
—— iii, 10: 108
—— iii, 11: 254
—— iii, 13: 75-8, 104
—— iii, 14: 241
—— iii, 19: 108
—— iii, 27: 149, 253-66
—— iii, 30: 21
—— iii, 30, 4-5: 102
—— iv, 5: 241
—— iv, 7: 4-7, 14-28
—— iv, 9: 87-9
—— iv, 12: 7-14, 96
—— iv, 13: 90-9, 101, 154
— *Satires* i, 2: 146
—— i, 2, 102-4: 148
—— i, 2, 123: 98
—— i, 5: 147
—— i, 9: 141, 147
Housman, A. E., 4-7, 18, 30, 131-2, 185

Howald, Ernst, 15, 100

Imperfect indicative, 125
infestus, 234
iniquus, 250
in somnis, 189
Interweaving, 212-16, 229
Irony in Horace, 256
—— Propertius, 188, 189, 196
—— Virgil, 231

Jäger, Felix, 239-40, 242

Kiessling, Adolph, 84
Knight, W. F. J., 50
Knights, L. C., 31, 57, 206-7
Knoche, U., 74
Kühner, R., and Stegmann, C., 221
Kukula, R. C., 240

Langbaum, Robert, 109
lassus, 189
Lawrence, T. E., 74
Leavis, F. R., 2
Lessing, G. E., 6, 255
Lewis, C. S., 63
Livy, 190
Löfstedt, Einar, 111-12, 205
Lonie, I., 135
Lucian, 68
Luck, Georg, 135, 155
Lucretius, 8, 183
— on love, 144-7, 150, 156
— i, 1: 23
— i, 1ff.: 8
— i, 2-4: 18
— ii, 14-34: 108
— iii, 894-6: 104-5
— iii, 912-15: 105
— v, 1392-6: 108
ludere, 93
Lusus Troiae, 137
Lyly, John, 70

MacInnes, J., 37
Mackail, J. W., 38, 50, 185, 198, 201, 205
—— a Romantic critic, 31-2
McKay, K. J., 194
Macron, 171
Marriage, Roman law of, 38
Marsh, Edward, 263
Marx, F., 137

Index

Meleager, 148, 172, 179, 240
Menander Rhetor, 239, 242
Mendell, C. W., 113
Mezentius, 212–14
militia equestris, 137
miser, 152
mollis, 133, 161
Moschus, 156, 255, 265
Mythology in Horace, 26–7, 139, 160
— — Propertius, 190, 195, 250–1

Narrator, function in epic of, 36, 54
nauis, 189
Nero, 114–29
niger, 191
Norden, E., 221

Occasional verse, 79, 87, 240, 256
Ovid, 135–6, 255
— attitude to love, 266
— compared with Propertius, 165
— *Amores* ii, 11: 248, 266–73
— — iii, 11: 266

Palinurus, 215
Palmer, L. R., 239
paraclausithyron, 241
Parallel narrative, 124, 233–4
Parthenius, 149, 240, 269
Pasquali, Giorgio, 8, 12, 86, 89, 137, 239, 253
Pease, A. S., 31, 36, 39
Penates, 209–11
pereo, 47, 186
Perret, J., 29, 35
Philodemus, 147–8
pius, 49
Plautus, 171, 173, 179
Pliny the Younger, 117–21
— — *Epistles* iv, 11: 117–18
Pöschl, Viktor, 41
Poetic thinking, 168
— tragedy, nature of, 56
Poetry and philosophy, 175
— — prose, difference between, 175–6, 238, 265–6
Ponchont, M., 137
Poppaea, 114–15
Postgate, J. P., 169–70, 175, 265
postquam, 220
potui, 52
Pound, Ezra, 100–1
Priam, 229–38

Propertius and passion, 74
— attitude to love, 149–53
— contrasted with Horace, 259–60
— — — Ovid, 188, 196–7
— date of earliest poems, 149
— difficulty of his verse, 130
— importance of, 130–41
— intellectual vigour, 167
— para-rational statement in, 130
— relations with Horace, 140–1
— i, 1: 131–2, 142, 150–1, 243–4
— i, 3: 151
— i, 5, 3–4: 152
— i, 6, 12: 156, 158
— i, 7, 1–8: 132–4
— i, 8: 151, 242–53
— i, 9, 17–24: 151
— i, 17: 240, 267
— i, 20: 149, 160, 254, 261
— ii, 1: 163–4
— ii, 2, 5–10: 67
— ii, 3: 164–5
— ii, 3, 9–16: 70–1
— ii, 6: 165
— ii, 8, 8: 156
— ii, 12: 168–82
— ii, 13b: 163
— ii, 15, 29–30: 158
— ii, 16: 243
— ii, 17, 9–10: 152
— ii, 22a: 162
— ii, 26a: 187–97, 240, 259–60
— ii, 27: 182–7
— ii, 29, 15–18: 176
— ii, 29b: 165
— ii, 30a: 180
— ii, 31: 165
— iii, 2, 8: 189
— iii, 8, 20: 158
— iii, 10: 165
— iii, 15: 254
— iii, 16, 11–18: 186
— iii, 21: 166
— iii, 23: 165
— iii, 24: 166, 180
— iii, 25: 166
— iv, 1, 28: 185
— iv, 6, 17: 189
— iv, 8: 92
pulcher, 67
puppis, 189
purpureus, 191
puto, 195

Index

Quintilian on elegy, 136

Rand, E. K., 9, 41
ratis, 189
rauus, 191
Reitzenstein, Erich, 134–5, 182
— Richard, 84, 86
Relative clauses, 96
Richards, I. A., 107
Romantic critics, 5–7
Romanticism and the classics, 63, 86
Rose, H. J., 171, 245
Rostagni, A., 149, 254, 272
Rothstein, M., 184, 194
Rudd, Niall, 3, 21, 26

Sappho, 65, 240, 259
Scholarly attitude to poetry, 62
Schuster, M., 134–5
seruitium amoris, 150, 180
Servius, 245
Sincerity, Roman notion of, 163
Snell, Bruno, 65
Sophocles, *Antigone*, 781–4: 94
Spengel, L., 239, 242
Statius, 240, 241
Stephanus of Byzantium, 239, 240
Suetonius, 121–2
Syme, Ronald, Chapter 5 passim

Tacitus, *Annals* xiii, 45, 6–7: 115
— — xiv, 8–10: 115–29
— *Histories* i, 49: 112–13
Tempo in Propertius, 186
— of epic, 35
— — narrative, 125
Tenses in Virgilian narrative, 220–38; historic infinitive, 221; historic present, 222–9; imperfect indicative, 221, 226–9; perfect indicative, 223–9
Terzaghi, N. O., 141
Tescari, O., 21
thalamus, 56
Theocritus, 240, 261
Tibullus, 136–7, 162, 163
— attitude to love, 153–4
— his love poetry criticized by Horace, 155–8
— i, 1: 154
— i, 2, 16–32: 186
— i, 3: 240, 267, 273
— i, 3, 1–2: 259
— i, 5: 155

Tibullus ii, 4, 1–10: 153–4
Tränkle, Hermann, 135
Tragic irony, 50
Trilling, Lionel, 2, 66
Tyrell, R. Y., 64, 99

uentosus, 175
uenus, 68, 96
uenustas, 68
uirilis cultus, 139–40
Ussani, V., 249
ut, 202, 220, 230
uulnis, 234

Valgius, 158–62
Verse and poetry, distinction between, 87
— epistle, 87
Vettii, house of, 171
Virgil as craftsman, 64
— impreciseness of narrative technique, 122
— Horace's Ode iv, 12 to, 7–14
— treatment of love, 148
— *Aeneid*, 23
— — archaism, 199
— — divine machinery in, 37
— — syntax, 199–201
— — i, 94–6: 210
— — i, 220–2: 49
— — i, 455ff.: 230
— — ii: 48
— — ii, 1–2: 224
— — ii, 50–3: 224
— — ii, 243: 224
— — ii, 252–3: 223
— — ii, 268–720: 207–11
— — ii, 274–5: 217–18
— — ii, 310–11: 216
— — ii, 491–5: 236–7
— — ii, 506–58: 229–38
— — ii, 526–32: 124
— — ii, 540: 48
— — ii, 540–3: 218
— — ii, 549: 200
— — iii, 1–5: 220–1
— — iii, 11: 238
— — iii, 11–12: 209, 211
— — iii, 62–8: 81
— — iii, 132–46: 227
— — iii, 332: 216
— — iii, 469: 216
— — iv: 29–58

Index

Virgil, *Aeneid* iv, 1–2: 180
—— iv, 69–73: 177
—— iv, 589–91: 202
—— iv, 685–92: 200–1
—— v, function of, 48
—— v, 1ff.: 48, 215
—— v, 1–11: 227–9
—— v, 45–71: 82
—— v, 139–47: 225
—— v, 211–12: 206
—— v, 294ff.: 214–15
—— v, 370–4: 219
—— v, 376: 21
—— v, 387–484: 203–6
—— v, 494: 206
—— v, 495–7: 219–20
—— v, 553–602: 226
—— v, 563–5: 215–16
—— v, 673: 206
—— v, 680–2: 223
—— v, 823: 194
—— v, 833–71: 215
—— vi, 231: 57
—— vi, 455: 41
—— vi, 494–534: 217–19
—— vi, 847: 106
—— vii, 647–8: 212
—— viii: 19
—— viii, 6–8: 212
—— viii, 407–53: 39
—— viii, 481ff.: 213

Virgil, *Aeneid* viii, 569–71: 213
—— ix, 230ff.: 214–15
—— ix, 521–2: 213
—— ix, 586–9: 213
—— x, 298–302: 126
—— x, 465: 41
—— x, 721: 185
—— x, 729–46: 213–14
—— x, 762–802: 226
—— xi, 26: 82
—— xi, 266–8: 233
—— xi, 708: 175
—— xii, 289–310: 224
—— xii, 848: 175
— *Eclogues*: 11
—— 10: 242, 245–6

Walker, B., Chapter 5 passim
White, R. E., 249
Wilamowitz-Moellendorff, U. von, 5–7, 30, 90, 253
Wili, Walter, 14, 86
Wilkinson, L. P., 4, 90, 149, 253, 255, 267
Williams, R. D., 137, 205, 221
Witt, N. W. de, 89
Wodehouse, P. G., 99
Woolf, Virginia, 3
Wordsworth, William, 30

Yeats, W. B., 67